Here is a challenging perspective on American social work that calls attention to current needs and new goals while contributing to refinements in methodology.

This compilation of papers treating some of the major problems and issues facing American social welfare and social work was prepared, at the invitation of the editor, Alfred J. Kahn, by a group of leading social work practitioners, researchers, and educators in important centers throughout the country.

After setting forth present-day views on the function of social work and the demands that may be made upon the field in the future, the authors look in detail at the knowledge and resources available for undertaking new roles. Drawing upon relevant social science concepts, the authors analyze specifically the issues and trends as they affect the various segments of American social work.

Among the topics considered are social work as a profession, the blending of psychoanalytic and social

les of
nteers,

aution
nethod
basic

rofes-
tential
itoma-
hange
.

York
or of
hn is
The
Vork,
or of

Issues in

AMERICAN

SOCIAL WORK

Edited by ALFRED J. KAHN

New York and London

COLUMBIA UNIVERSITY PRESS

FOREWORD

This is a book about social work and social welfare. It deals with trends, with problems—and, above all, with issues. For American social work seems about to make some vital choices, and it is in a position to make them in the light of deliberate consideration of their implications.

The editor argues, in the first paper, that the needs of American society would best be served if social work were to adopt an "institutional" rather than a "residual" concept of its role. Social work, in this view, should regard itself as an essential component of modern society, serving the "normal" as well as the disadvantaged, involved in planning the better life as well as in meeting pathology and social disorganization.

As the reader will note, this is not necessarily the point of emphasis of the authors of all the succeeding papers. The latter did not have access to the editor's formulation prior to their writing. They were selected either as experts in their respective fields or as creative contributors from among the newer social work scholars and teachers. Nonetheless, despite individual differences of emphasis and orientation, they tend to stress a broad rather than a delimited concept of social work. They see need for social work in a social policy role at the same time that the methodology of individual and group adjustive services is refined and its practitioners become more skillful.

Particularly interesting in this group of papers is the dramatic demonstration that social work is ranging widely in its borrowing of conceptual and theoretical frameworks from relevant social and behavioral sciences, while it continues to add to its indigenous knowledge. The reference here is not merely to statements to the effect that this would be a desirable development: these have been heard with fair frequency for more than a decade. More significantly, the analyses which follow employ directly a variety of new frameworks and analytic approaches. The extent to which the perspectives of sociology, social psychology, anthropology, and the newer ego psychology contribute to our task is here seen firsthand. Yet, at no point is there any evidence of need to give up that which social work has created as its own base.

What, then, are the central issues? While each paper is an independent entity, the volume as a whole also represents an effort to develop perspective on major problems to be dealt with, and choices to be made by, American social work. Some receive far more attention than others. They may be summarized as follows:

1. *Issues relating to social work's function and role.* These range from the basic question of the place of social work in modern society to questions about the specific areas in which social work may make a special claim to competence. They include, too, issues of professional strategy, relationships with other groups, and the response to public expectations which arise as social work seeks to develop to its full potential.

2. *Issues relating to the social work knowledge base and to the content and manner of application of knowledge from the social and behavioral sciences.* The basic question deals with the knowledge available to fulfill the roles defined, but several components and aspects of the knowledge require examination. These matters are pursued in many of the papers. Involved, too, is the question of the relationship between

knowledge-skill-attitude in any one area of social work practice and the requirements of other areas of practice. In what
sense is social work theory "generic"—and what is the nature
and value of the "specific"? Of highest priority to several of
the authors is the development of more comprehensive practice
theory in a "middle range," as a more direct guide to the professional worker than the broad statements of principles and
goals which now must frequently be relied upon.

3. *Issues relating to nonprofessional social work roles.* Given
a broad, institutional concept of social work what is the place
of the subprofessional, the volunteer, the citizen? These questions become exceedingly important as the professional practitioner tends to become more highly trained and specialized.

4. *Issues relating to the sound development of the social
work profession.* There are many questions about recruitment, training, supervision, definition of professional roles and
of "professional self" which require careful consideration in a
period of great demand for social workers. The solutions accepted will affect social work's expansion potential.

5. *Issues relating to the organization and structure of
services.* How is the nature of the service rendered affected
by the way in which the agency or institution is structured?
What forms of organization are most likely to promote achievement of social work objectives?

The papers contain clear evidence, in their approaches, in
their content, and in the explicit views expressed, that casework, group work, and community organization are at three
different stages of development and must address themselves
to different priorities in the immediate future. Nowhere is
there defensiveness about this fact, however, and the authors
dealing with these fields share a receptivity to new tasks as
well as to new theoretical contributions from the social and
behavioral sciences.

The volume does not seek to discuss, specifically and comprehensively, major social policy questions currently facing social work. Even if limited to three or four major subjects in the fields of social security, housing, public assistance, delinquency prevention, mental health, urban renewal, or leisure time, for example, the task would require and deserve a full book. There is much to be said about major American social problems and potentialities. We seek, here, rather to suggest the nature of social work's relationship to changing need and to social policy. One source of the differences in emphases as between the papers is the extent of preoccupation with problems of professional social work methodology or with some of the broader issues facing social work as a social institution. Of this, more in the text.

The book is devoted to *American* social work not out of lack of concern for problems beyond our borders and not because we do not conceive of social work as having a contribution to make elsewhere. Here, too, it was necessary to face the fact that adequate treatment would have required more attention than was possible in this work.

It need hardly be added that while the individual authors deserve full credit for their substantial contributions, the editor is, alone, accountable for any defects in the conception and structure of the volume.

New York City   A. J. K.
1959

CONTENTS

THE CONTRIBUTORS

HARRIETT M. BARTLETT is currently engaged in several professional projects concerned with examination of social work practice. She was most recently professor at the Simmons College School of Social Work, where she directed the program in medical social work.

BERTRAM M. BECK has been the Associate Executive Director of the National Association of Social Workers since the organization was founded in 1955. Prior to that he was Director of the Juvenile Delinquency Project in the United States Children's Bureau.

NATHAN E. COHEN is Dean of the School of Applied Social Sciences, Western Reserve University. He was the first president of the National Association of Social Workers and is the author of *Social Work in the American Tradition*.

JOSEPH W. EATON is Professor of Social Work Research at the University of Pittsburgh and Visiting Professor at the University of California at Los Angeles. His most recent book is *Culture and Mental Disorders*.

ALFRED KADUSHIN is an associate professor at the School of Social Work, University of Wisconsin. His professional papers have appeared in major social work and mental health publications.

ALFRED J. KAHN is Professor of Social Work at the New York School of Social Work, Columbia University, and staff consultant, Citizens' Committee for Children of New York City, Inc. He is author of *A Court for Children* and *For Children in Trouble*.

SAMUEL MENCHER is an associate professor at the Graduate School of Social Work, University of Pittsburgh. His major research interests include the relationships of governmental and voluntary services.

HENRY J. MEYER is a professor of social work and of sociology at the University of Michigan. He is co-editor with Edgar F. Borgatta of *Sociological Theory: Present-Day Sociology from the Past* and co-author of a monograph, *An Experiment in Mental Hospital Rehabilitation*.

NORMAN POLANSKY is a professor at Western Reserve University, a lecturer at the Smith College School for Social Work, and Director of Research at the Bellefaire Regional Child Care Center and Service. His major research interests include group dynamics in treatment milieus and the helping process.

WILLIAM SCHWARTZ is an associate professor at the University of Illinois School of Social Work, Chicago Branch. He is currently engaged in a study of the nature of the helping process in education and social group work.

ISABEL STAMM is Associate Professor of Social Work at the New York School of Social Work, Columbia University. She was also one of the authors of *A Conceptual Framework of Social Casework*.

ROBERT D. VINTER is an associate professor at the School of Social Work, University of Michigan. His most recent publication is *Staff Relationships and Attitudes in a Juvenile Correctional Institution*.

Issues in AMERICAN SOCIAL WORK

THE FUNCTION OF SOCIAL WORK
IN THE MODERN WORLD

ALFRED J. KAHN

In 1942, inspired by Malinowski's functional anthropology, Helen L. Witmer undertook an analysis of social work as an institution. She concluded, in brief, that it is important to distinguish between *social welfare* and *social work*. The former may be seen as organized society's provision "to fill up gaps in the usual institutional arrangements of our society"; if social welfare services did not exist, basic needs of considerable numbers of people would not be met. Thus, the public assistance program is the organized means of dealing with extreme poverty, and the foster care agency concerns itself with the fact that some children lack adequate families. Social work, on the other hand, is seen as the institution which gives "assistance to individuals in regard to the difficulties they encounter in their use of an organized group's services or in their own performance as members of an organized group." [1]

Social work, in this view, is "an institution that serves other

---

[1] Helen Leland Witmer, *Social Work: an Analysis of a Social Institution* (New York: Rinehart and Co., Inc., 1942), p. 121. For a recent variation see Kermit T. Wiltse's characterization of social work as a method of helping people solve their problems in meeting their needs through the typical social institutions. To Wiltse, social services refer to all health, education, and welfare, while social welfare services focus on helping people with identifiable problems. Wiltse, "Social Casework and Public Assistance," *Social Service Review*, XXXII (1958), 41–50.

institutions." While people other than social workers function within social welfare programs, social work has a clearly delineated role in such programs and also in helping individuals in their social roles in all areas of individual and group living. The child guidance worker seeks to help parents and children with their problems of functioning within the family, while the school social worker seeks to assist students in making optimum use of school facilities and resources. Similar interpretations may be made of medical social work, probation, and other fields of social work practice.

Witmer's writing contributed to a number of efforts to conceptualize social welfare and social work in a manner which would encompass both a field involving diverse programs and a profession demanding a range of skills. Nonetheless, because social work had other preoccupations in the 1940s, her leads were not fully pursued. Certainly there was need to ask whether the newer post-depression developments in family casework or child guidance were truly encompassed by a view of social work solely as promoting adjustment to, or functioning within, social institutions. To some, at least, casework's emerging psychotherapeutic role, with its emphasis on individual personality correction or change, was not adequately described in these terms. Nor were social action or community organization undertakings seen as oriented to helping adjustment to the status quo, or facilitating change only of social welfare institutions. Environment could be the object of change, too.

Thus, while some refinements might have been suggested in discussion, Witmer's general view of social welfare and social work continued to be influential. The United Nations Social Commission, surveying social work education throughout the world, for example, found it most useful to conceive of social work as: (a) a *helping* activity (directed to problems which affect economic and social well-being; (b) a *social* (nonprofit) activity; and (c) a *liaison* activity (concerned with facilitating use of community resources). This formulation, too, stresses social work's contribution to social adjustment, and gives much emphasis to the social worker's role and skill as an integrator, whose objective is to assure that "individuals, families, and groups may derive full benefit from the facilities and services available in the community for promoting and maintaining social well-being." [2] It adds a new ingredient, however: social work is seen as also having the role of fixing attention on social ills, pointing to the need for remedial and preventive services, and maximizing resources for well-being. It is not clear whether a social planning or a social reform task is given emphasis in this U.N. formulation.

While efforts to conceptualize the field of social welfare and the institution of social work thus moved toward a broader view, social work practitioners and scholars sought a unifying "core" which would establish conceptually the validity of what was becoming a widely acknowledged reality, i.e., the substantial overlap in social work practice of method, skill, and value systems between casework, group work, and community organization. Already available and of some influence were earlier suggestions about common cores in method by Mary Richmond and Mary Jarrett and the view, clearly articulated in the 1929 Report of the Milford Conference, that the various casework specialties had a generic base.[3] This had had

[2] United Nations, Department of Social Affairs, *Training for Social Work: an International Survey* (New York: United Nations, 1950), p. 13.

[3] Mary Jarrett, "The Psychiatric Thread Running through All Social Case Work," in *Proceedings of the National Conference of Social Work, 1919* (Chicago, 1920), pp. 587–93. Mary Richmond stressed personality development as the basic social work aim, according to Nathan E. Cohen, *Social Work in the American Tradition* (New York: Dryden Press, 1958), pp. 138–39. For the Milford Conference Report see *Social Case Work, Generic and Specific* (New York: American Association of Social Workers, 1929).

little attention for almost two decades, however. Now, it was as though a thread lost after the Milford Conference could be picked up again after the forced interruptions of the great depression, the refugee problem, the defense mobilization, the war programs, the postwar adjustments. As will be seen, this tendency exerted influence on behalf of a narrower concept of social work.

Key organizing concepts came, first, from psychoanalytic theory alone, a natural enough development since Freudian psychiatry had from the early 1920s provided the foundation for the development of social casework, long the major social work method. Full success could hardly be found in this direction since the concepts did not encompass all of casework, and certainly not much of group work or community organization. As the field sought to "return to the social" after the Second World War it found new help from the revitalized social sciences. Those who would define the conceptual unity of social work methods now required models which could account for psychological as well as sociocultural dimensions. In the experimentation which has inevitably followed, one formulation, apparently inspired by Seyle's stress theory, defined social work as concerned with the "prevention and alleviation of the socially and psychologically damaging effects of crisis situations" (i.e., the personal and social stress).[4] There has also appeared the tendency to seek the conceptual and psychological unity of social work method around the "problem-solving" process, as though this could be the province of any one profession (or could be monopolized by professionals, as differentiated from all thinking and acting—i.e., all living—individuals). Others have stressed concern with, and help through, relationship as the central social work core; at times,

[4] For example, see Henry S. Maas and Martin Wolins, "Concepts and Methods in Social Work Research," in Cora Kasius, ed., *New Directions in Social Work* (New York: Harper, 1954), especially p. 215.

concern with the goal of improved social functioning and special understanding of, and skill with regard to, person-in-situation and group-in-community have been described as social work's unique perspective.[5]

The unifying conceptual key to all social work method has not yet been identified and, as will be seen, the search for it may be comparable to the ancient alchemist's search for the philosopher's stone—valuable, the source of many innovations and discoveries, however unreal. In the interim, important progress has been made in identifying the cores currently common to each of the major social work concentrations (casework, group work, community organization), the elements of knowledge, attitudes, and skill they may share (at least on some levels of generality), and the nature of the requirements of some fields of practice (corrections, medical social work, school social work, and so on).[6] The social work profession has made important gains, as a result of all of this, in the form of a unified professional association, plans to cease accrediting "specializations" which do not merit such designation, facilitation of interchange of personnel and experience between fields of practice, and the ability to mobilize maximum resources to face new problems.

Inherent in all this, however, is a significant danger: Social work is a complex institution, a scientific art, and a profession. Much of its essence is lost if we seek to conceptualize its func-

[5] For recent formulations see Werner W. Boehm, "The Nature of Social Work," *Social Work*, III, No. 2 (1958), 10–18, Katherine Kendall, "Services to Individuals and Families," *The Social Welfare Forum, 1957* (New York: Columbia University Press, 1957), pp. 9–14; Helen Harris Perlman, *Social Casework, a Problem-solving Process* (Chicago: University of Chicago Press, 1957).

[6] Harriett Bartlett reports the current efforts in "Toward Clarification and Improvement of Social Work Practice," *Social Work*, III, No. 2 (1958), 3–9; also see Ruth E. Smalley, *Specialization in Social Work Education* (New York: Council on Social Work Education, 1956).

tion, its future, its contribution to social welfare solely in terms compatible with, in fact derived from, a temporarily popular (or even temporarily valid) unifying notion about social work methods. The social work institution involves goals, values, beliefs, apparatus, techniques, as well as its professionals' chief method or methods at a given time. Method is thus only the conscious, goal-directed application of technique by trained personnel—it is not all of social work.

To be even more explicit, Witmer helpfully differentiated between social welfare and social work. We would do well to recall that social work is not only a professional method but is also an institution whose characteristics and functions are not encompassed by the scope of its professional specializations or transitional preoccupations. Since the conceptual keys proposed tend, at least at present, to be based in individual or group adjustive or therapeutic services, this kind of approach inevitably overemphasizes what Wilensky and Lebeaux call the "residual" rather than the "institutional" conception of social welfare and ignores the substantial historical evidence that the nature and specific function of social work (and thus the methods of social workers) must, in fact, reflect the given, changing social situation. Both of these matters require some elaboration.

Witmer's 1942 view of social welfare will be recognized as fitting the description of a residual conception: "social welfare institutions should come into play only when the normal structures of supply, the family and the market, break down." [7] It is true that a holder of this view may emphasize humanitarian values in the service of individuals who need help in adjusting to, or functioning in, social institutions, but the basic assumption is that all things being equal, individuals will do

[7] Harold L. Wilensky and Charles N. Lebeaux, *Industrial Society and Social Welfare* (New York: Russell Sage Foundation, 1958), p. 138; see also the remainder of that chapter.

well without these special welfare services. We need social welfare if institutions or individuals do not function adequately or if problems arise in their interrelationships. Given such a conception, methods directed to relieve stress, solve individual problems, help people use services, or promote adjustment seem to be the unique, characteristic, appropriate, and sole social work claim to professional competence.

Such a view, it has been pointed out, hardly takes account of the newer attitudes to security in our culture since the great depression and the increasingly popular notion that "welfare services . . . [are] normal 'first line' functions of modern industrial society." [8] Social workers, among others, see social welfare provisions and programs as essential components of modern life, as "normal" and "proper" as the more traditional social institutions. We argue for educational services, health agencies, housing programs, income maintenance provision, as matters of right in the modern world and as social inventions essential to all complex societies. In effect, social workers tend to believe in this institutional formulation of social welfare, rather than in a residual role, on the basis of their conception of society and of human rights. Our definitions of social welfare and social work and our methodological conceptualizations, however, lag. The profession will not meet the demands of the future unless it sees the residual function as one already far too narrow and pursues the ramifications of a social structure in which so-called "welfare services" are part of basic institutional arrangements. Social work, it is true, may be a profession largely (but not solely) concerned with serving social welfare programs, but we understate our functions if ours is a residual view of social welfare programs, or if our conceptualization of the social work profession assumes such a view.

[8] *Ibid.*

Needs, Rights, and Social Work

The conviction that this is the direction derives from analysis of the interrelationship between needs and rights and consideration of major social dynamic factors in modern society. Most discussions of social welfare programs inevitably develop a "needs" rationale, but the literature, unfortunately, shows substantial confusion in concepts. The difficulty is compounded by the fact that social planning councils and community organizations require one of several kinds of operational definition of needs, depending on the situation at the time, while casework and group work practice generally have another orientation.[9]

Clarity for purposes of the present discussion may be achieved if we avoid the usual debates as to which are the universal, basic human needs and begin instead with the sociological-anthropological notion of functional prerequisites to group survival. Most such discussions agree that human groups tend to survive and to thrive in accordance with the degree to which they successfully organize appropriate institutions and activities to:

1. Maintain the biological functioning of group members (provision of food, shelter, clothing, and resolution of biological drives).

2. Produce and distribute goods and activities ("economic" activities).

3. Reproduce new members (social rules and arrangements).

4. Socialize new members into functioning adults.

[9] Maas and Wolins, *op. cit.*; Genevieve W. Carter, "Practice Theory in Community Organization," *Social Work*, III No. 2 (1958), 49–57; Charlotte Towle, *Common Human Needs* (New York: American Association of Social Workers, 1952).

5. Maintain internal order and order between the group and outside groups.

6. Maintain meaning and motivation (religion, philosophy, aspects of culture, and so forth).[10]

Obviously, the content of these activities must vary with such factors as history, geography, technology, and culture and with the relations between a group and its neighbors. Moreover, the activities are closely interrelated. For example, a relatively simple society may subsist with a primitive technology, relatively isolated, with simple social group and governmental structures. Its socialization system raises children whose physical and social appetites are conditioned by the group's potentials and experiences.

A modern society cannot survive unless its citizens are raised to master a much more complex technology, thereby producing food, shelter, clothing, and other requirements of survival. Arrangements for socialization—education, rules about reproduction and creation of new families, and systems of motivation—are correspondingly appropriate to the new situation.

Looked at from the perspective of the psychology of the individual, one might say that the selfsame biological drives are differently directed for members of different social groups. (For the moment, our reference is to different societies; it might just as well be to different social subgroups in one society.) The goals toward which biological drives are directed are affected by resources, technology, and the many other factors affecting the requirements of the society at a given moment. The body restlessness or discomfort that is recognized as hunger may be directed at a corn-meal cake or at caviar, at fried grasshoppers or at roast guinea hen. Given a period of tension-relief through achievement of a given goal,

---

[10] There are many such listings. For one, see John W. Bennett and Melvin M. Tumin, *Social Life* (New York: Knopf, 1948), Ch. IV.

however, the drive is converted into a motive. Now tension and energy are mobilized and selectively directed.

We may all need x calories, but the kind of food which makes us salivate is determined by our experiences in a group. The group, in turn, molds those experiences by its possibilities, its resources, its prerequisites to survival. It can, for example, make fish our major food or a taboo food, depending on its own requirements. Similarly, one group may satisfy its clothing demands through animal skins, another through cottons, a third through the use of grasses.

Social groups, sharing common developmental conditions, train and educate their members to have common motives. The illustrations in relation to food and clothing may be duplicated in relation to social rules and arrangements (i.e., whom does one seek to marry); economic institutions (i.e., what is the model of a successful provider); systems of socialization (i.e., what kind of education is to be required of all); methods of maintaining order (i.e., what crimes are most serious); and systems of religion and motivation (i.e., what patterns of conduct lead to salvation).

For present purposes, and in somewhat oversimplified and schematized fashion, it is enough to note that the forms which group prerequisites to survival take are determined by the many conditions surrounding the group and that these, in turn, find their way into the psychology of the individual by the ways in which drives are converted into motives. In short, a universal biological restlessness and tension eventually becomes a *need*. From this perspective, we all have minimum biological requirements, but at the level of consciousness the individual has needs which have been socially molded, shaped, and defined. The need is the manifestation in the individual of a group's functional prerequisite to survival, as shaped by that group and brought to consciousness through group experience.

Needs, in this sense, change with changes in the fate, orientation, and technology of the social group.

It is thus possible to identify a dynamic process with the following components:

1. As a group's experiences develop in any given area, more and more individuals successfully channel drives in a specific way and accept the goal involved; the motive becomes common (i.e., to behave in a certain way, receive certain recognition, have certain shelter, eat specific food).

2. The motive is articulated and appropriate, supportive attitudes are attached to it. (One *ought* satisfy the drive this specific way).

3. The attitudes become widespread, and we talk of a general or universal *need*, meaning both that the goal is the appropriate way for the drive to be channeled and that all people *should* have the need met (i.e., have ways of achieving the goal).

Cardoza illustrates the process in these words in *Helvering* v. *Davis*, a case supporting the constitutionality of Title II of the Social Security Act: "Nor is the concept of social welfare static. Needs that were narrow or parochial a century ago may be interwoven in our day with the well-being of the nation. What is critical or urgent changes with the times . . ." [11]

4. The next step in the process is the legal guarantee that the need will be met in the recommended way (i.e., the legal establishment of a *right*): the society has set up ways to assure the meeting of the need, and the individual's need satisfaction is backed by law.

(The discussion is confused by the the fact that we sometimes talk of "moral right," which is another way of describing the "ought" phase in identification of need. Another source of confusion arises because legal rights are not always enforced.

[11] *Helvering* vs. *Davis*, 301 U.S. 619 (1937).

Nonetheless, the crucial thing about a right is that it is justiciable.)

At this point in the discussion it becomes possible to describe a function of social work which is at the core of the institution in the middle of the twentieth century. In addition to staffing direct services (many of which are outgrowths of the residual functions Witmer describes so well), social work devotes a substantial portion of its professional and lay energies to the identification and recognition of needs which emerge in society as a whole or in social subgroups, with changing social conditions. Social work articulates the need, studies its characteristics and its implications. Social work plays its role, along with other professions and citizens at large, in assuring the creation of institutional structures (sometimes but not always social welfare services) for need satisfaction and, where appropriate, assuring legal guarantees of need satisfaction, that is, assuring the translation of needs into rights.

When needs are not met within the existing institutions and require new institutional provision, the consequence is sometimes new social welfare services. The latter are best conceived, not in Witmer's terms as services to fill gaps in usual or "normal" institutional arrangements, but as social inventions to meet new situations and, themselves, new parts of what become the *usual* institutional arrangements. Other segments of society are also alert to needs and develop ways to meet them; sometimes through normal market channels, at other times through educational, religious, or other institutions. The distinctive characteristics of social welfare solutions as suggested by Burns, Wilensky and Lebeaux, and others are:

1. Formal organization—an organized social response to need.

2. Social sponsorship and accountability—purposes and methods are socially sanctioned and there are mechanisms to express public interest and to assure that the service is ac-

countable to the larger community. Services may be public or voluntary.

3. Absence of the profit motive—the criteria and motives of the market economy do not prevail.

4. An integrative view of human needs, whereas many other social institutions have a segmental approach to people— individual agencies are specialized, but the social welfare field is inclusive. It has a comprehensive view of the individual's personality and his requirements and does not limit itself to one phase of human life. (This would exclude the schools.)

5. Concern with human consumption needs—as contrasted, for example, with those governmental services which, while performing vital functions (Army, post office, conservation), are involved only indirectly in the fate of the individual.[12]

This does not deny the role of welfare services vis-à-vis the broader economy but stresses the aspect which is essential to qualification as social welfare. Nor does this underemphasize that newly developed needs must sometimes be met outside social welfare. There is no reason to assume that the remainder of the institutional structure will remain static.

Social welfare services require many kinds of resources and personnel. A children's institution, for example, may need cottage parents, doctors, maintenance staff, psychologists, cooks, secretaries, and personnel in many other categories, in addition to social workers. Similarly, another program may require technicians and case aides as well as professionally trained social workers. Social work as a whole is, nonetheless, devoted to manning social welfare services and to creating both new social welfare services and new arrangements for meeting need through other institutional arrangements. Its uniqueness derives not from any one methodology; for its

[12] Wilensky and Lebeaux, *op. cit.*, pp. 140–47; and Eveline M. Burns, "How Much Social Welfare Can America Afford?" *The Social Welfare Forum, 1949* (New York: Columbia University Press, 1950), pp. 57–78.

practitioners, like members of all professions, are constantly developing, improving, and changing its methodology. Nor does it have a monopoly on the democratic value core or humanitarian tradition which sets its direction, since these are widely shared. As in the case of social welfare as a whole, however, crucial to social work is an integrative view of needs. The U.N. survey stressed that other programs and institutions are able

to exclude all save certain specific aspects of the socio-economic environment from their purview. . . . The social worker, on the other hand, cannot exclude from his consideration any aspect of the life of the person who seeks help in solving problems of social adjustment . . . [or any] of the community's social institutions that might be of use to the individual . . .[13]

The real commitment, and the unique nature of the entire social work institution, its professionals and lay supporters, its technicians and its volunteers, is not to any one method or even to one concept but rather to human need in the sense indicated. The role is dynamic—and never completed. The danger is the loss of that flexibility essential to the recognition of new horizons and the undertaking of consequent responsibilities.

A Dynamic Profession

For as long as society grows and changes, individual need will change. Changing need must be articulated, interpreted, and established as legitimate. Where primary social institutions or the institutions of the market place are unable to respond, social welfare services must be established, given form and content, and manned. These do not become residual services,

[13] *Training for Social Work: an International Survey*, p. 13, as quoted by Wilensky and Lebeaux, *op. cit.*, p. 144.

supplementary services, or "last-resort" services, however, but part of the normal arrangements in a modern society. In all of this, social workers may serve in therapeutic roles, through direct service, in group leadership positions, or as administrators, policy personnel, researchers, social actionists, and planners.

To use the phrasing of E. H. Carr, government in our age and, we might add, all of society, has passed from a "night watchman to a social service or welfare state, dedicated to equality of opportunity, freedom, protection of the rights of all and to provision of a basic underpinning to essential needs." [14] Social work is committed, in this evolving scene, to encourage implementation of needs in a manner consistent with concern for individual dignity, legal rights, democratic institutions, and that maximum self-realization of people which does not infringe on the rights of others.

As long as society continues to hold such values high it is possible to predict a broad and important role for social work. Because, in our search for security, we would not lose the values which motivate the search, we face complex problems of organization and professional methodology. The recipient of public assistance will become a more responsible member of society and not a passive, "pauperized" sponger on the public—but only if public assistance is well-administered. The probationer in a court dedicated to rehabilitation and individualization will not see in his experience evidence that the community is "soft" and "dumb"—but only if the service is well-manned and led.

Social work must remain humane, never losing its concern for the condition of man, and flexible, so that major new needs do not escape it. Its task is never completed, but it functions

[14] Edward Hallett Carr, *The New Society* (Boston: Beacon Press, 1957), p. 87.

on progressively new levels, as man's aspirations and potentials grow. It is truly "science at work in furthering human values." [15]

What situations now confront Americans? What are the new factors conditioning American social work?

The Scene

Despite the stress on new situations and new needs one should perhaps emphasize that not all the well-known gross social problems have been solved, and it is far from true that all Americans now enjoy the much sought "health and decency" standard of living. We write and talk as though there were one social situation everywhere, when even if the horizon is limited for the moment to the American scene alone, there is tremendous range and variation. We cannot, for example, ignore the reports that 9,000,000 children under eighteen years of age live in families with the completely inadequate annual income of $2,000 or less. Nor is it possible to minimize the consequences of the fact that while the annual per pupil expenditure for public education was $535 in the highest ranking state in 1957–58, the lowest ranking state spent $164.[16]

Similar data might be cited about housing. Seventeen million Americans reside in dirty, rat-infested buildings decayed beyond rehabilitation. Much remains to be done in relation to infant mortality, a field in which the national rate is 26.0 deaths per 1,000 live births per year, while in some states the rate is considerably higher, and the nonwhite national rate is 42.1. In fact, the rate for nonwhites is more than three times that for whites in several states. There is no shortage of causes

[15] Eduard C. Lindeman, as quoted by Nathan E. Cohen in "Professional Social Work Faces the Future," *Social Work Journal,* XXXVI (1955), 85.

[16] Research Division, National Education Association, *Estimates of School Statistics, 1958–59* (Washington, D.C.: the Association, 1958), Table 10, p. 27.

around which to rally if some children are born under circumstances which lead to 35.9 deaths per 1,000 (New Mexico as a whole), or 89.8 per 1,000 (Wyoming nonwhites, 1956), while others are born where the rate is 20.1 per 1,000 (Nebraska or South Dakota, 1956).[17] Data might also be presented to show unequal access to basic resources, opportunity, or services in other fields.

Basic services have been created in very few places to deal adequately with mental illness and delinquency. Criminals and mentally ill persons are only now being recognized as victims or products of forces in their social environments and worthy of individual consideration and real treatment. The required facilities and skills are seldom brought together for a scientific rehabilitative effort. Even where public attitudes support such an approach, knowledge is incomplete and resources are in short supply.[18]

Medicine, too, has had to renew its old fights and to render its basic, initial services while at the same time turning to new horizons. Not ignoring the extreme, long-known needs not yet met, social work must continuously take account of newer elements in the scene. While the present context permits only a relatively brief, impressionistic statement, the following seem particularly relevant at present:

1. *Our population is changing in its age composition through high birth rates and increases in longevity.* In the immediate future, a relatively smaller proportion in the "middle" group will have to produce, economically, enough to support and supply larger numbers of young (and the not-so-young whose education is extended) and old (who live longer but whose

[17] "Infant Mortality," U.S. Department of Health, Education, and Welfare, *Vital Statistics*, XLVIII (September 29, 1958), 351.

For housing data, see Editors of Fortune, *The Exploding Metropolis* (New York: Doubleday and Co., Inc., 1958).

[18] Alfred J. Kahn, "The Untried Weapon against Delinquency," *Federal Probation*, XXII, No. 3 (1958), 11–15.

productivity either ceases or decreases). This will demand, in fact already demands, a variety of social inventions, institutional arrangements, and new services ranging from pension and retirement plans to provision for young children while mothers work, from leisure-time programs for senior citizens to efforts to help the "new" families consider the roles of, and their own relationships to, their senior family members.

2. *Rates of internal population mobility continue to mount.* How can we have stable families and neighborhoods when one family in five, on an average, moves each year and household relocations range over the entire country? The changes brought about by the new age composition of population require family cohesion, mutual support and dependence, yet population mobility pushes us in other directions. What are to be the new sources of family and neighborhood cohesion? Where is the continuity in norms and value integration to be based?

3. *Rates of technical and social acceleration seem constantly to increase.* In the words of Charles Frankel, ours has become an "age of acceleration." Is it possible, somehow, to affect or to overcome constantly increasing gaps in perception and appraisal of social situations on the part of young people and their parents, teachers, or authority figures in general? What of the differential rates at which social change affects various population subgroups? If we do not deal effectively with such matters, there is little hope that school tensions will be resolved, or that the high rates of delinquency and rejection of the educational experience will be decreased.

4. *Population mobility and increased availability of mass media (particularly television) tend to decrease regional differences and to create a national community.* Will regional and cultural diversity decrease rapidly? If so, is this to be resisted? How? If, on the contrary, the process should be encouraged, how and to what ends?

5. *This is the era of the great metropolitan centers.* The

bulk of the American population has moved from the countryside to the town, to the city. Now the movement is out of the
city to "the urban fringe that rings each of the great cities and
extends far into the countryside." How long it will go on, nobody knows. The new suburbanite may reside in or near a
semirural area, but his cultural orientation is to the large city to
which he commutes [19] and the city continues to "explode" in
the sense of both expansion and disintegration. Certainly, there
will be need to organize our structure of government and
system of financing all governmental services to take account
of this new situation. Even the location and interrelationship
of community services need examination, but we must not
delay efforts to grasp the implications for daily living. Will
the suburb create new primary group forms and thus make up
for the frequent separation from relatives and neighborhood
friends? Can this process be facilitated? Will the new residential areas fail to recreate the primary group values which
once characterized the town? What of the attack on the
suburb as an instrument of excessive conformity which replaces
some of the positive aspects of the privacy and multiple relationships of the city? [20]

6. *Rapid technological change, particularly the development
of automation and of atomic power, requires high competence
from, and extended training of, ever larger proportions of the
labor force.* Moreover, there will be major changes in work
organization, supervision, and systems of payment. There are,
consequently, major problems of motivation, of preserving interest in the humanities while specialization continues, of use
of leisure time, of protecting the dignity of less specialized or

[19] Rockefeller Brothers Fund, Special Studies Project, *The Pursuit of
Excellence: Education and the Future of America* (Garden City, N.Y.:
Doubleday and Co., Inc., 1958), p. 5.
[20] William H. Whyte, *The Organization Man* (Garden City, N.Y.:
Doubleday Anchor Books, 1957), Part VII.

less complex occupational roles.[21] All of this gives emphasis, too, to a problem long central to a democratic society, that of assuring equality of opportunity in a manner consistent with encouraging the pursuit of excellence.[22]

7. *All these influences have so affected primary group relationships as to cause high rates of personality disturbance and breakdown.* Social workers know the phenomena firsthand. How are these effects to be prevented and/or treated? Are the new institutions such as counseling, guidance, advice, and treatment services prepared for their major roles technologically and philosophically?

8. *Our society is facing a great shift in concepts and patterns of intergroup relations.* Although there are numerous forms to this development, its two major manifestations are the legal establishment and national enforcement of the right to integration of Negroes in education and public services and the trends toward their more complete social integration in large cities outside the deep South. The process is characterized by reversals, tensions, conflicts, setbacks—and by significant gains. Democratic society faces no greater challenge and no more complex problem. Have we the knowledge and skill to deal with its human aspects, to overcome the consequences of prejudice, discrimination, hysteria—and entrenched institutional practices?

9. *Our complex, specialized society requires comparably complex organization to assure synchronization, order, continuity, dependability.* "Bigness" in industry, labor, education, community size, and all other aspects of life seems to follow.

[21] A full discussion of the implications of automation is outside our scope here. See, for example, "Social Consequences of Automation," a special issue of the *International Social Science Bulletin*, Vol. X, No. 1 (1958). There are many other possible ramifications for social welfare than those to which we have alluded. The problem of new work incentives is clearly put by Carr, *op. cit.*, chap. iii.

[22] Rockefeller Brothers Fund, *op. cit.*, pp. 15–17.

How are basic goals and values to be protected against the perversions which occur when essential bureaucratization goes to pathological extremes? Is it possible to guard individual creativity and initiative in an environment full of "hidden persuaders" who encourage an "organizational man"? [23] Whether one thinks of social welfare programs or of society at large, it is clear that ways must be found to balance the needs of the organization with the integrity of the person. Provision for the effectiveness of the group must be considered along with measures to give play to the creativity of the individual. There are certainly some implications in all of this, many of them not yet clear, for systems of organization, for group programs, for education.

Speaking to the National Conference on Social Welfare, Max Lerner said: "If we are to expand the functions of social welfare, we can do it only by bringing the human personality and the human condition back into the center of human concern." [24] What knowledge, means, programs, does social welfare have for this task? What can the social work profession offer?

In prior periods, social work settlements, charity organization societies, "child-saving" agencies, and others dealt with the earlier consequences of immigration, urbanization, and industrialization. They were modern society's response to the breakdown of primary group supports and to the consequences and demands of modern life. They played, for the most part, what we have called "residual" roles. The great depression which began in 1929 was the occasion for the transition to a broader perspective with which social work confronts the newer social dynamics outlined above.

[23] *Ibid.*, p. 14; also Whyte, *op. cit.*, and Vance Packard, *The Hidden Persuaders* (New York: David McKay Co., Inc., 1957).

[24] Max Lerner, "What Kind of American Civilization?" *The Social Welfare Forum, 1957* (New York: Columbia University Press, 1957), p. 47.

It is not yet clear whether the trends outlined are completely out of control and, as yet, unmastered, or whether they already contain the seeds of new solutions and positive forces, as Wilensky and Lebeaux hold. The latter point to new patterns and sources of stability and new tendencies toward integration in American society: new forms of primary group life in the city; rapid adaptation by internal migrants; personalization even of market relations; new family patterns which contribute to solidarity; the tendency of bureaucratic industrial organization to regularize other areas of life; the additional stability provided by large secondary associations (church, trade union, veterans' organizations); the "filtering" of mass media by local influences.[25] Ohlin adds:

The social organization of our society is so complex that total integration and control is virtually inconceivable in the face of a constantly growing population. The internal and external pressures toward change in American society are . . . demanding. . . . The fact is that organizational requirements of ideological conformity in our time are matched by the necessity to furnish the conditions for personal and social growth so that the creativity needed to maintain organizational integrity in times of rapid social change will be fostered . . .[26]

Not many hours away, if one computes by the standards of the jet age, there is the evidence that other "solutions," which violate our basic values, continue to be offered as alternatives. Thus, while it is good to have a statement of some of the major social issues and problems of the day balanced with these positive notes and sources of reassurance, none can hold that modern society will master satisfactorily the newer forces enumerated without constant reaffirmation of, and rededication

[25] Wilensky and Lebeaux, *op. cit.*, chap. v.
[26] Lloyd Ohlin, "Conformity in American Society," *Social Work*, III, No. 2 (1958), 64.

to, basic democratic, humanistic values, as well as planning, legislation, new programs, new social inventions. There will be roles for government and for voluntary associations. Many disciplines, professions, and segments of society will contribute in their specialized ways. The social work profession too will have to adapt to these new requirements if it is to continue to play its role as a profession attuned to emerging needs.

Directions for Social Work

Social work's potential contribution will be realized only as it makes itself felt, and finds ways to function, in relation to a wide range of social situations. There are, first, the social work agencies and programs (i.e., where social work is the "host" profession), then the broader social welfare services in which social work has played essential leadership or adjunctive roles in the past. The changing social scene makes it essential, however, that social work contribute to new social institutions and new phases of community life.

To use a rather obvious analogy, medicine would lose major ground if it put all its efforts into refinement of general practice and strengthening of hospitals alone, even though these activities continue to require the major portion of its personnel on all levels, as well as the bulk of its funds. Public health, preventive medicine, and medical research are recognized parts of American medicine, if one thinks of it in institutional terms, and these fields of work have clear claims on personnel and resources. (Nor, incidentally, to refer to another point, is it considered essential, except on a high level of generality, to establish that the concepts and methods in public health or medical research are identical with those of the general practitioner. Moreover, the practice of medicine and the development of medical programs is recognized as requiring professionals other than physicians, in addition to subprofessionals, technicians, aides, and volunteers in a variety of categories.)

None of this justifies deprecation of the professional practice of social work as a scientific art, or suggests that the traditional areas of social work service or practice are any less important than they have been. Social work's broader impact on society should be based on a deepening and an enrichment of competence in the more traditional areas, lest the new forces of the day inundate what has been developed in the past. The role projected, in fact, requires many more well-trained professional social workers. Rather, the task is, first, one of constant strengthening and expanding basic social work services which have emerged in the past (child welfare, family casework, child guidance, group work in community centers, and so forth), incorporating new knowledge and skill, and assuring the responsiveness of services to social milieus. Second, it is necessary that social work appropriately deploy professional personnel in the light of a strategy related to the total demands upon it. Third, it is essential that we not assume that all those issues or factors unrelated to the technical aspects of practice by professionally trained personnel are of only peripheral concern to social work.

Social work's unique orientation, in its broad sense, grows out of a value core and perspective which we have described as characterized by concern for person-in-situation, and group-in-community, community-in-society, or, in short, an integrative view of the individual or the human situation. This, rather than one methodological key, is what is crucial. Social work has concentrated its efforts in social welfare programs which are, as noted, formally organized under social, nonmarket auspices; accountable to the public; concerned with consumption needs, broadly conceived. The social work potential for a unique contribution to other social institutions resides in this selfsame orientation. The social worker in local government, foreign service, city planning, recreation, urban renewal, education, community development, or in any of the new or forthcoming areas, begins with whatever is applicable from the core of knowledge and skill available to casework, group work, and community organization. Eventually, new developments in social work method and process, relevant to these new centers of activity, will take place and become part of the general sum of social work knowledge and skill. The social worker in these newer settings becomes only one more staff member if his performance does not grow out of, and base itself on, his special perspective.

Prior to a more specific discussion of roles which already appear appropriate to social work, we might note that social work, as an institution, and services rendered by social workers, obviously ought to be constantly examined and evaluated from a social work viewpoint, as should all major institutions affecting the daily well-being of many people. Reform begins at home. Growth in size of programs and organizations and increased specialization in service hold the same hazards for social work as for other segments of American society. Planning, close supervision, and much coordination become vital to survival of programs, yet they, in turn, may "produce a ritualistic and compulsive adherence to detailed rules and regulations which is so characteristic of the bureaucratic organization and its dominant personality types." An alternative solution is the creation of close ideological or value conformity within staffs.[27] Yet, the consequences may be the stifling of essential flexibility and creativity, internal conflicts within staff members, and inadequate concern for the client because of the requirements of the "system."

There has been far too much evidence that clients and opportunities to serve clients are often "lost," not because in-

[27] *Ibid.,* p. 60.

dividual agencies do not wish to act responsibly and not because individual practitioners are lax. Rather, we have not countered some of the pathological consequences of bureaucratization of social services through: development of devices for client-centered accountability (so that a "case," once "found" is retained on a community roster and assigned to a responsible agency until there is a common decision to close it); systems of coordination appropriate to the service concerns of the programs; educational means of emphasizing that the social worker's success is to be judged ultimately by the outcome of the service and that the evaluation of professional process is only a step en route to that. Finally, the ultimate conquest of the problem demands a constant review, highlighting, and redefinition of community goals in establishing programs and the nature of the agency responsibility involved in them. Or, to return to the phrasing of an earlier section, the major preoccupations should always be: What are the central needs to which the program is addressed? What individual rights are being implemented? What new social developments require creative, goal-oriented responses?

The Variety of Roles

Social work's tasks and objectives imply readiness to discard old, inappropriate roles and to assume new ones with the changing requirements of the times. Any listing must, therefore, reflect both long-established and still valid responsibilities, as well as some predictions as to what may, or should, come into being. The following would seem to have claim on social work energies, resources, and manpower on all levels:

1. *Individual and group corrective, adjustive, and therapeutic services.*—This catchall title may serve to encompass much of what has long been the core and, quantitatively, the bulk of social work services. Many of these services are well

conceptualized by Witmer's notion of services to help individuals solve their difficulties within social groupings (family, peer group, and so on) or in adjusting to, or making use of, social institutions and services (school, hospitals, recreation, etc.). For the moment, we need not explore the issue of whether the psychotherapeutic aspects of these endeavors are adequately conceptualized in Witmer's formulation. Certainly, much of the work here is with people under stress, people facing difficulties in relationships or in use of social resources, people who must deal with the realities of deprivation and unmet need, children in need of substitutes for family care, people often encountered initially because of problems in social functioning.[28] Both individual and group methods are appropriate. The setting may be the home, foster home, agency office, a group residence, or a variety of social institutions.

2. *Services whose major contribution is to normal socialization and social control.*—The group worker may be in either a therapeutic or an adjustive relationship, as above, or may develop a program which seeks to enrich group experience in a manner which takes account of individual differences and needs and, at the same time, promotes sound group goals. Family agency staff may conduct parent education programs designed to facilitate sound child rearing and healthy family life. Other social workers may staff neighborhood self-help programs or encourage the launching of tenant organizations in housing projects as a contribution to healthy community activity and relationships. In short, this type of individual, group, or direct community service should be differentiated from the first category to emphasize social work's concern for, and contribution to, *normal* individuals, groups, and communities. This realm of action has, too often, been appended to discussions of social work activity through inclusion of "prevention" as a role. It is far more satisfactory to state directly

[28] For example, see Kendall, *op. cit.*, p. 10.

that social work considers itself qualified to contribute to individual socialization and enrichment of experience in certain phases of community life—without the fiction that this is only justified because otherwise maladjustment will follow and adjustive services will be necessary. This is another way of repeating that social work has more than a residual social role.

3. *Planning and coordination services, related specifically to social welfare.*—Social work goals and ideology require coordination of services as well as constant planning in relation to changing needs, availability of resources, new knowledge, and new methods. Agency methods, functions, and responsibilities require adjustment and change as required by the times. Programs must be periodically evaluated and their effects measured. There is need, too, for assurance of integration of services to the individual case, on the operational level, as between agencies, and provision for agency case accountability vis-à-vis the community.[29] A variety of functions is involved, including community organization, research, administration, case supervision, and some aspects of individual casework.

4. *Services which contribute to the formulation and implementation of social policy.*—The reference here is not to the responsibility of every practitioner to be alert to newly emerging need, resource lacks, problems in agency programs. Such responsibility is certainly basic to the social work tradition and ethic. The reference is rather to a specialized social work role long established on a small scale, but obviously of extreme importance and requiring major expansion if the premises of the early part of this discussion are correct. The central concern of professionals in this area has to do with the ways in which major social policies affect the well-being of individuals and communities.

Traditionally, social workers have given their attention to

[29] Alfred J. Kahn, *For Children in Trouble* (New York: Citizens' Committee for Children of New York City, Inc., 1957).

government policy in relation to the social insurances and public assistance. Some other social welfare areas, such as health and housing, have also had both attention from, and some staffing by, social workers. There are many other fields and assignments crucial to social policy which have used social workers occasionally or which could make use of them on a significant scale. Social workers may, for example, serve as consultants to housing authorities in tenant selection and development of services in public housing, or as consultants in development of programs of improved intergroup relations. Some social workers may be social welfare attachés in American embassies, learning of foreign developments of value and interpreting our programs abroad. In the past, problems of civilian defense and evacuation policy required participation of some personnel with social work orientations.[30] Social workers in other roles may contribute to a variety of areas of government and community life, from public policy with regard to school-leaving age, child labor, or handling of young offenders to urban renewal strategy, tax policy as it affects wage earners, consumer problems, and keeping local government attuned to community needs.

However broad this listing may seem to be, it follows from the premises that social work has a distinct responsibility and contribution in relation to need-recognition, need-articulation, and need-implementation, and that social work has a distinctive perspective on society out of which emerge suggestions for policy and its implementation. The functions performed by social work professionals in these areas might include consultation, research, administration, public education, social planning. Social workers might, too, staff social action or community organization agencies which develop and promote social policies, as well as participate in this field through the

[30] Richard M. Titmuss, *Problems of Social Policy* (London: His Majesty's Stationery Office and Longmans, Green and Co., 1950).

social work professional associations. Social work agencies will also require the services of other disciplines and considerable lay support in this work as well.

5. *Research activities essential to evaluation of services and their ultimate improvement.*—Research has been described elsewhere as a component of professional accountability.[31] Social workers are under obligation to measure the consequences of their activities. As professionals who rely on the adequacy of their theory about people and situations, they have need to elaborate, test, and expand their knowledge core. The substantive implications of this are dealt with elsewhere in this volume but we might note two components which ultimately merge: (*a*) studies of people, groups, situations, and problems which add understanding of the nature and extent of need and the form which should be taken by the variety of direct and indirect services which social work renders: (*b*) studies of the consequences of methods, process, and their subcomponents, designed to increase the effectiveness of social worker intervention or of other services. Some of these studies may use social science conceptual tools and, in turn, contribute to social science theory. Others may rely largely or solely on the conceptualizations developed within social work and may contribute to their validation and elaboration. At various levels, practitioners, supervisory personnel, members of other disciplines, and social work research personnel may be involved in these research activities.

This type of classification of social work roles may encompass no more than Boehm's listing of social work functions as "restoration," "provision of resources," and "prevention." [32] It probably parallels the suggestion of the Commission on Social

[31] Alfred J. Kahn, "Facilitating Social Work Research," *Social Service Review*, XXX (1956), 331–43.

[32] Werner W. Boehm, "The Nature of Social Work," *Social Work*, III, No. 2 (1958), 10–18.

Work Practice of the National Association of Social Workers that social work practice seeks: (*a*) to resolve or minimize individual or group problems arising from disequilibrium with the environment; (*b*) to identify and prevent potential disequilibrium; and (*c*) to strengthen individual, group, and community potential.[33] If the listing has any justification, then, it derives from the stress on social work's commitment to the normal as well as to the disadvantaged and the maladjusted, and from the effort to demonstrate that social work's internal logic should carry it into a wider circle of social institutions, given the present tendencies of modern society. Modern social work is neither "poor law" nor "charity organization." It is not "child saving" or "corrections." It is an institution which has evolved out of all of these and encompasses their present forms, but it is also a key instrument for what might be called the "humanization" of the superurban society in the age of the atom, automation, and the organizational man.

A Dream or a Program?

How much of this is possible? Does social work have the manpower, resources, support, prestige, and competence to undertake these broad roles, these many functions? Would it not be wiser to narrow the perspective and to urge a more modest program?

As has already been suggested, although not articulated as such, the recent tendency has been in the direction of the more modest outlook. Despite some major exceptions and important deviations, the line of development in American social work from the 1920s to the 1950s has involved a concentration on "function" rather than on "cause," in Porter Lee's sense,[34]

[33] Bartlett, *op. cit.*
[34] Porter R. Lee, *Social Work as Cause and Function and Other Papers* (New York: Columbia University Press, 1937).

and the consequent preoccupation with the shaping and refinement of method.[35] The latter effort has played a major part in the strengthening of social work services and education and the growth of the profession as a whole. One of its most recent by-products, as noted earlier in this discussion, has been the movement to find a central core, a unifying key, around which a social work theory and method might be formulated. Since the range of services, situations, roles, and relationships of social work demands more than could possibly be encompassed by a theory so derived, we have tended to narrow our horizons to what could be so conceptualized. The institution of social work, as depicted through the resultant efforts in the major social work methods of group work and casework, is narrower in responsibility, potentiality, and scope than what is possible, desirable, or actually observable! While all are and have been ready to agree that the picture of one worker helping one client, under stress, through a controlled relationship, is not the only social work pattern, it is a model which has continued to determine major directions of the field in education, research, and writing.

Many social workers have found this tendency attractive, because intensive cultivation of any one vineyard may yield much—and also, perhaps, because a number of professions close to social work have moved toward specificity of function. Range and change mean uncertainty; new roles require new beginnings. It may be easier to hold onto what is good, valuable, accepted, and obviously much needed, and to leave all the rest to other groups.

This view has its obvious appeal, but consideration of the line of social development in the United States suggests that if social work will not encompass its appropriate roles in relation to broader phases of community and national life, if it will not give new and adequate attention and energies to social

[35] Cohen, *Social Work in the American Tradition,* chap. v.

policy, planning, community organization, and social action, new professional groups will have to appear. There are needs to be met, services to the created, vital functions to be filled. Moreover, the internal requirements of such new professional groups might very well lead them to parallel social work in many ways and, eventually, to join with it or to compete with it for the right to service. There is already a series of such situations confronting the profession. For example, large segments of the field of intergroup relations are staffed by personnel deriving from backgrounds in human relations, social science, or education.

The view that the direction outlined for social work thus seems almost inevitable does not relieve us of the many problems which stand in the way. Most crucial, of course, is the matter of whether social work actually has, or is in a position to develop and adapt, the value orientations, knowledge and variety of skills essential to the tasks at hand. Brief and definite answers are not possible, but there is impressive evidence in many of the papers in this volume, and in the operating programs which they reflect, that social work can meet the challenge on this level.

New undertakings of this scope require new resources, too. Are these possible? There is every reason to believe that a society oriented ever more to consumer needs and increasingly receptive to new individual and group services, as it is to new technology, will not permit its core values to be lost through failure to provide for the new social instruments demanded by the times. Social work will have to forge its new roles by demonstration, interpretation, and the rallying of support, however. It will have to begin by taking on that which it is able to do, in the conviction that community organization programs will, in time, win backing for social planning services, and that the latter will demonstrate the need for new functions in growing communities. Similarly, successful social action endeavors by a professional social work association and the allies it is able to rally may, in turn, lead to the employment of consultants and social policy personnel whose own work may prepare subsequent steps. Resources may be provided through individual philanthropy, foundation support, and government programs, but only gradually as the claim is justified by demonstrable results, clear achievement, and public backing.

There are other professions and social institutions with knowledge, skill, experience, and large-scale programs in some areas which parallel, overlap, or offer alternatives to social work endeavors. The scope of this development is suggested by an incomplete listing:

1. Marital counseling programs which are staffed by personnel trained in psychology, education, or sociology serve clients also within the scope of family agencies.

2. Educational and vocational guidance services have developed on a large scale in areas in which school social work has sought to function.

3. The boundaries between group work and recreation are far more clear in textbooks than in practice.

4. A number of professions claim competence to perform an integrating role in community development.

5. Members of a variety of professions and academic disciplines are functioning in some of the social policy areas discussed above.

6. There are major inconsistencies and differences of opinion in relation to the appropriate roles and emphases of psychiatry, psychology, and social work in many settings in which they work side by side.

Some of these confusions and unresolved matters are perhaps desirable by-products of valuable experimentation, diversity, and freedom. Some may be inherent in the fact that the helping professions share a "village common" of concepts and procedures. Others will require resolution in the interest of efficiency and the conservation of resources. Social work would do well, in its discussions, experiments, and studies, to clarify for itself where it belongs, and in what roles; it might do this on the basis of what it knows and can offer and consideration of the relationship of any given area to its other areas of activity. The new definition would, however, be in relation to the broader context, not to the residual social welfare concept. We must, of course, also look at what others are able to bring to a situation. Not that the analytic process will, of itself, resolve all these issues; it might, however, help in the design of a social work platform and strategy for direction of de‐ velopment and deployment of resources. It would guide the profession in the decision as to when and how to seek to establish and maintain a claim in a given area, to request essential resources, and to invite new recruits for training.

The ability to attract thousands of young people annually to social work professional training and to involve others as volunteers on many levels and in many capacities may, in the long run, be the only important test of the program here out‐ lined. The issue of "voluntaryism" is discussed elsewhere in the volume. We must face the facts that in many parts of the country it has not been possible to staff major social work programs with qualified personnel and that social work schools train far too few graduate social workers annually to man even the programs characterized as "adjustive" and "thera‐ peutic." It would be the height of irresponsibility to urge that these long-established programs give up personnel to permit the development of new roles. Obviously, recruitment efforts in casework and group work, and for current community or‐ ganization programs, require both support and expansion.

No, it is another perspective that is here projected. Let us continue the appeal that has attracted good personnel to social work in recent decades, but let us also put forth another kind of call as well. There are other people, perhaps even some other kinds of people, who might wish to devote themselves to some of the newer areas. They would have to be appraised by new criteria and, when we know just how, perhaps even trained in new ways. If welcomed, supported, and permitted to develop, they would give substance to these new directions and attract others. The great social changes of our era have had a variety of effects on the youth of our time. Is there not some basis for the hope that new needs will produce new recruits to man's constant effort to translate technology and organizational structure into happiness? We must discover and welcome these recruits, as social work seeks to evolve in accord with the requirements of the modern world.

Tufts concluded, in his pioneering study of social work education, that "the moral would seem to be that the conception of the field of social work should above all be kept fluid in order to maintain in this profession at least an open mind towards humanity's changing needs and the best methods or agencies for meeting them." [36] In a new era, in which the pressures to codification and delimitation continue strong, we would do well to heed this advice. Our methods must be goal-conscious and our goals responsive to changing needs. If we find ways to achieve this, the results will surpass the smaller, better defined, more immediate prospects to which the pressures of the day constantly lead. Those who began social work and led its development would have no question about the choices.

[36] James H. Tufts, *Education and Training for Social Work* (New York: Russell Sage Foundation, 1923), pp. 30–31, as quoted by Cohen in *Social Work in the American Tradition,* p. 148.

THE KNOWLEDGE BASE OF SOCIAL WORK

ALFRED KADUSHIN

The knowledge base of social work is a comprehensive topic which encompasses the facts and theories, skills and attitudes, necessary for effective, efficient practice. The literature which details what the social worker needs to know, to do, and to feel is almost embarrassingly rich.

Within the last thirty years there have been two reviews of social work education throughout the world.[1] There have been some five general studies of social work education in the United States.[2] Since 1932, when the first curriculum statement was adopted by the American Association of Schools of Social Work, we have had a series of statements embodying changing conceptions of the knowledge base of social work from the national organization primarily concerned with the requirements of sound professional education.

[1] Katherine Kendall, *Training for Social Work: Second International Survey* (New York: United Nations Bureau of Social Affairs, 1955); Alice Solomon, *Education for Social Work* (Zurich: Verlag fur Recht und Gesellshaft, 1937).

[2] James Tufts, *Education and Training for Social Work* (New York: Russell Sage Foundation, 1923); Sydnor Walker, *Social Work and the Training of Social Workers* (Chapel Hill, N.C.: University of North Carolina Press, 1928); James E. Hagerty, *The Training of Social Workers* (New York: McGraw Hill, 1931); Edith Abbott, *Social Welfare and Professional Education* (Chicago: University of Chicago Press, 1931); Ernest V. Hollis and Alice L. Taylor, *Social Work Education in the United States* (New York: Columbia University Press, 1951).

We have had summarizations of the required knowledge base of caseworkers [3] and group workers [4] in particular and a more comprehensive summarization of the knowledge base of social workers in general.[5] The professional organizations concerned with specialized areas of practice, now organized as sections of the National Association of Social Workers, have published statements outlining the required knowledge base of practice in their particular specialization.[6] The American Public Welfare Association has formulated a series of statements outlining the required knowledge base of specialized practitioners in public welfare.[7] There have been special studies of the knowledge base of social workers in specific settings—family service, for instance.[8]

There is a plethora of articles on social work education, supervision, and in-service training which discuss, in varying

[3] American Association of Social Workers, *Social Case Work, Generic and Specific*, a Report of the Milford Conference (New York: the Association, 1929).

[4] "Professional Education for Group Work Practice," *The Group*, IX (1947), 6–9.

[5] American Association of Schools of Social Work, *Towards an Integrated Program of Professional Education for Social Work: Summary and Findings of Four Workshops* (New York: the Association, 1952).

[6] The American Association of Medical Social Workers, *Education for Medical Social Work—the Curriculum Content* (Washington, D.C.: the Association, 1953); National Association of Social Workers, "Essentials in Professional Education for Psychiatric Social Workers, 1955" (New York: the Association, n.d.; mimeographed).

[7] American Public Welfare Association, *The Child Welfare Worker's Job in the Public Welfare Agency* (Chicago: the Association, 1954); American Public Welfare Association, *The Public Assistance Worker* (Chicago: the Association, 1952); American Public Welfare Association, *The Local Administrator in the Public Welfare Agency* (Chicago: the Association, 1958); American Public Welfare Association, *The Medical Social Worker in the Public Welfare Agency* (Chicago: the Association, 1955).

[8] Maurice J. Karpf, *The Scientific Basis of Social Work* (New York: Columbia University Press, 1931).

degrees of comprehensiveness, the knowledge base of social work. We have available a number of articles which explicitly examine the subject.[9]

Moreover, as of this writing, the curriculum study of the Council on Social Work Education, directed by Werner Boehm, is preparing its analysis of the curriculum content of schools of social work. The plan for the study indicates that a need more clearly to delineate knowledge used in social work practice was one of the reasons for the undertaking.[10]

In reviewing the materials at hand, one is struck by their repetitiveness. Old friends appear over and over again in one listing after another. There are differences, of course, especially as we move from statements regarding the required knowledge for one method to another, but the similarities heavily outweigh the differences.

The consensus may be a result of the level of generality at which most listings are pitched. For example, the statement that all social workers need to understand agency function is so general that all would agree with it; this says very little, however.

Perhaps the similarities in the listings may be a consequence of a second characteristic of the statements. With one exception, they appear to have been formulated on the basis of agreement of experts acquainted with practice. They did not evolve out of a detailed analysis of practice. The experts are

[9] Alfred J. Kahn, "The Nature of Social Work Knowledge," in Cora Kasius, ed., *New Directions in Social Work* (New York: Harper, 1954), pp. 194–214; Isaac L. Hoffman, *Toward a Logic for Social Work Research* (St. Paul: Amherst H. Wilder Department of Research and Statistics, 1952), pp. 23–27; Henry S. Maas, "Use of Behavioral Sciences in Social Work Education," *Social Work*, III, No. 3 (1958), 62–69; Harold J. Dumain, "Professional Problems Contingent to Theory," *Journal of Psychiatric Social Work*, XXIV (1954), 47–54.

[10] Werner W. Boehm, *The Plan for the Social Work Curriculum Study* (New York: Council on Social Work Education, 1956; mimeographed), p. 92.

generally professional social workers who, having shared a similar educational experience, are likely to have developed some uniformity in their perception of what social workers need to know.[11] Only Karpf in his study of the knowledge base of the family caseworker attempted this.[12] Perhaps, however, the most cogent explanation for the repetitiveness, and hence near unanimity, regarding the content of the listings lies in the fact that a common core of knowledge exists and is required for effective service in all areas of practice.

In discussing this core, it might be helpful to use, as a framework, the curriculum statement of the Council on Social Work Education.[13] The statement indicates that the knowledge base of social work—the facts and theories, the skills, the attitudes—can be separated into three major areas: social services; social work practice; and human growth and behavior. The social service area is concerned with the organization, administration, and operation of social welfare programs and services, the interrelationship of agencies, historical development of such programs, the nature of the human needs served by such programs. Social work practice is concerned with the actual

[11] The need for a study of practice, rather than the use of expert opinion, as a basis for developing a statement regarding the knowledge base of social work is clearly indicated by Karpf's study. He was able to formulate on the basis of expert opinion a reasonably unanimous statement about what caseworkers in family agencies needed to know. However, an examination of practice failed to show that the practitioner ever employed much of the knowledge he supposedly needed to know.

[12] Other statements may have been based on a detailed analysis of practice, but if so they have not been reported. One might perhaps note Fenlason's attempts to study the knowledge base of casework practice on the basis of a forty-five-page questionnaire. The questionnaire listed units of knowledge, and the worker was asked to evaluate the relative importance of each unit of knowledge to practice. Results were reported in *Studies in Higher Education, 1938–40* (Minneapolis: University of Minnesota, 1941), pp. 156–66.

[13] Council on Social Work Education, *Curriculum Policy Statement* (New York: the Council, 1952; mimeographed).

process of helping the client (individual, group, or community), the techniques of helping, the resources for helping, the appropriate attitudes which enable helping. The third area, human growth and behavior, is concerned with the material necessary for understanding the client in his problem situation, normal and deviant personality development and behavior, the dynamics of individual and group behavior.

Knowledge in all three areas consists of an amalgam of materials both indigenous to social work—developed by social workers for social workers—and borrowed from other disciplines. The interrelationship of borrowed and indigenous material is so inextricably compounded that it is often difficult to distinguish one from the other. Borrowed material is translated, amended, reshaped for use often beyond recognition of the discipline which conceived it. As a matter of fact, there is some contention that the differentiating factor regarding social work knowledge is its unique synthesis of borrowed material. But the nature of the balance, of the ratio, between indigenous and borrowed material differs greatly for the three principal areas outlined above.

The largest knowledge components in the social service and practice areas have been developed by social work for social work. These have been supplemented by borrowing from medicine, political science, economics, sociology, law, and so forth. In the area of human growth and behavior the situation is reversed. Here we depend to the greatest extent on borrowed knowledge, principally from psychoanalytic psychology.

Knowledge Developed by Social Work
for Social Work

To illustrate specifically and exhaustively the nature of the knowledge developed by social work for social work would require the equivalent of a long, detailed syllabus. It might be well, therefore, to illustrate the point by listing such knowledge on three ascending levels of increasing generality and decreasing specificity: on the level of a specific task in a specific setting; on the level of a particular method; and on the level of the total profession.

To illustrate on the most detailed level of specificity, one might inventory the knowledge which the social worker needs, and what he should be able to do and feel, about one specific problem (adoption), in one specific agency (a public child welfare agency), in contact with one specific client (the adoptive applicant), at one specific point in the contact (the screening interview).

In order to offer effective service the worker needs to know the agency regulations regarding age, fertility examinations, and health conditions of applicants. She needs to know the rationale of such requirements and she needs to have achieved some acceptance of them. She needs to know the desirable physical conditions of a good adoptive home, of a good adoptive neighborhood. She needs to know and understand something about the optimum age differential between adoptive parents and child. She needs to know something about the attitudes and feelings which the clients are likely to have regarding the need to come to such an agency, about the likely reactions to the family's sterility, likely responses toward adoption as a way of achieving parenthood. She needs to know what feelings she should appropriately convey so as to free the clients to communicate openly. She needs to know how to implement these feelings by the appropriate verbal and gestural responses to the clients' productions. She needs to know what specific information the agency considers most helpful in arriving at a prompt decision regarding the clients' acceptability and needs to have developed some conviction about the value of such information. She needs to be able to phrase, and intone, the questions soliciting such information in a way that will help the clients to answer fully and truthfully. She must know some of the questions about adoptions, and adoption procedures, which are likely to be troubling the clients and have the skill to answer such questions in a manner which is both understandable to, and accepting of, the client. She needs some knowledge of motives for adoptions and a detailed knowledge of the relationship between certain specific motives and the likelihood of success or failure in adoptions. She needs to know: the diagnostic significance of information regarding the applicants' developmental history, work history, health history, the history and current functioning of the marriage; the clients' conceptions of parenthood, expectations as to the rewards and deprivations of parenthood, expectations about the child they hope to adopt, and their age, sex, nationality, and class preferences in relation to the child they hope to adopt. She must know how the agency came to have guardianship over the children, the procedures of the adoption study, the procedure of matching applicants and children. She needs to know how to pace the interview so that it does not start, or end, on too high an emotional level. She needs to have a knowledge of community resources and the mechanics of making a referral, and the skill to make a referral. She needs to know and accept the significance of her own feelings regarding adoptions and parenthood, her bias in favor of, or against, the children seeking to be adopted and/or the parents seeking to adopt.

Screening interviews can be, and are, conducted by personnel with lower levels of knowledge but not, we feel, with the desired competence. The social worker would need to know, feel, and be able to do all of this and more to render the best service possible. And a substantial part of the knowledge listed has been developed by social workers. One could formulate comparable listings for an impressive number of specific situations in specific settings.

Moving up to a higher level of specificity, one might, illustratively, recapitulate the knowledge, much of it developed by social work, which is thought necessary for effective practice within a particular social work method. Thus, the group worker needs to know something about: the history and development of group work agencies; the functions they currently serve in the community; the structure of group work agencies; the administration of such agencies; the relationship of the agency to the neighborhood, to other social agencies, and to non-social work community agencies. He needs to know how to differentiate his function from that of recreation and adult education. He needs to know about the nature and variety of groups that are likely to use such agencies and the process of formation of such groups. He needs to know about: group cohesion, group morale, group-leadership interaction, group control, subgroup formation; effects of cliques, pairs, isolates; group status structure, group decision-making, group contagion, differential group roles, rejection-acceptance patterns in groups. He needs skill in developing program activities, skill in leading program activities, skill in helping groups plan program activities. He needs to know the activities appropriate for each age level and the patterns of association at each age level. He needs to know the effect on individuals of differentiated group activities and processes and to have skills in helping the individual to use the group constructively.

On a still higher, more general level of specificity, one might illustratively inventory the knowledge and skill developed primarily by social work, which we think all social workers need to have regardless of setting or methodological affiliation. These include: knowledge of the history of social work and the relationship of social work, as a profession, to the society in which it operates; knowledge of social agency organization, administration operation and function; skill in interpreting social welfare programs and services; knowledge of community resources relevant to problems that clients bring to social agencies; knowledge of the nature of human needs which social welfare programs are designed to meet; knowledge of the relationships between the different units of the network of social services in the community and skills in using this network in behalf of the social agency client; knowledge of appropriate professional behavior in relation to clients, colleagues, and other professional persons; knowledge, and acceptance, of the values and philosophical orientations of social work and of the ethics of the profession; knowledge and acceptance of the role of social work, and the social worker in relation to the client; skills in developing, sustaining, and managing a relationship with clients of social agencies; skill in the application of the scientific method—study diagnosis and treatment—in helping the social agency client; skills in interviewing, discussion leadership, committee chairmanship in a social agency setting for social work purposes; skills in constructively using social work supervision and consultation and knowledge about such supervisory, consultative relationships; skill in recording in line with the agency's needs.

We stress these components because of the conviction that they are associated with effectiveness. Once again it can be seen that the listing, although not exhaustive, is heavily weighted with material developed by social work for social work.

In general, the content of the component of the knowledge base of social work developed by social workers is concerned with the specialized facts, theories, skills, and attitudes necessary for helping in a particular way (through social work processes) a particular group of people (social agency clients) around particular problem situations (the problems for which social agencies have accepted responsibility) in a particular frame of reference (social agency setting and service).

One can make the same point, that social work has developed a large component of the knowledge base of social work, by an analysis of the contributions to social work journals. Social workers contributed 78.8 percent of the articles appearing in *Social Work* in the period between 1956 and 1957, in *Social Casework* between 1955 and 1957, in the *Journal of Psychiatric Social Work* between 1952 and 1955, and in the *Social Service Review* between 1955 and 1957.[14] Thus, in reading the literature, social workers turn to other social workers for help in answering their questions.

Furthermore, we are members in good standing of clinical teams in a number of different settings. It is reasonable to suppose (although it may not be true) that we are on the team because we contribute some knowledge which other disciplines cannot contribute—some knowledge which is unique to social work. We are on the teaching staffs of other professional schools, such as medicine and nursing, supposedly, once again, for similar reasons.

Some Characteristics of Knowledge Developed by Social Work for Social Work

The component of the knowledge base of social work which is derived from social work presents some disturbing characteristics. There has been no systematic attempt to validate this knowledge. The border line between social work hypothesis and fact is often tenuous. A seemingly truthful, self-evident hypothesis achieves the status of a fact by sheer repetition. Yet the history of science is strewn with the debris of self-evident propositions.[15]

[14] Clifford R. Roach and Paul G. Zarbock, "A Survey of Selected Social Work Journals to Determine the Influence of the Various Social Sciences" (unpublished Master's thesis, School of Social Work, University of Wisconsin, 1958), p. 114.

[15] One might note, in mitigation, that such a problem regarding knowledge grounded in practice is to be expected. The practitioner faced

For instance, the proposition that adoption frequently has an effect on fertility seems generally accepted among social workers. A study attempting a systematic examination of this hypothesis resulted in its rejection.[16] Yet many workers "know" of instances where conception followed adoption and can cite examples. Do we "know" in those cases what factors other than the adoption were operating to increase the chances of conception? Do we "know" the frequency with which conception does not follow adoption?

To illustrate the point further, one might note the general acceptance of the hypothesis that the client shows a high component of negative ambivalence in applying for financial assistance. Once again the literature is replete with substantiating anecdotal accounts of client reaction. Research gives us a firmer reason to believe, however, that this is true for some groups of clients but not true for other groups.[17]

Involved here is the difference between knowledge based on experience and casual observation as against knowledge formulated on the basis of rigorous, critical, systematic examination.

We are, however, making an attempt to meet the deficiency in systematic validation of the practice wisdom of the profession. Investigations of client motivation and strengths as related to the use of service, conducted at the University of

---

with a client who has serious problems cannot wait for definitive answers. He must use what he has, even if the best has doubtful validity. Nor can he afford constantly to remind himself of the tentativeness of his answers. The practitioner converts hypothesis into certainties because only in this way can he work with the necessary security and assurance. Skepticism about one's tools and a conviction in one's practice are incompatible attitudes.

[16] Frederick M. Hanson and John Rock, "Effect of Adoption on Fertility," *American Journal of Obstetrics and Gynecology,* LIX (1950), 311–19.

[17] Ivor Svarc, "Client Attitudes toward Financial Assistance—a Cultural Variant," *Social Service Review,* XXX (1956), 136–46.

Chicago, might be cited as an example of such efforts. Another heartening example is Polansky's work on the process of relationship-formation in initial interviews.[18]

A second characteristic of knowledge developed by social work for social work lies in the lack of consistent effort to conceptualize such knowledge. This, too, is likely to be more true for the past than for the future.[19]

Failures in this direction deprive the field of knowledge which might be but has not been made explicit. We know more than we know we know. Much effective social work is practiced on the basis of a knowledge which the social worker has not explicitly communicated, not even to himself. Maas's investigations, cited by Polansky,[20] in which interviewers are asked to react to selected interviewing situations and then questioned as to what they would do and why, is a fruitful beginning in making such knowledge explicit, hence communicable, hence transmissible.

Furthermore, and perhaps most important, the conceptualizations which derive from such research are in the lower and middle ranges of levels of abstraction where our needs are most pronounced. For instance, we have, to some extent, systematized some high-level abstractions regarding the worker's approach to the client—concepts such as acceptance, noncondemnation, client self-determination. We have developed

[18] Lillian Ripple, "Motivation Capacity and Opportunity as Related to the Use of Casework Services—Plan of Study," *Social Service Review*, XXIX (1955), 172–93; Norman Polansky and Jacob Kounin, "Clients' Reactions to Initial Interviews—a Field Study," *Human Relations*, IX (1956), 237–62.

[19] Werner Lutz, *Concepts and Principles Underlying Case Work Practice* (Washington, D.C.: National Association of Social Workers, 1956); Eleanor E. Cockerill, ed., *Conceptual Framework for Social Case Work, a Suggested Outline* (Pittsburgh: University of Pittsburgh, 1952).

[20] Norman Polansky, "Getting Down to Cases in Case Work Research," Howard J. Parad, ed., *Ego Psychology and Dynamic Casework* (New York: Family Service Association of America, 1958), p. 275.

some broad treatment typologies—social therapy, supportive treatment, insight therapy. However, between a high-level abstraction, such as self-determination, and the worker's sitting in a room with a client—individual or group—there is a gap in the identification and systematic validation of our knowledge.

Comprehensively to teach a truly professional approach toward applying the abstraction, self-determination, we need to fill this gap. We need to know the specific, repetitive kinds of behavior engaged in by the worker (caseworker, group worker, community organizer) which are the results of his conscious, explicit application of this abstraction. Having identified such units of behavior we would need to know, specifically, the kinds of response which different clients make when they are encouraged to be self-determining. Are they pleased, worried, disappointed, puzzled, uncomprehending? Do they accept it readily, resist it, accept it reluctantly? What is the client's perception of the basis of the worker's offer? Does he see it as indifference, rejection, respect for his autonomy, a result of the worker's inability, or refusal, to provide a solution? What factors are associated with what kinds of reactions to an atmosphere conducive to self-determination—factors such as personality variables exhibited by the client in his characteristic approach to problems (dependent-independent, passive-aggressive, systematic-unsystematic, etc.); factors such as the client's presenting problem; factors such as sociocultural, age, and sex affiliation of the client; factors such as differences in client expectation regarding agency function, operation, and worker's behavior? What differences in reaction are associated with various points in the history of the contact? To what extent are differences in the client's reaction associated with the way the worker makes the offer—explicitly; implicitly in relation to a specific request; formally; informally with sincerity and conviction; as an announcement of agency procedure?

How is worker adherence to self-determination related, not only to the immediate reaction, but to more remote outcomes —client return, client problem-solving, client satisfaction in the relationship? What factors in the personality make-up, group affiliation, education and experience of the worker, are associated with differences in attitudes toward, and approaches to, implementing client self-determination? What is the worker's expectation as to client response and to what extent do these expectations condition client response and the worker's perception of client response? What are the elements in the worker's perception of her role in relation to the client, her definition of appropriate behavior, which relate to her implementation of client self-determination? In short, what we need to know are the specifics of implementation of the abstraction in a particular way with a particular client so that we achieve a particular result.

One might formulate a similar list of questions related to just one aspect of one of the broad treatment typologies currently employed: for instance, the use of money as a sociotherapeutic resource.

The principal point is that we need to fill in the details of our more generalized abstractions. Greenwood's statement that the "prime need in social work today is the construction of diagnostic and treatment typologies"[21] calls, in effect, for filling in the details of our highest level abstraction of process —study, diagnosis, and treatment.

There is no intimation that this is easy. There is merely the conviction that the development of concepts of more limited generality is necessary. As long as we continue to talk only at the two extreme levels—at the level of very general abstraction and at the level of the particular and unique case situation

[21] Ernest Greenwood, "Social Science and Social Work—a Theory of Their Relationship," *Social Service Review,* XXIX (1955), 28. See also Alfred J. Kahn, "Some Problems Facing Social Work Scholarship," *Social Work,* II, No. 2 (1957), 55.

—we will be safe, but not so effective as we might otherwise be.

A third characteristic of knowledge developed by social work for social work lies in the fact that it has a tendency to be noncumulative. Both Little and Goldstine have noted this in their examination of social work literature.[22] Goldstine says:

A review of the literature of medical social work over the last 45 years, as published in various professional journals leads to the conclusion that it shares in the common failure of the social work profession to communicate its experience and thinking by cumulative analysis and synthesis rather than by accretion.[23]

One might speculate about the relationship of this characteristic of the knowledge developed by social work for social work and the fact that, until very recently, Hamilton's textbook was the only one available on social casework, the most highly professionalized method of social work practice.[24]

The noncumulative nature of social work knowledge can be related to the characteristics cited above. If what we know is not clearly established, we cannot with confidence build on it. The tendency is to accumulate and use knowledge piecemeal rather than to make previously established knowledge the base for a further contribution. If what we know is not conceptually organized, we cannot know clearly how to relate any new contribution to those already available.

We can, however, attempt more systematic reviews of what we do know, or think we know. Biestek's [25] review of the prin-

[22] Roger W. Little, "The Literature of Social Case Work," *Social Casework*, XXXIII (1952), 287–90; Dora Goldstine, "The Literature of Medical Social Work: Review and Evaluation," *Social Service Review*, XXVII (1953), 316–28.

[23] Goldstine, *op. cit.*, p. 316.

[24] Gordon Hamilton, *Theory and Practice of Social Case Work* (2d ed., rev.; New York: Columbia University Press, 1951).

[25] Felix P. Biestek, *The Principle of Client Self-Determination in Social Case Work* (Washington, D.C.: Catholic University of America Press, 1951).

ciple of client self-determination as it appears in the casework literature over a period of thirty years is an example of the kind of stock-taking which needs emulation.

The Component of the Knowledge Base Which Is Borrowed

Let us now focus on the nature and problems of the borrowed component of the knowledge base of social work. The ratio of borrowed to indigenous knowledge is heavily weighted in the direction of borrowed knowledge for the third basic area of the curriculum as defined by the Council on Social Work Education, that of human growth and behavior. We owe the greatest indebtedness by far, in this sector of the curriculum, to psychoanalytic psychology or its derivatives. From it we derive our principal knowledge and understanding of normal and abnormal personality development, the dynamics of normal and abnormal behavior, the anatomy of personality, and the mechanisms of adjustment.

Within the last decade there has been a gradual shift in the unquestioned dominance of psychoanalytic psychology as the source of our borrowing for understanding of growth and behavior. Material from the social sciences has been gaining greater recognition and acceptability.

It may be instructive to sketch briefly the shifts in influence of psychoanalytic psychology and social science on social work. These are shifts in an important part of the knowledge base of social work.

The profession of social work is, like all professions, an occupational subculture embedded in the matrix of the larger culture. The dominant ideas and moods of the enveloping culture exert a subtle, but inexorable, influence on the ideas and moods that social workers, as social workers, regard as right and proper.

The period between 1890 and 1915 was characterized, in America, by a great enthusiasm for social reform. It was during this period that a great body of reform legislation was sought to curb the most obvious abuses of capitalist exploitation. Sharp criticism of social institutions was wedded to a buoyant, optimistic attitude in the possibility, and desirability, of improving man's environment.

Social work was, inevitably, responsive to the spirit of the period. Although it was recognized, in a dim, inexplicit manner, that every problem was psychosocial in nature, the emphasis was placed on treatment of the social component of the problem situation. Social work, like society generally, looked to the establishment of a more favorable, more benign environment as the means of helping people to achieve happiness.

Social work, therefore, faced outward and sought to change the client's social environment. Concern with the intrapsychic aspects of the client's situation was not absent; it was merely muted. The prevailing mood of American thought during this period made a sociological orientation the logical approach for social work.

The period of the 1920s was sharply different. It was a period characterized by relative indifference to social reform and apathy toward social problems. The primary focus was on the internal problems of the individual. The generation of the twenties turned its eyes inward.

Wish, an American historian, recapitulating the contrast between prewar and postwar America, says: "Just as the dominant prewar note was sociological, that is, committed to the ideal of social reform by means of cooperative action, so the new era of individualism ushered in a preoccupation with self that was psychological in emphasis." [26]

Once again social work was responsive to the prevalent

[26] Harvey Wish, *Contemporary America* (New York: Harper, 1945), p. 333.

mood of the larger culture of which it was only a part. As always, a process of selective perception operated. Now, because of the atmosphere of the period, social workers were sensitized to "see" more readily the psychological component of the client's problem and to emphasize this. The social component was not absent; it was merely muted. At this time a psychological approach to the problems of the client was more relevant, more culturally pertinent, than the earlier sociological orientation.

Social workers in the smaller world of their professional responsibilities experienced problems which seemed to reflect the truthfulness of the *Zeitgeist* and reinforced the predisposition to adopt a new approach. Many clients seemed inexplicably incapable of responding to the more favorable environment provided by social workers. Reduction in social pressures was somehow not enough.

Consequently, social work was at this time searching for, and congenial to, a psychological approach, and psychoanalytic psychology was the approach of choice. The fact that many considerations combined at this time to make the culture generally, and the occupational subculture in particular, sympathetic and receptive to psychoanalytic psychology had lasting significance for the profession. This was the period during which the pace toward professionalization of social work was greatly accelerated.[27]

The profession, at this time, created a definite organizational structure and apparatus. Many aspects of the profession became codified and institutionalized, with the growing rigidity and resistance to easy reformulation that such structuring im-

[27] One might note that the emphasis on a treatment methodology as against a reform orientation made professionalization possible. We lacked then, and lack today, any adequate scientific base that would make possible professionalization of a social action approach. Psychoanalytic psychology, in offering a scientific base for the professionalization of methods of helping, encouraged the possibility of professionalization, which in turn strengthened this orientation.

plies. Social work was self-consciously developing a professional self-image, a self-image which incorporated indentification with Freudian theory as a component. And, like all self-images of the formative years, this was likely to be persistent.[28]

The direction which American social work took during the twenties was confirmed during the 1930s. Unlike most Western European countries, America did not adopt a comprehensive system of social security until 1935. This permitted the establishment and growth of a rich network of voluntary agencies. Until the late 1930s, tax-supported, governmentally administered social work did not exert any significant influence on professional developments in the field. The apparatus of professional social work was largely dominated and controlled by private, voluntary agencies, and most professionals were trained for work in such agencies.

When the Federal Government, in adopting its social security program in 1935, refused to channelize financial aid through the private family service agencies, these agencies were forced to emphasize functions other than relief granting. They chose to stress help with personal problems, for which a psychiatric orientation was supposedly most effective. Stating this same point somewhat differently, Wilensky says the fact that public agencies took over financial assistance freed "large numbers of the professionally-minded in voluntary agencies from the responsibility of dispensing relief and gave them the opportunity of developing still further their technical interest in the psychology of the individual." [29] A focus on this function

[28] Neither social group work nor community organization, both of which might have been expected to keep social work more sharply oriented toward the social environment, was sufficiently professionalized during the greater part of this period actually to exert any appreciable influence.

[29] Harold L. Wilensky and Charles N. Lebeaux, *Industrial Society and Social Welfare* (New York: Russell Sage Foundation, 1958), p. 327.

meant a continued, more intensive focus on psychoanalytic theory. Since the demands of the generally private casework agency "shaped the curriculum of schools of social work" [30] and since the curriculum of the school shaped the thinking of the professional social worker, the demands of the private casework agency ultimately confirmed the orientation of the field— an orientation sympathetic to psychoanalytic psychology.[31]

The Rediscovery of the Social Sciences

Once having been initiated, trends such as the reliance of social work on psychoanalytic psychology achieve functional autonomy, and no further explanation is needed to account for continuation. The practice is institutionalized in the organizational apparatus, the literature, the education of the profession; and in the process of being socialized to the occupational subculture, new recruits are educated to an acceptance of this body of theory. The fact that the orientation is accepted explains continued acceptance. Change takes place, but it is generally as a revision rather than a rejection of the old.

American social work has been undergoing such a revision during the past ten years. During this decade, social work has been actively seeking to borrow from the social sciences, particularly sociology, anthropology, and social psychology. Eaton notes that until "recently training in general personality theory [in schools of social work] was largely restricted to psychoanalysis. Since World War II, however, other behavior science approaches are being added." [32]

The literature of the field has seen a rash of articles on the

[30] Hollis and Taylor, *op. cit.*, p. 12.

[31] The exclusiveness of the tie to psychoanalytic psychology is overstated. Social science exerted a constant, if attenuated, influence on social work between the two world wars.

[32] Joseph Eaton, "Whence and Whither Social Work?" *Social Work*, I, No. 1 (1956), 15.

relationship of social science to social work.[33] Studies have been made which have attempted to apply sociological principles to social work practice.[34] A book of readings of social work and the social sciences has been published, as has a case book on sociocultural elements in casework.[35] A limited number of articles by sociologists is appearing in social work journals. Coyle indicates that "an examination of the curricula of fifty-two accredited schools of social work in the United

[33] Henry S. Maas, "Collaboration between Social Work and the Social Sciences," *Social Work Journal*, XXXI (1950), 104–9; Research Department, Welfare Council of Metropolitan Los Angeles, "Social Sciences and Social Work," *Special Report Series No. 28* (Los Angeles: the Council, 1951); Stanley P. Davis, "The Relation of Social Science to Social Welfare," *Social Work Journal*, XXXII (1951), 4–8; Kimball Young, "Social Psychology and Social Casework," *American Sociological Review*, XVI (1951), 54–61; Elizabeth Herzog, "What Social Work Wants of Social Science Research," *ibid.*, pp. 68–73; Werner W. Boehm, "Social Work and the Social Sciences," *Journal of Psychiatric Social Work*, XXI (1951), 4–7; Boehm, "Social Work and Social Sciences," *Mississippi Quarterly*, IX (1956), 43–55; Otto Pollak, "Exploring Collaboration between Case Work and Social Science in Practice," *Social Work Journal*, XXXIII (1952), 177–83, 209; Grace L. Coyle, "New Insights Available to the Social Worker from the Social Sciences," *Social Service Review*, XXVI (1952), 289–304; Donald Young, "Sociology and the Practicing Professions," *American Sociological Review*, XX (1955), 641–48; Greenwood, *op. cit.*, pp. 20–33; Herman D. Stein, "Social Science in Social Work Practice and Education," *Social Casework*, XXXVI (1955), 147–55; Arthur Hillman, *Sociology and Social Work* (Washington, D.C.: Public Affairs Press, 1956); Alfred J. Kahn, "Sociology and Social Work: Challenge and Invitation," *Social Problems*, IV (1957), 220–27; Grace L. Coyle, *Social Science in the Professional Education of Social Workers* (New York: Council on Social Work Education, 1958).

[34] Otto Pollak, *Integrating Sociological and Psychoanalytic Concepts* (New York: Russell Sage Foundation, 1956); Pollak *et al.*, *Social Science and Psychotherapy for Children* (New York: Russell Sage Foundation, 1952).

[35] Herman D. Stein and Richard A. Cloward, *Social Perspectives on Behavior* (Glencoe, Ill.: Free Press, 1958); Council on Social Work Education, *Socio-cultural Elements in Casework: a Case Book of Seven Ethnic Studies* (New York: the Council, 1953).

States reveals that a considerable body of knowledge drawn from sociology and anthropology is now being introduced into their curricula." [36] There have been a number of workshops at annual Council on Social Work Education meetings devoted to the cultural component in the social work curriculum.[37] Some agencies are beginning to use social scientists as consultants, and schools of social work now frequently include on their faculties social workers who have advanced training in the social sciences. The doctoral programs of schools of social work frequently offer a heavy concentration of social science courses.

What accounts for the change? One explanation lies in the claim that it is the social sciences rather than social work which have changed. American sociology and anthropology of the post Second World War period are supposedly less preoccupied than previously with classification, quantification, and questions of method. Many of the concerns of the social scientist today are closer to the professional concerns of social workers than were the interests of the social scientist between the two wars.

Secondly, many reputable American anthropologists and sociologists have themselves been greatly influenced by psychoanalytic psychology. Although often not acknowledged as such, and sometimes directly repudiated as such, many currently discussed social science ideas owe a great debt to the concepts of psychoanalytic psychology.

Two leading American sociologists stated that "in the deepest

[36] Coyle, *Social Science in the Professional Education of Social Workers,* p. 25.

[37] American Association of Schools of Social Work, *Workshop Report—the Cultural Component in the Social Work Curriculum* (Milwaukee: the Association, 1950; mimeographed), American Association of Schools of Social Work, *Workshop Report—the Cultural Component in the Social Work Curriculum* (Toronto: the Association, 1951; mimeographed).

sense our debt is to the work of the great founders of modern social science, among whom we may single out Durkheim, Freud and Max Weber." [38] The war both accelerated a more utilitarian orientation on the part of the social scientists and developed their familiarity with psychoanalysis. Hinkle says:

While participating in government projects during World War II, many sociologists became familiar with other behavioral sciences. They engaged in interdisciplinary research of such war related problems as army life, German national character, leadership, war morale, propaganda and communication. Not uncommonly, psychoanalytic concepts and theories were introduced into description and interpretation of these studies.[39]

Consequently, social workers do not have to move far when they move from an orientation focused on psychoanalytic psychology to one which borrows more liberally from contemporary social science.

A third explanation lies in the fact that social work has not changed but contemporary psychoanalytic psychology *has* changed. Since the war, psychoanalytical psychology has discovered social science, and social work has followed psychiatry in this shift of interest.

American psychoanalytic psychology has moved steadily from a concentration of focus on instinctual problems to a consideration of ego problems. The greater emphasis on the ego prompts a greater interest in the social environment of the patient. This prompted the psychiatrist to become more sociologically oriented. Weisskopf notes that "psychoanalysis has become a naturalized American citizen by undergoing marriage to the social sciences. The Americanization of psychoanalysis

[38] Talcott Parsons and Edward Shils, *Toward a General Theory of Action* (Cambridge, Mass.: Harvard University Press, 1951), p. 52.

[39] Gisela S. Hinkle, "Sociology and Psychoanalysis," in Howard Becker and Alvin Boskoff, eds., *Modern Sociological Theory* (New York: Dryden Press, 1957), p. 596.

meant its 'socialization.' " [40] Similarly, Sanford states that "the story of our relations with Freud's ideas is the Americanization of Freudian psychology. Our own particular version of Freudian psychology . . . is less biological and more social." [41]

The *rapprochement* between social science and psychiatry, noted above, was thus reinforced by the *rapprochement* between psychiatry and the social sciences. This is evidenced by growing interdisciplinary research (particularly in social psychiatry, which is now recognized as a legitimate subfield of sociology) and by interdisciplinary conferences.[42] As a consequence, "the union of the two makes the social science of today more compatible and more useful to social casework." [43]

A further explanation lies in the increasing confusion as to clearly defined roles between the psychiatrist and the social worker as they work closely together—especially in child guidance clinics. Out of an attempt clearly to establish their uniqueness, many social workers began, in their thinking, to return to the traditional role of the social worker—the role of the expert on the social aspects of the case situation. The role requires a more sophisticated, more detailed knowledge of the social science material. Putting the "social" back in social work called for a *rapprochement* with the social science.

A fifth explanation lies in the impetus given to the awareness of what the social sciences can contribute to social work given by the program sponsored by the Russell Sage Foundation, an organization which for a long time has been close to American

[40] Walter Weisskopf, "The Socialization of Psychoanalysis," *Contemporary American Psychoanalysis and the Future* (New York: National Psychological Association for Psychoanalysis, 1957), p. 51.

[41] R. N. Sanford, "Freud and American Psychology," *Sociological Review*, VI (1958), 50.

[42] *Culture and Personality—Proceeding of an Interdisciplinary Conference* (New York: Viking Fund, 1949); Francis Hsu, *Aspects of Culture and Personality* (New York: Abelard-Schuman, 1954).

[43] Charlotte Towle, *Some Reflections on Social Work Education* (London: Family Welfare Association, n.d.), p. 18.

social work. The Foundation decided to give "main emphasis . . . to the improvement of the relation of research to practice in the disciplines and professions concerned with social behavior." Pollak's studies [44] exploring the contribution social science could make to the child guidance clinic were encouraged and supported by the Foundation. The Foundation, moreover, provided the services of a social anthropologist in cooperation with the New York School of Social Work to explore the contribution of anthropology to social work education and later added important backing to the social science and research components of the doctoral program of the School.

At the School of Applied Social Science, Western Reserve University, the Foundation sponsored a three-year project "whose purpose was to explore the potential contribution of the social sciences to the school's program of education for the profession of social work." [45]

A sixth explanation lies in the fact that the sector of the field concerned with public welfare programs has gradually achieved sufficient respectability and sufficient power in the apparatus of the profession so that the demands for its particular training needs must be accorded respectful attention. Public welfare has always felt that the reliance on psychoanalytic psychology was not the most relevant to its own responsibilities. It pressed for a greater emphasis on social science content. The case for such content grew stronger as the position of public welfare in the field of professional social work grew stronger.

Perhaps a further explanation lies in the impact of the Second World War on social work. The prolonged depression of the thirties had called insistent attention to the social environment of the client. In itself, the depression did not seem to be

[44] Pollak, *op. cit.*; Pollak *et al.*, *op. cit.*
[45] Coyle, *Social Science in the Professional Education of Social Workers*, p. 1.

sufficient to force a reorientation of social work. The depression was reinforced by the war. The social environment, once again, clamored to be recognized as a factor contributing to difficulties in social functioning. What the depression alone could not accomplish, the depression plus a war helped to achieve.

This perhaps lengthy digression into history is of significance in establishing an important point regarding borrowed knowledge. The point is that the criterion of relevance to the profession's principal functions—the functional importance of knowledge we seek to borrow—has been only one, and not always necessarily the principal one, of the many factors which determine the source from which we borrow.

The shift from an almost exclusive dependence on psychoanalytic psychology for an understanding of growth and behavior does not involve a major reorientation of the focus of social work. The personality, clinical, and therapeutic orientation is still dominant. Social science material is being used primarily to enhance a more comprehensive understanding of personality development and behavior rather than to reemphasize social action. In the Preface of a book on readings from the social sciences for social workers,[46] the editors note that they are presenting "salient materials on the social environment which provide a deeper understanding of human behavior," materials which give a "socio-cultural perspective to our understanding of human behavior."

The personality, behavioral focus is evident also in the nature of the social science materials most frequently cited as candidates for our attention. These relate to the sociocultural determinants of behavior—culture and subculture, role, social stratification, the concept of the reference group. Both F. Kluckhohn and Teicher have advanced culture as an important concept for borrowing. Maas and Treudley have explicitly

[46] Stein and Cloward, *op. cit.*, pp. xv–xix.

delineated the applicability of the concept of role to social work practice.[47] The services of the child guidance clinics have been studied with respect to the effect of class position on client behavior.[48] Concepts borrowed from the social sciences have been applied to the culture of social work itself.[49]

Group work has begun an adaptation of material on group dynamics, small groups, and social stratification.[50] Community organization is receptive to material from the sociology of social organizations regarding the power structure of the community and the bureaucratic structure of complex organizations as well as to material regarding intergroup relations.

[47] Florence Kluckhohn, "Cultural Factors in Social Work Practice and Education," *Social Service Review*, XXV (1951), 38–47; Morton I. Teicher, "The Concept of Culture," *Social Casework*, XXXIX (1958), 450–54; Research Department, Welfare Planning Council, Los Angeles Region, *Building Social Work Theory with Social Science Tools* (Los Angeles: the Council, 1954), Special Report No. 41; Mary B. Treudley, "The Concept of Role in Social Work," *American Sociological Review*, IX (1944), 665–70.

[48] Henry Maas *et al.*, "Socio-cultural Factors in Psychiatric Clinic Service for Children," *Smith College Studies in Social Work*, XXV (1955), 1–90; Herman D. Stein, "Socio-cultural Factors in Psychiatric Clinics for Children," *Social Service Review*, XXX (1956), 9–19.

[49] Otto Pollak, "The Culture of Psychiatric Social Work," *Journal of Psychiatric Social Work*, XXI (1952), 160–65; Research Department, Welfare Council of Metropolitan Los Angeles, *Toward a Sociology of Social Work* (Los Angeles: the Council, 1953), Special Report No. 37.

[50] Grace L. Coyle, *The Relation of the Research Center for Group Dynamics to the Practice of Social Work* (New York: American Association of Group Workers, n.d.; mimeographed); Ronald Lippitt, "Applying New Knowledge about Group Behavior," *Selected Papers in Group Work and Community Organization*, National Conference of Social Work (Raleigh, N.C.: Health Publications Institute, 1951), pp. 7–17; Gertrude Wilson and Gladys Ryland, "Social Classes: Implications for Social Group Work," *Social Welfare Forum, 1954* (New York: Columbia University Press, 1954), pp. 169–86.

Problems Regarding Borrowed Knowledge

There are some recurrent problems associated with borrowing knowledge. My principal concern here is not with the repeatedly noted barriers to borrowing, such as the difficulties in communication due to the fact that each discipline develops a specialized vocabulary of useful terms or gives idiosyncratic meanings to words in general use. Nor do I wish to review the nature of the barriers due to difficulties in communication resulting from differences in thought ways between the scientist's striving for basic generalizations as against the technologist's concern with specific application, or the concern of the academician with explicit degrees of reliability as against the clinician's readiness to accept and use whatever is helpful without worrying about its reliability. These are aspects of the basic scientist's orientation toward the development of knowledge for its own sake and the orientation of the practitioner toward usable answers [51] and action.[52] My concern here is more with the hazards of borrowing than with the barriers to borrowing.

One hazard lies in the fact that interdisciplinary movement of knowledge is likely to involve a greater time lag than intra-

[51] For detailed discussion of such problems see: David G. French, "The Utilization of the Social Sciences in Solving Welfare Problems," in *Proceedings of Symposium—Social Work Practice in the Field of Tuberculosis,* Eleanor E. Cockerill, ed. (Pittsburgh: School of Social Work, University of Pittsburgh, 1954), pp. 15–30; Robert C. Angell, "A Research Basis for Welfare Practice," *Social Work Journal,* XXXV (1954), 145–48.

[52] Along these lines, Merton's perceptive analysis of the differences between the American and the European approach to knowledge may be pertinent. Social work, influenced by psychoanalytic psychology, has a tendency to be in the European tradition, and some of our impatience with the American social scientist's concern for "adequacy of empirical data at any price" may stem from this. See Robert K. Merton, *Social Theory and Social Structure* (Glencoe, Ill.: Free Press, 1957), pp. 439–55.

disciplinary movement of the same knowledge. We are therefore more likely to borrow yesterday's knowledge than today's
knowledge. For instance, the excellent compilation of readings
in the social sciences for social workers mentioned above includes a study, first published in 1946, of the effects of class
and caste affiliation on child rearing practices.[53] More recent
studies have, however, resulted in modifications of the conclusions of this report.[54]

Secondly, we are likely to endow borrowed knowledge with
a greater degree of certainty than is granted it by the discipline which originally developed this knowledge. We are often
not aware of the intense disagreements among different sectors
of the "lending" discipline regarding the validity of the knowledge we borrow. For instance, social workers regard asthma
as a primarily psychosomatic complaint, giving emphasis to
the psychological component as the crucial etiological factor.
Yet a host of medical experts differ enthusiastically with the
psychiatrists on this.[55]

We are avidly borrowing the concept of culture and, presumably, we have accepted some definition of this, yet Kluckhohn [56] was able to collect some 257 different, and sometimes

[53] Stein and Cloward, *op. cit.*, pp. 419–31.

[54] E. E. Maccoby and P. K. Gibb, "Methods of Child Rearing in
Two Social Classes," in W. E. Martin and C. B. Stendler, eds., *Readings
in Child Development* (New York: Harcourt Brace Co., 1954); Allison
Davis and R. J. Havinghurst, "A Comparison of the Chicago and Harvard Studies of Social Class Differences in Child Rearing," *American
Sociological Review*, XX (1955), 438–42. A comprehensive review
of the material on class differences in child rearing is contained in
Urie Bronfenbrenner, "Socialization and Social Class through Time
and Space," in *Readings in Social Psychology*, E. E. Maccoby, T. M.
Newcomb, and E. L. Hartley, eds. (New York: Henry Holt and Co.,
1958).

[55] D. Leigh, "Asthma and the Psychiatrist; a Critical Review," *International Archives of Allergy*, IV (1953), 227–46.

[56] A. L. Kroeber and Clyde Kluckhohn, *Culture: a Critical Review of
Concepts and Definitions* (Cambridge, Mass.: Peabody Museum, 1952).

contradictory, definitions, developed by social scientists, of this concept.

A third hazard lies in the fact that we are likely to borrow a simplified version of the truth—and one falsified to the degree that it is simplified. Bowlby's study *Maternal Care and Mental Health* [57] has been warmly received by social workers. The book, however, either ignores or mutes many of the complexities of the problems of mother-child separation—complexities which are clearly recognized and discussed by Bowlby and his associates elsewhere.[58]

The last two mentioned dangers—those of certainty and simplification—derive from the fact that the borrower is not in the best position critically to evaluate the knowledge he borrows. Yet we have, perhaps, the responsibility of being as critical as other borrowers. For instance, Spitz's work on "hospitalism" [59] has made its way, through many sources, into the literature of both social work and psychology. Psychology, however, in contrast to social work has attempted a highly critical examination of Spitz's research.[60]

Coyle points to the danger of "confusion of identifications which seem to be a common result of inter-professional borrowing" [61] —a confusion which is intensified when we borrow teachers as well as knowledge from the "lending" discipline. There are even now occasional warnings that we will have

[57] John Bowlby, *Maternal Care and Mental Health* (Geneva: World Health Organization, 1951).

[58] Mary D. Ainsworth and John Bowlby, "Research Strategy in the Study of Mother-Child Separation," *Courier,* IV (1954), 105–31.

[59] René Spitz, "Hospitalism: an Inquiry into the Genesis of Psychiatric Conditions in Early Childhood," in *Psychoanalytic Study of the Child* (New York: International Universities Press, 1945—), I, 53–74.

[60] Samuel R. Pinneau, "The Infantile Disorders of Hospitalism and Anaclitic Depression," *Psychological Bulletin,* LII (1955), 429–62.

[61] Coyle, *Social Science in the Professional Education of Social Workers,* p. 12.

only a minor achievement if we move from being little psychiatrists to being little social scientists.

A further hazard lies in the danger that the borrowed material will remain an undigested lump in the body politic of social work, interesting but unintegrated and unused. To ensure its use the applicability of the borrowed material to the practitioner's work will have to be demonstrated.

As a technology we are concerned with achieving "controlled changes in natural relationships via relatively standardized procedures that are scientifically based." [62] As a species of the genus technology, practice is concerned with changes in human beings. As the subspecies social work, in the species practice, in the genus technology, we are concerned with changes in the social relationships of human beings.

Sociology and anthropology are also concerned with social relationships, but as basic sciences they are not directly concerned with the problems of change. Selected subdivisions of the basic sciences, however, which are in the nature of derived sciences standing between the basic sciences and the technologies, are more directly concerned with the problems of change in social relationships. Medical sociology, social gerontology, industrial sociology, social psychiatry, the sociology of social disorganization and social control, correctional sociology and penology, are examples of such subdivisions.

By sharpening our focus and selecting for examination those subdivisions of sociology, or of other social sciences, which are concerned with problems paralleling those faced by specialized social services, we can increase the degree of significance of the material to the practitioner to ensure its use. Some of the social science subdivisions are beginning to develop technological interests which should increase for us the meaningful-

[62] Greenwood, "Social Science and Social Work—a Theory of Their Relationship," p. 24

ness of borrowing from these particular areas. For instance, 12 percent of the members of the American Association of Marriage Counselors are sociologists whose sociological subspecialization is in the field of marriage and the family. They are attempting to relate social science concepts to the counseling situation.[63]

The highest levels of abstractions, the kind we might borrow from the basic sciences, are perhaps less useful at the present time than more limited theories closer to the empirical base of our actual current practice.

While all social workers have need for a common core of knowledge and, consequently, can look to the same sources for some material, the differentiation of function between casework, group work, and community organization requires that each group look to different sources for pertinent material of special interest to the method. There may be elements within one area of social work—casework, for instance—which are specific to it, of little practical importance to other social workers, but which are held by caseworkers in common with other professions—clinical psychology, vocational counseling, educational guidance, and counseling. Interchange between caseworkers and these professions may, therefore, be particularly fruitful for casework; interchange with the same professions may have less relevance for other social workers. Hence, to ensure meaningfulness we need more specificity as to the most profitable sources of borrowing for each of the principal methods of social work.

Similarity in the nature of the problem situation of mutual interest to social work and the area to which we might look for help is one kind of similarity that should guide borrowing so as to ensure usefulness.

[63] See, for instance, A. R. Magnus, "Role Theory and Marriage Counseling," *Social Forces,* XXXV (1957), 200–209.

Similarity in the skills employed to promote change should be another guide to borrowing. Recognizing the differences in setting and purpose between social work interviews and other kinds of interviews, studies by sociologists and social psychologists on the specifics of interview interaction contain many valuable leads for social workers.[64]

Similarity in the process employed to promote change should be another guide to borrowing. Recognizing once again that there are differences between casework and counseling, guidance, psychotherapy, it can be maintained that there are many similarities as well. On the basis of the similarities in the helping process we can turn to these sibling fields for meaningful borrowing.

Meaningfulness is a function of relevance. Borrowing is meaningful because it can be related to our needs. The last hazard in borrowing which I would like to make explicit is the hazard that what we borrow, or fail to borrow, may be a function of factors other than our needs.

Here I should like to pick up the point I made at the conclusion of the historical digression on the direction of our borrowing. The point made was that the criterion of relevance to the profession's functions—the functional importance of the borrowed knowledge—has been only one (and not always necessarily the principal one) of the many factors which determine what we seek to borrow. This I think is true today.

Are we fitting our needs to our borrowing, or are we borrowing to fit our needs? Is the movement in the direction of incorporation of social science material in answer to a felt need

[64] K. Merton, M. Fiske, and P. Kendall, *The Focused Interview* (New York: Bureau of Applied Social Research, Columbia University, 1952); Herbert H. Hyman *et al., Interviewing in Social Research* (Chicago: University of Chicago Press, 1954); Robert L. Kahn and Charles F. Cannel, *The Dynamics of Interviewing—Theory, Technique and Cases* (New York: John Wiley and Son, 1957).

on the part of the practitioner? Has a study of practice demonstrated that there were gaps in understanding for efficient, effective service which the material would fill?

My own bias lies in the belief that this material is helpful. I cannot substantiate the belief at this point by pointing to the fact that social workers educated to an awareness of this material (for example, at agencies which have had sociologists on their staff) are, as a result, performing more efficiently and effectively. However, I am not making the point to decry the currently more sympathetic response to social science.[65] I am making it principally to call attention to the fact that because factors other than relevance to need are operating, we seem to be denying ourselves access to knowledge which might be valuable.

It is difficult to prove a negative fact. Yet the lack of any apparent organized effort to borrow from clinical psychology, an effort which is clearly apparent as regards the social sciences, may support the contention that the knowledge coming from this area has for us little perceived availability.

Hoffman, in discussing the relationship of social work to the social sciences, says:

What impresses me is that there has been relatively little cross fertilization between clinical psychology and social work in its common areas of concern except on an essentially procedural and operating-structure basis. . . . In terms of logical connection and interdisciplinary relationship the areas of common concern as well as of difference are far greater for social work and clinical psychology

[65] I would feel much more secure in my bias regarding the usefulness of social science to social work if I knew that we had studied our practice, identified our gaps in knowledge, raised a series of questions which we want answered, and were approaching the social sciences with these practice questions in mind. My own guess is that we are apt to be disappointed in the knowledge borrowed from social science because it deals with questions relative to the social sciences rather than questions formulated by social work.

than they are for any of the other professions with which social work has contact.[66]

As a practice technology grounded in a basic science concerned with controlled changes in the area of interpersonal relationship, knowledge from clinical psychology might have much relevance to our needs. But, as noted above, other factors operate to determine what we do, or do not, seek to borrow.

The nature of the other factors in this instance are speculative. Zander in his study of the role relations in the mental health professions points to the alliance of social worker and psychiatrist against the psychologist.[67] Does the competition with psychology for acceptance by psychiatry lead us to minimize the potential contribution of clinical psychology to our knowledge base? We seek to maintain a clear differentiation from the psychologist. Would borrowing from the clinical psychologists emphasize our identification with them and consequently make more difficult the efforts at differentiation?

We have accepted considerable knowledge about the nature of a helping relationship and the helping process from psychiatry. Do we hesitate to turn to psychology for additions or amendments to such knowledge because this might be regarded as a betrayal of, or disloyalty to, psychiatry, a betrayal and disloyalty not involved in borrowing from sociology and anthropology? Are we threatened by valid divergencies between knowledge about process borrowed from psychiatry, which we have already incorporated, and what we might learn from psychology? Do we regard psychology as a Johnny-come-lately to the clinical setting and so tend to an *a priori* derogation of any contribution it might make to our knowledge base?

[66] Isaac L. Hoffman, "Research, Social Work and Scholarship," *Social Service Review*, XXX (1956), 29.

[67] Alvin Zander, Arthur E. Cohen, and Ezra Stotland, *Role Relations in the Mental Health Professions* (Ann Arbor, Mich.: Institute for Social Research, 1957), p. 123.

Psychologists are, it seems to me, doing imaginative research on the process of therapy [68] and the outcome of therapy,[69] on the components of the counselor's contributions to the therapeutic relationships,[70] and on the characteristics of the good counselor both with individuals [71] and groups,[72] on the effects of factors such as age and sex on therapy [73] and the effect on the client of certain specific procedures employed by the interviewer; [74] on the counselor's ability to recognize the nature of the client's feelings,[75] on the values and limitations of interview recording,[76] and on methods of systematically analyzing the content of interviews.[77] I would venture to guess that

[68] Carl Rogers, "The Case of Mr. Bebb—the Analysis of a Failure Case" and "The Case of Mrs. Oak—a Research Analysis," in Carl R. Rogers and Rosalind F. Dymond, eds., *Psychotherapy and Personality Change* (Chicago: University of Chicago Press, 1954).

[69] E. I. Sheerer, "An Analysis of the Relationship between Acceptance of and Respect for Self and Acceptance of and Respect for Others in Ten Counseling Cases," *Journal of Consulting Psychology*, XIII (1949), 169–75.

[70] Hans Strupp, "The Psychotherapist's Contribution to the Treatment Process," *Behavioral Science*, III (1958), 34–67.

[71] Fred E. Fiedler, "The Concept of the Ideal Therapeutic Relationship," *Journal of Consulting Psychology*, XIV (1950), 239–45.

[72] Morris Parloff, "Some Factors Affecting the Quality of Therapeutic Relationships," *Journal of Abnormal and Social Psychology*, LII (1956), 5–10.

[73] Desmond S. Cartwright, "Success in Psychotherapy as a Function of Certain Actuarial Variables," *Journal of Consulting Psychology*, V (1955), 357–63.

[74] D. V. Bergman, "Counseling Method and Client Response," *Journal of Consulting Psychology*, XV (1951), 216–24.

[75] Dorothy K. Ried and William Snyder, "Experiment on Recognition of Feeling in Non-directive Therapy," *Journal of Clinical Psychology*, III (1947), 128–35.

[76] Bernard J. Covner, "Studies in Phonographic Recordings of Verbal Material; Four Written Reports of Interviews," *Journal of Applied Psychology*, XXVIII (1944), 89–98.

[77] F. Auld and E. Murray, "Content Analysis Studies of Psychotherapy," *Psychological Bulletin*, LII (1955), 377–95. Some of the best studies done by psychologists on the process and outcomes of therapy

few articles in the journals of sociology would evoke more emphatic responses from social workers, in all settings, than, for instance, Rogers's article on the nature of the helping relationship [78] or the symposium by psychologists on a social work movie, "Head of the House." [79]

If relevance to our needs were the primary factor in determining the direction in which we turned for help, we—at least casework—should currently be developing a more active interchange with psychology. The answer may, however, lie in a more fundamental question. Relevance to our need may not be the primary factor in determining borrowing simply because we are not clear as to what is relevant. This is a perennial problem of social work and the fundamental problem in establishing a firm knowledge base. In 1931 Karpf noted that it was necessary to answer the question of what is social work and who is a social worker "if the processes and procedures of social work were to be analyzed for determining the type of knowledge on which they are based." [80] Yet the answer was not available then. Nor is it available today.

Both clarity about the nature of our professional functions and an examination of practice in terms of those functions are necessary before we know what knowledge is relevant to the task we set ourselves—what knowledge developed by social work we need to systematize, conceptualize, and validate and what knowledge we need to borrow. Does the triteness of this

---

are contained in the following three compilations: Arthur H. Brayfield, ed., *Readings in Modern Methods of Counseling* (New York: Appleton-Century-Crofts, Inc., 1950); Carl Rogers and R. Dymond, eds., *Psychotherapy and Personality Change* (Chicago: University of Chicago Press, 1954); and Hobart O. Mowrer, ed., *Psychotherapy— Theory and Research* (New York: Ronald Press, 1953).

[78] Carl Rogers, "The Characteristics of a Helping Relationship," *Personnel and Guidance Journal*, XXXVII (1958), 6–16.

[79] "Behavior Theories and a Counseling Case—a Symposium," *Journal of Counseling Psychology*, III (1956), 107–24.

[80] Karpf, *op. cit.*, p. 2.

statement make it any less true? Clearly, the urgency of the problem is greater. Perhaps, too, there is basis for the hope that we are ready for an answer.

Society has sanctioned the organization and support of agencies to deal with recurrent social problems, problems which arise out of man's relationship to his world of social institutions and other men. This represents the institutionalization of society's offer of help to individuals, groups, and communities.

Society does not dictate the definition of a problem situation —it may be in terms of dysfunction or it may be in terms of enhancing an already adequate functioning. The emphasis is largely for the profession to decide. Society has not granted social work exclusive jurisdiction over the areas with which it is now concerned. Conversely, we are not restricted to the areas for which we currently have responsibility. Acceptance of responsibility for other and as yet unforeseen problems is largely a matter for the profession to decide.

Nor does society dictate how we should help in these situations. We may choose to emphasize social action, individual therapy, prevention, and so on, or a flexible combination of all possible approaches. This once again is largely the profession's decision.

The one demand that society does make of social work, as well as of every other profession, is that we do our job more efficiently, more effectively, more expertly, than if a layman were to do it. This is the only justification for the existence of a profession. The professional engineers a better bridge, or performs a better operation, or designs a better motor—incontestably better than would a nonprofessional assigned to the same task.[81]

[81] I am aware of the importance of values and ethics to a profession. But these are, I think, secondary to technical proficiency. Formulation of a beautiful, coherent set of values without the skill to implement them is an exercise in futility. As a matter of fact, society, it seems to me, is concerned that a profession have values and ethics because

There is no question of the need for social work services. If all child welfare agencies should disappear tomorrow they would have to be reorganized. But the certainty of the need for a service does not guarantee the need for a profession to offer such service. A profession is needed to offer the service if it can be demonstrated that as a result of prolonged rigorous training during which a base of knowledge is acquired, a degree of skill is achieved which is clearly superior to the commonplace skills of the layman, whether this be helping an individual or a group, getting a child placed, or developing a program for better housing.

This is why the question of a firm knowledge base is more urgent now than it was thirty years ago. The necessity to prove ourself to a patient society is greater now. The failings of childhood are not excusable in the young adult. Are the consequences of intercession by the trained social worker in the life of the client—individual, group, or community—significantly different from the results achieved by the layman or untrained worker? Maybe this is so and we cannot effectively prove it. However, the evidence which is available is equivocal. Our inability clearly to answer in the affirmative is partly a result of our inadequate knowledge base.[82]

But if there is greater urgency there is also greater hope. Thirty years ago we did not have an organized group of social workers concerned with research. Since 1947, when the Western Reserve Workshop on Research in Social Work was held,

---

it fears the consequences of misdirected expertness. Ordinary social controls are sufficient for the layman with a knife. The expert whose knife is a scalpel has so much more power for evil and good that further controls in the form of professional values and ethics are necessary.

[82] Our inadequacies, such as they are, reflect to a considerable extent the inadequacies of the behavioral sciences generally. The knowledge which would permit us to succeed most often with the client is not available. There is a lot of truth in the old quip that social work is an art based on a science which has not been invented yet.

we have had a growing number of social workers devoting themselves to research projects and training. Furthermore, due to the increase in the size of the doctoral programs in social work we now have a greater number of social workers capable of formulating and conducting sophisticated research projects.

Thirty years ago a large percentage of social work research was concerned with the needs of agency operation and administration, and sufficiently parochial in nature that only the sponsoring agency learned anything. While this is perhaps still true for much social work research, there has been an increase in the amount of basic research being done. There is a growing tendency, too, for even operational research to be more broadly formulated so that the conclusions have wider applicability.

Within the last few years, research centers have been developed in schools of social work at Chicago, the New York School of Social Work, the George Warren Brown School of Social Work, Bryn Mawr, and the University of California at Los Angeles, and there has been active exploration of social work research in such units as the Interdisciplinary Faculty Seminar on Research in Social Welfare at the University of Michigan. Some social agencies have developed research units such as the Institute of Welfare Research of the Community Service Society of New York.

Both Polansky and Greenwood have reviewed the recent impressive developments in social work research, documenting the results of the increased research-mindedness of the field.[83]

Of particular significance, perhaps, to the broad question under discussion is the fact that the Commission on Practice of the National Association of Social Workers is engaged in activity which may result in a comprehensive direct study of

[83] Polansky, "Getting Down to Cases in Casework Research"; Ernest Greenwood, "Social Work Research—a Decade of Reappraisal," *Social Service Review*, XXXI (1957), 311–21.

practice. A research proposal for such a study has been formulated.[84]

Hope rests with these developments. While we advance with the behavioral sciences toward a more systematic understanding of social processes, we still are solely responsible for social work knowledge. The field cannot burden the practitioner with the primary responsibility of systematizing, conceptualizing, and validating social work knowledge. Only with the intensification of social work research, such as we are witnessing today, can this be accomplished and a firmer knowledge base established.

[84] Margaret Blenkner and Genevieve Carter, "Research Proposal for Development of Methodology and Instruments for a Study of Social Work Practice" (New York: National Association of Social Work, Commission on Social Work Practice, n.d.; mimeographed).

EGO PSYCHOLOGY IN THE EMERGING THEORETICAL BASE OF CASEWORK

ISABEL L. STAMM

There is a vigorous, searching spirit abroad in casework today, as in all social work. This is a stimulating period of development in practice, marked by assessment of the results of long practice and by a rapid expansion of relevant theory originating from within the profession and imported from a wide range of scientific sources. From the challenge to utilize in practice the various newer concepts and the principles they generate, three crucial tasks emerge: (1) "new" theory must be evaluated and mastered; (2) "old," or familiar, theory must be reappraised and placed again within the context of present knowledge; and (3) both new and old theory must be applied and tested in specific case practice to assure both the translation of theory into improved practice and the further development and integration of theory.

In the course of this process special attention must be paid to ego psychology. It provides concepts about intrapsychic aspects of personality and has also come to include concepts about the individual's total functioning, the ways he handles the complex needs and demands both from inner forces and from forces in his sociocultural environment. The newer ego concepts are compatible with theory developing in the social sciences and offer to casework practice a link between psychoanalytically oriented personality theory and theory from the social sciences.

Perspectives

During the past three decades casework's efforts to assemble and to understand the meaning of specific case data in terms of scientific concepts have centered largely upon the intensive study and application of theory imported from psychoanalysis and medicine. The resulting enrichment to practice is a familiar part of the history of casework's development.[1]

Psychoanalytic theory taught us first that the client's problems in relation to his social reality could not be explained exclusively in terms of external factors or in terms of the physical organism, but must also be understood in terms of instinctual strivings and needs. Initially, psychoanalysis provided us with facts and hypotheses about unconscious mental processes, some aspects of psychic conflict, and the characteristics and development of instinctual drives, particularly the libidinal drive, through the stages of psychosexual development. It provided concepts about anxiety, transference phenomena, the interaction of the past and present, the repetition compulsion, to name a few. Psychoanalytic theory thus added a new and much needed psychological dimension and stimulated casework to further conceptualization. Soon it became possible to conceive of casework as psychosocial, a practice based upon multidimensional diagnosis which was formulated from observations and assumptions ordered to theory.

During the initial period of vigorous assimilation of psychoanalytic theory, casework had to resolve a number of problems which arose in the application of this theory to practice. Some

[1] Annette Garrett, "Historical Survey of the Evolution of Casework," *Journal of Social Casework*, XXX (1949), 219–29; Gordon Hamilton, "A Theory of Personality: Freud's Contribution to Social Work," in *Ego Psychology and Dynamic Casework*, papers from the Smith College School for Social Work, Howard J. Parad, ed. (New York: Family Service Association of America, 1958), pp. 11–37.

problems were those inherent in applying new theory from any source to the specifics of a given case. For example, at times we began with a concept and sought only data which fit it. The new insights about unconscious conflict sometimes led us to observe and elicit only data relevant to emotional factors, while giving merely passing attention to the environmental reality situation. At times a piece of observed behavior, a derivative of unconscious conflict, was confused with the unconscious conflict itself. This assessment then led to a premature focus upon the core conflict. We failed to grasp the necessity for assembling sufficient data about a range of incidents, relationships, and their meaning to the client. We learned by experience that by securing significant data about all the relevant factors in a given case we could avoid the pitfall of trying to fit case findings to a theory which at the time was not itself sufficiently well developed or broad enough to give meaning to all that we saw in a case.

There were further problems in application stemming from the promise that the new understanding of personality seemed to offer in the solution of human problems and the enthusiasm with which we absorbed theory and identified with our psychiatric teachers. We, therefore, had to answer again and again questions about whether this theory was needed in all casework or only in some instances of "intensive treatment" of clients whose problems were defined in emotional terms. We had to distinguish between the application of psychoanalytic concepts in our own casework activities and the use of the psychoanalytic technical procedures which were initially developed for investigating unconscious parts of the mind and especially the conflicts which existed there. The difficulty of making such a distinction between the technical procedures of casework and those of psychoanalysis led to the adoption of certain ways of working without an adequate test of their relevance to casework practice, such as, at times, an exclusive focus on the individual client, particularly his underlying emotional conflicts, a reduction in home visits, an avoidance of direct intervention when the client did not ask for it, and, upon occasion, the attempted use of psychoanalytic techniques during case study and treatment.

Similarly, we had to differentiate between using psychoanalytic theory to advance casework aims, on the one hand, and adopting the aims of psychoanalytic treatment, namely, the resolution of internal structural conflict, on the other. The status and value we accorded to goals of resolving unconscious conflict for a time slowed up examination of differences between the goals of the two professions and our own formulations of goals appropriate to, and characteristic of, casework. Eventually we arrived at some clarity and agreement: psychoanalytic concepts were necessary in the assessment of personality structure and functioning; an assessment which, in turn, was necessary if we were to achieve casework goals.

During these decades the social sciences had not yet developed an equally dynamic set of theoretical constructs about environmental dimensions. To fill the gap the caseworker used some segments of borrowed theory and some indigenous descriptive definitions about the environment.[2] It was often necessary for the individual caseworker to rely largely upon his own experience and his intuition about the social milieu in which clients were living. However effective this was in a particular instance, casework as a whole lacked a framework by which to integrate assumptions about a total personality–whole-situation constellation. In actual fact, our specific case formulations about diagnosis and treatment were inevitably slightly out of balance in favor of psychological factors, although we never lost sight of the fact that our therapeutic in-

[2] Alfred J. Kahn, "The Nature of Social Work Knowledge," in Cora Kasius, ed., *New Directions in Social Work* (New York: Harper, 1954), pp. 198–201.

tervention must always be psychosocial, resting upon a multi-dimensional yet integrated psychosocial diagnosis.

Our difficulties in integration have been reflected in our efforts to classify the modalities of casework treatment. Treatment has at times been described [3] as though it were a continuum with measures designed to reduce environmental stress at one end, measures to support and strengthen adaptive functioning somewhere in the middle, and, finally, at the other end a precious therapeutic segment dedicated to the resolution of instinctual conflicts. By implication, psychosocial diagnosis was not fully formulated in the first category, but progressively increased in breadth and depth as the relationship between psychological and situational causative factors were more apparent. A psychological assessment based on psychoanalytic concepts often lost sight of the family unit and omitted the significant social-psychological situational factors. In effect, treatment in the first group had the "old-fashioned" focus on the situational problems facing a family and the management of daily tasks, which did not include evaluation of the effect of such intervention upon basic, long-standing problems. At the other end of this treatment continuum, preconscious material about libidinal conflicts and their effect on current relationship difficulties was the focus of attention, with limited attention to relevant situational manifestations in the family's daily life.

Thus, in cases where the reduction of environmental stress was the central treatment, the client was presumed to have a reasonably well-integrated personality structure capable of adaptation if stress were removed. When the central measures were designed to support and strengthen adaptive functioning it was presumed either that the client's personality structure was sufficiently well integrated so that he could manage if sup-

[3] Florence Hollis, "The Techniques of Casework," *Journal of Social Casework*, XXX (1949), 235–44.

ported through crisis, or that the client's pathology was such that measures designed to strengthen defenses against internal conflict were required. Finally, at the other end of the treatment continuum the client's personality was presumed to be sufficiently strong to benefit from clarification and insight about certain parts of his conflict. Such classification did not take sufficient account of the fact that casework treatment might involve all these modalities in different phases of treatment. It did not include variations in capacity of the ego to handle unconscious conflict and external stress, depending upon the nature of pressures and support in the social-psychological environment. Such classification focused upon individual-centered treatment, and failed to include casework intervention designed to alter or improve the interaction between several individuals within the family or other primary groups.[4]

These conceptual efforts to identify treatment method and goals were important landmarks in the ongoing work of moving from descriptions of activity in a given case to some formulations about practice in terms of the diagnosis. The concept of casework as psychosocial has stimulated constant reexamination of goals and method and has kept casework receptive to new developments in theory on which to base a truly psychosocial practice. Today the boundaries of knowledge in the behavior sciences have been extended. We are "in the midst of plenty" since we have the products of long professional practice waiting to be fully summed up. At the same time there are many more theoretical constructs from many sources to illuminate the broad area of our professional concern. Con-

[4] Gordon Hamilton, *Theory and Practice of Social Casework* (New York: Columbia University Press, 1940), chap. ix; Lucille Austin, "Trends in Differential Treatment in Social Casework," Cora Kasius, ed., in *Principles and Techniques in Social Casework* (New York: Family Service Association of America, 1950), pp. 324–38; Eleanor Cockerill *et al.*, *A Conceptual Framework of Social Casework* (Pittsburgh: University of Pittsburgh School of Social Work, 1952).

cepts, developed from practice, will guide us in our use of the theory which we incorporate from elsewhere.

Central to the integration of newly available knowledge, and the major focus of this discussion, is the emerging ego psychology. During the last three decades psychoanalytic researches into the development and functioning of the ego, in particular, have extended knowledge about personality structure and its interrelationship with social reality. Research and theory-building have illuminated normal behavior as well as pathology. These, in turn, also influenced many earlier hypotheses and constructs about anxiety, instinctual drives, and the cathexis of energy.[5] By now it is clear from the discussion of ego psychology that we cannot understand personality, either normal or pathological, in terms of emotions, drives, and impulses alone. If we are to know people we must understand the functions of the ego organization (the ego and superego), the relationship of the parts of the personality to each other, and their relationship to external reality. In this same period psychoanalytic researches have been closely integrated with findings by psychologists about certain ego functions.

During these decades remarkable developments in sociology, social psychology, and cultural anthropology have contributed new insights about value systems rooted in the social environment and in cultural and religious heritage, about social roles and social stratification, about the structure and functioning of social institutions, and about the psychological significance of social change. There is a trend toward closer working relationships in research on the part of representatives of all these disciplines, and we may look forward not only to further developments in theory but also to greater integration of theory.

The practitioner who must attempt daily solutions to con-

[5] Heinz Hartman, "Comments on the Psychoanalytic Theory of the Ego," in *The Psychoanalytic Study of the Child* (New York: International Universities Press, Inc., 1950), V, 74–96.

ceptual problems cannot, of course, await the completion of all researches or the fully satisfactory exposition of convincing theory which would seem to represent at a givent moment the integration of what is known. Yet as we use theory in practice we must make some attempt to correlate and merge the various theoretical constructs into a systematic whole, and we must seek a bridge between the specific in a given case and the relevant theoretical constructs. It is never easy to "place" either various highly organized pieces of observed behavior or even our own treatment activities within an existing theoretical structure. It is even more of a struggle when this general theory is rapidly expanding and when it is far from being fashioned into a systematic form.

The client who needs help with various problems describes these in terms of everyday behavior and attitudes. Everyday behavior is a complex psychosocial phenomena. We must analyze it in various ways—as a social role and as family interaction, as an expression of ideals and values, as physical processes, as an expression of psychological processes, such as instinctual drives and defensive operations. Casework practice requires that we use all these frames of reference. Yet a simple addition of these various dimensions can provide only a static sum which does not adequately blend and synthesize all these aspects into a description of living, functioning people, interacting in an equally dynamic sociocultural situation.

It is at this point that ego psychology arrives to claim a significant place in scientific theory basic to casework. It is an integral part of theory about personality structure and functioning, which provides one set of theoretical constructs from which to explain our case findings. In addition, however, concepts about the functioning ego form a connecting link between concepts about instinctual drives and unconscious conflicts and concepts about social role and its ties to the structure and functioning of social institutions. Intrapsychic factors determine the psychological meaning of events and circumstances and, at the same time, situational factors influence ego needs, roles and adaptive patterns. As we perceive the significant relationship of theoretical constructs about these covariants of intrapsychic structure and the social-cultural environment, we are aided in better organizing our case findings and in drawing inferences and hypotheses in our diagnostic and treatment formulations.

Central Concepts

While the present context does not permit full discussion of all aspects of ego psychology, and while it is known that almost daily new elaborations and innovations in practice are reported, some description is valid if only to highlight the fruitfulness of such study and application in casework.

1. *The ego, a substructure of the personality, is defined by its functions.* The term "ego" is a theoretical construct, and in that sense we never "see" it. What we do see are manifestations of many interdependent functions. A listing of functions as found in psychoanalytic literature [6] would include: (*a*) perception and appraisal of the outer world; (*b*) adaptation to the outer world; (*c*) perception and appraisal of the self, of instinctual drives, of superego demands; (*d*) specific functions which mature independently of, although interrelated with, id and superego, including control of motor and sensory functions, language, conscious ego interests. (For example, between the random movements of the infant and the sensitive fingering of the violinist there has been an intervening period of growth and experience in which undifferentiated motor and sensory activity has come under ego control. Once under such control

[6] Heinz Hartman, "Notes on the Reality Principle," in *ibid.*, XI (1956), 31–53; David Beres, "Ego Deviation and the Concept of Schizophrenia," in *ibid.*, XI (1956), 164–235.

it can be purposefully directed to the development of skills and conscious interests compatible with expectations and demands determined by the superego and by society); (*e*) thought processes; (*f*) defense functions; (*g*) object relationships; and (*h*) the function of synthesis or of creating priorities and order between various ego functions and between the several parts of the personality.[7] Obviously, these functions cannot be separated from their organic base. Clearly, the manifestations of ego functions take place within a living body, and some occur in interaction with the social milieu or as a response of the organism to the physical environment.

An all-round view of the ego of any one person is obtained only by adding up impressions gained from investigating the variety of ego functions. Anna Freud describes the care she had to exercise when investigating the defense mechanisms of the ego in order not to stress one function at the expense of others. She cautions against partial concepts and emphasizes both the initial basic unity of the id and ego and the unity of ego and superego (the ego organization) when their aims coincide.[8] Understanding manifestations of ego functions, therefore, cannot be separated from the understanding of other parts of the personality and of conditions in external reality which nourish or impede ego functions.

Casework method relates to the functioning ego in its capacity to form relationships, to perceive and act upon reality, to make some self-observations about the meaning of circumstances, relationships, attitudes, and subjectively felt internal pressures, aims, and values. We observe behavior patterns and ways in which our clients adapt to reality situations. They describe to us their feelings, and the significance to them of

[7] See also Fritz Redl and David Wineman, *The Aggressive Child* (Glencoe, Ill.: Free Press, 1957), pp. 58–194.

[8] Anna Freud, "The Mutual Influences in the Development of Ego and Id: Introduction to the Discussion," in *The Psychoanalytic Study of the Child*, VII (1952), 45–46.

life events and relationships. Concepts of ego functioning give meaning to what might otherwise be considered data about superficial daily behavior. All the details of family life—of work, of marriage, of the daily minutiae of activities and relationships, of illness, loss, and other sources of stress which must be handled—are seen as ego tasks and manifestations of the operations of the ego organization as well as derivatives of instinctual drives and unconscious conflicts. This sharpened understanding provides a scientific base to the oldest and most familiar aspect of casework practice wherein we roll up our sleeves, figuratively speaking, and become professionally involved in the "bread-and-butter" concerns and specific problems of a family.

Although casework relates to the total personality through the ego, we must not forget that most intrapsychic aspects of ego functioning are unconscious. They cannot be observed directly or asked about, but can only be inferred. A full assessment of ego functions depends upon collaboration with psychiatry and psychology which, by their own characteristic methods, may more directly explore intrapsychic functions and structure.

2. *Ego development is both a maturational process and a learning process.* Both constitutional and sociocultural environmental factors exert specific influences in varying proportions at each stage of growth.[9] The ego, it is postulated, forms initially out of the same undifferentiated biological base as the id; ego operations are, for the most part, unconscious and preconscious. Concepts about various phases and tasks of the ego are closely related to, but not identical with, concepts about psychosexual development and libidinal drives and needs. If the process is smooth and unimpeded, the result will

[9] Heinz Hartman, Ernst Kris, and Rudolph M. Lowenstein, "Comments on the Formation of Psychic Structure," in *The Psychoanalytic Study of the Child*, II (1946), 11–38; Beres, *op. cit.*, p. 171; Gerald H. J. Pearson, *Psychoanalysis and the Education of the Child* (New York: W. W. Norton, 1954), pp. 96–235.

be an ego which is autonomous, that is to say, is relatively independent of inner and external pressures, strong enough to control and flexibly mediate between conflicting internal and conflicting external forces. Without elaborating the concepts of primary and secondary ego autonomy, suffice it to say that ego formation is complex, with each stage dependent upon successful progress during the preceding ones.

Ego impairment so that energy and equipment are not brought under ego control may occur for any of these reasons:

a) The equipment for sensory perception, motor activity, and memory may be defective.

b) There may be failure in the normal development of libidinal and aggressive drives.

c) The child may receive too much or too little gratification and frustration of a degree and kind appropriate to his maturation. Since the immature ego needs both supportive stimuli and protection from overwhelming amounts of inner and outer pressure, either of these possibilities will seriously impede growth.

d) There may be insufficient or inadequate opportunities for identification with parents, teachers, peers, and other models whose real and unconscious attitudes toward reality and toward instinctual drives are apparent in adequate performance and enjoyment of a variety of roles, relationships, and beliefs compatible with the society of which they are a part.

e) It is also necessary that there be a successful resolution of conflicts between instinctual drives and reality demands.[10] (Not only ego functions but also the superego functions, it might be added, depend upon these same factors, particularly processes of identification and the successful resolution of conflicts.)

Casework has traditionally been family-centered because it

[10] Freud, *op. cit.*, p. 47; David Rapaport, "The Theory of Ego Autonomy," *Bulletin of the Menninger Clinic*, II (1958), 16–17.

has known that what happened to families happened to children. This was clear long before concepts about growth and developmental needs provided precise understanding of the significance to a child of a warm, stable, affectionate environment with parents who could "make sense out of life" for themselves, and who could cope in a reasonably constructive way with life circumstances and pressures. These concepts do, however, now illuminate the underlying therapeutic significance of casework's specific efforts to make details of life more reasonable and more comfortable for parents whose ego functioning is threatened by the tasks confronting them.[11]

These concepts give importance to the reciprocal interaction of parents with children, and children with each other. For example, parents both have an important role with their children and are themselves also affected in important ways by the relationship to their children, as well as by the vicissitudes of life. Therefore, we cannot center our efforts upon only one individual if by doing so we ignore the meaning of the psychosocial environment and the important needs and roles of others in the family.

Caseworkers have a great many opportunities to meet families at the point of some crisis, either severe or transient. We meet members of some families in hospitals or clinics, in family or children's agencies, in schools, courts, and various institutions. Initially, the client or someone in his environment has identified a specific problem affecting the family about which something helpful needs to be done as soon as possible. From our present knowledge, we conceive of this as one facet of the problem with which the family is coping. We are well aware that some clients may not perceive or be able to discuss their difficulty. Except for what has occurred in the immediate situ-

[11] Erik H. Erikson, "Growth and Crisis of the Healthy Personality," in Clyde Kluckhohn and H. A. Murray, eds., *Personality in Nature, Society and Culture* (2d ed.; New York: Knopf, 1953), pp. 185–225.

ation, their problems may be ego syntonic, that is, causing some discomfort but not perceived as "problem." For example, from initial clues in one of these cases, and with the use of our present theoretical knowledge, we may have concluded that the adults in a family have certain impaired ego functions, such as poor perception of reality, poor ability to control instinctual impulses, or limited capacity for object relationships. The developmental needs of their children may well stimulate in such parents tension and aggression beyond their capacity to control. The children may lack a stable, relatively conflict-free milieu in which to identify with, and learn from, their parents. In reaching such a conclusion, we must, of course, guard against distortions in our own perceptions due to a sociocultural orientation different from that of the client family. The issue in practice is whether we offer casework only to meet the facet of the problem of immediate concern to the client, in ways which will be generally helpful in terms of the postulated underlying problem. Or should we, rather, use this casework opportunity to enlist the family's participation in the further assessment of its capacity to meet the needs of its children and in clarification of ways in which improved care might be facilitated?

In making such an assessment, the caseworker may be deeply concerned and frustrated both by the difficulty of reaching such a family which neither perceives nor seeks help with its problem on these terms and by the unavailability of community services. It might be easier to confine diagnostic understanding to the presenting problem, or to conclude that the data we have are not sufficient to confirm our assumptions that the children's ego development is jeopardized by the family's problem, or to decide that, because of other work and the objectives of the setting, we cannot further extend our professional responsibility to include such a broadly conceived diagnostic function. Nevertheless, the possession of knowledge and the opportunity to use it do add up to professional responsibility in the interest of safeguarding healthy development of children, if we believe it is essential to "find" early those cases where children are not likely to receive the nurture necessary to the mastery of those ego tasks described by Erikson as central to each stage of development.[12] The expansion and integration of community services are furthered by the exercise of just such casework responsibility based upon present theory.

3. *Some ego functions are the products of maturation* and do not have their sources in conflict during the process of early growth. These include sensory perception, motor activity, memory, language. Also, it is postulated that the increasingly mature ego has control over energy which is no longer tied to instinctual drives, but becomes available for purposeful useful activities and interests.[13] These concepts emphasize the adaptive potential of the ego and highlight the importance of assessing ego functions of the client which are free from conflict and the nature of the impairment in those functions which are not conflict-free.

During the course of later development ego functions conceived of as initially conflict-free may become involved in critical conflict. Capacity to learn, perception of reality, language, and other functions may, in the latter instance, be affected.[14] When conflict or pathology exists, it is essential to assess the extent to which the total personality is involved.

[12] Erik H. Erikson, *Childhood and Society* (New York: W. W. Norton, 1950), p. 234; "Ego Identity and the Psychosocial Moratorium," in Helen L. Witmer and Ruth Kotinsky, eds., *New Perspectives for Research on Juvenile Delinquency,* Children's Bureau Publication, No. 356 (Washington, D.C.: U.S. Department of Health, Education and Welfare, Social Security Administration, 1956).

[13] Hartman, "Comments on the Psychoanalytic Theory of the Ego," in *The Psychoanalytic Study of the Child,* V (1950), 90–92; Hartman, "Ego Psychology and the Problem of Adaptation," in David Rapaport, ed., *Organization and Pathology of Thought* (New York: Columbia University Press, 1951), pp. 362–96.

[14] Freud, *op. cit.,* pp. 48–50.

The clinical diagnoses of neuroses, psychoses, or character disorders are central to psychosocial diagnosis, since they estimate the effect of the illness on ego capacities and functions. That some damages are irreversible is true; but the fact that the damage may not be total and that there may be conflict-free areas and latent potentialities for correction of distorted and underdeveloped capacities opens the door to further experimental work with each of these categories.

4. *Some tentative estimation of ego strength and weakness can be reached* by a detailed evaluation of various ego functions in relation to the whole personality in specific situations.[15] The caseworker sometimes generalizes about ego strength and weakness without specifying to what functions he is referring. Do we mean that the ego has insufficient energy to control instinctual impulses and selectively to direct the discharge of tension? Are we referring to an ego dominated by, or at the service of, aggressive impulses or to a primitive or distorted superego? Do we mean that the ego makes a poor choice of defensive reactions or defense mechanisms to handle a problem? Do we mean that such functions as the perception of reality or thought processes are not at a level appropriate to age and constitutional equipment? Or are we attempting to describe the general level of ego organization? Again, since the ego is, for the most part, unconscious, and since many intrapsychic functions cannot be observed or assessed by casework methods, the full and precise evaluation of ego strength or weakness requires collaboration with psychiatry and psychology.

5. *The concept of the mature, autonomous ego merits consideration.* This involves the flexibility with which ego functions mediate between the unconscious impulses and reality demands in order to obtain optimum gratification for the individual without arousing anxiety or increasing serious guilt

[15] Beres, *op. cit.*, p. 228.

feelings, and to assure that energy becomes available for relationships, activities, interests, and creativity. The autonomous ego is comparatively independent of inside or outside pressures; it is relatively well able to handle these pressures and achieve gratifications within social-psychological reality.[16] Casework defines its broad goals as involving the support of the right of each individual to have a mode of living which respects his worth and provides him with opportunities to mold his own life creatively; the latter implies opportunities for the individual to influence, responsibly with others, the wider social environment of which he is a part.

The objectives of casework, therefore, have not only a philosophical, ethical base but also a scientific one as defined by ego psychology. Casework practice is directed toward the goal of ensuring a social-psychological environment which promotes the development of mature autonomous ego functions, so that each individual is capable of "exercising freedom under the law." [17] Casework is also directed to helping individuals resolve their problems of adaptation through measures designed to support and strengthen ego functions as well as to modify overwhelming stress or threatening demands in their social reality. We cannot settle for a goal of adjustment to an impossibly difficult, even detrimental, social situation; and we must not underestimate the strength and potential capacities of individuals when primary relationships and social milieu support ego functions.

Working with the Ego

Ego psychology thus brings us back to the scenes of everyday life. Although casework has always had this focus, we see

[16] Rapaport, *op. cit.*, pp. 13–16.
[17] Robert Knight, "Determinism 'Freedom' and Psychotherapy," *Psychiatry*, IX (1946), 251–62.

new depths and meaning to the client of his daily behavior, attitudes, and relationships. It is from his living situation that we draw inferences about the tasks which his ego faces and his characteristic ways of handling them, as well as his capacity to manage conflicts or pressures from without and within, and to secure gratifications. The gathering of this material—by observing the client's behavior, by discussing his concerns and worries, by perceiving what he describes of his interests, problems, recollections of other situations and other feelings, and how he describes them—may seem deceptively uncomplicated, but actually it demands the greatest skill. It is the characteristic casework task and the core of casework method. It is different from group work method, in which clients are directly and repeatedly observed in interaction with each other and with the worker, and it is also different from certain characteristic tasks and methods of psychiatry.

Our clients usually begin by describing in specific, everyday terms a problem in which their adaptive efforts are not effective. We may react with frustration to such apparently simple details or to the slow pace of elaboration of such details. We may take some short cuts and prematurely focus upon a core conflict our client is handling so ineffectively, thereby feeling a rise in our own self-esteem because we had such a "good interview" and "got so much dynamic material." Without data about the client's ego capacity to handle resulting anxiety we can neither evaluate the timeliness of this procedure nor deal with our own rationalizations for undertaking it. We may focus only upon certain functions of the ego which are clearly tied to the problem, such as defenses. In so doing, however, we may give insufficient attention to those activities or interests which represent autonomous, conflict-free functions of the utmost significance in the assessment of the client's potential adaptive capacity.

If we wish to perceive and understand, we begin with what

the client perceives in reality, and his conscious sense of who he is and what his situation is. Through this we gain glimpses of what this all means to him, what his fantasies and deeper emotional conflicts are. We seek to understand what it is like to live in his home, to work next to him on the job, to meet him when he is having fun. We hope to learn what triggers off a "blowup," what it looks like, or sounds like. We focus, necessarily, upon no one person in a household, but upon the interaction of all members of the family. The client tells us the story of repeated situations of frustration, patterns of reaction, and ways these are tolerated by various family members. Incidents with children, spouse, parents, or the boss, give clues to individual patterns which have resulted defensively from unresolved childhood conflicts. They tell about a client's expectations of himself and others, and of the ways he gratifies impulses during the day's activities. From specific incidents we may see how the client's perception of reality is distorted upon occasions when feelings of fear, anxiety, or insecurity run high. From these incidents we may perceive what relationships, situations, or other gratifications provide a feeling of self-esteem, what contributes to a period of calm functioning, and what goes on then. We gain clues to how he learns and the kinds of relationships he creates or can manage.

Only gradually and indirectly is the client able to share some painful material. A person cannot perceive directly his emotional needs and conflicts which are expressed in behavior permitted by the ego. For example, a parent's behavior and attitudes may be hurtful to his child, but are so necessary to his own preservation and so cemented into his characteristic patterns that these are not discussed or felt as a problem. A parent may "do all the right things" with no feeling of empathy with his child, or in ways which prevent his child from becoming independent of the parent-child bond. Similarly, the client may not be able to perceive the significance of situational factors. For the most part, there is substantial variation in the meaning of situational factors to various individuals as well as variation in their way of handling the social reality, due to both psychological and sociocultural forces.

During this mutual exploration of specific situational and relationship difficulties at the client's pace and in terms which have meaning for him, the client is also learning. He perceives what value the caseworker places upon understanding who he is and what he has to cope with. He learns what is considered important to discuss. The client senses the essential safety for him in this activity which is carefully designed not to heighten anxiety beyond his capacity to control, but to promote his ego functioning and to provide external support and control. Some clients, as a result of this work, may be stimulated to see new meaning in the details of life or to perceive the significance of childhood conflicts in relation to present tasks. On the other hand, such intellectual insight may never occur or even be essential to the improvement in ego functioning. A precondition to psychological insight is the adequacy of the client's various ego functions to this task.

Caseworker-Client Relationships

Basic to all aspects of casework is the planned establishment of a relationship between caseworker and client, defined in terms of the client's capacities and needs. Repeatedly, our "hard-to-reach" clients will have none of this. Even clients whose motivation to secure casework help with some aspect of their difficulties appears to be strong vary in their "readiness to use help." Assumptions and loose generalizations about relating technique to the characteristics of the client and specific ways of developing, and directing a relationship need to be reexamined in terms of the contribution of ego psychology. Such examination and further experimentation in direct practice are underway, but clearly require even more development.

By way of illustration, one of the crucial periods in the caseworker-client relationship is the initial study phase. The professional relationship is a task of the functioning ego for both the client and the caseworker. This has been interpreted to mean that the relationship should be a logical, orderly process of mutual discussion in a "warm, accepting" atmosphere about the problem with which the client is concerned. Discussion, in this view, would then gradually extend to the client's other concerns, his capacities, his family, and their situation. Yet this requires of the client a capacity for reality assessment, self-perception, and adequate control over tensions. The client's defenses must be in reasonably good working order to handle the potential mobilization of core conflicts resulting from a focus of his own problems in this new relationship. This is clearly a task which can be accomplished only by a fairly stable, well-functioning ego. To require the client to have such functioning capacity before he initiates a request for casework, unnecessarily excludes people who need help and who will be helped by casework.

Many of our clients have suffered vicissitudes and deprivations as a result of which they are unable to meet the demands of the casework relationship. We must be prepared to develop a relationship which does not ask too much or too little of the client, and which does not hamper the capacities and motivating energy which he has at a given time. When a client is a child in years we know that his ego is immature and that ego functions of reality appraisal and self-perception are not well established. We then begin very slowly, flexibly modifying our methods in ways appropriate to his capacities and limitations and evaluating our strategy as we proceed. Similarly, we must vary our technical procedures when the client is an adult in years but has marked ego disturbances and a poorly integrated personality. The stereotype of "beginning where the client is" must be broadened to include "in relation to what the client is," if we are to offer the client a relationship he can use.

The fact that large parts of the ego are unconscious suggests that the client does not know what is wrong and therefore cannot tell the caseworker logically about his problem. The client will, in fact, inevitably protect himself by conscious attitudes, characteristic ways of behaving, and by unconscious defense mechanisms from a relationship which is too rapidly or too sharply focused upon problems or upon problem-solving. He will protect himself from heightened anxiety, from threatened loss of ego control, or even from loss of part of a problem deeply felt as an inherent part of himself.

Anxiety and major social pressures cause reactions that distort established and latent ego capacities so that the client cannot involve himself. In some instances immediate and active intervention by the caseworker is necessary in a reality situation which would be overwhelming to anyone, or which appears to be particularly stressful to a particular family. At times the client may perceive the relationship as one in which he can trust only as he receives support from the caseworker's own stable ego. The latter may be demonstrated through reality assessment, anticipatory planning to prevent difficulties for the client, selection of effective ways to manage immediate pressures or to limit unacceptable behavior.

The client's characteristic ways of functioning and coping with the world will color his use of the relationship. His attitudes and behavior in the relationship provide clues to basic conflict areas and problems and to his adaptive patterns and ways of mastering his tasks. He may initially view discussion of his problems as censure, as an effort to show him how to improve what he did wrong. He may need to have depleted supplies of self-esteem restored, or to achieve mastery of some part of his difficulties before he is ready slowly to become more involved with the casework relationship. He may relate only in extremely demanding, disorganized, unrealistic ways because of excessive deprivation. Or he may be communicative and well related to the caseworker only if their work together always makes sense to him on his own terms: if it is directed to his own conflicts and needs by way of doing something about specifically defined problems of others, such as his child, wife, or parent, as though only with the "safety" of such a screen could he bear to relate to, and use personally the help of, the caseworker.

For the caseworker, ego functions of perception, cognition, and empathy are not easily put to full use when the caseworker's own ego organization differs markedly from that of his client's with respect to values, acceptable behavior, or feelings about social status. The client's conflicts and patterns of handling instinctual behavior may heighten the caseworker's own defenses against conflict reactivated by the requirements of the professional relationship. These problems affect what the caseworker sees, hears, and does, what inferences he draws about his clients, and what casework plans he develops. If the caseworker is not aware of and able to manage his own part in the relationship, the client quickly senses that the worker "does not talk his language," that the frustrating concerns of the client's life for which he seeks solutions are not exactly what casework is about, or that his particular caseworker finds it too taxing or too painful to move slowly on his own level of perception.

It should not be a matter of apology that in practice each caseworker cannot manage an equally effective relationship with all clients. It should be of concern when we project such failures upon the client and fail to assess all the factors in the relationship in a given case. Casework has from time to time described both general eligibility requirements for treatment and also the vicissitudes of the professional relationship as if clients were all well motivated, had substantial capacity to perceive their own part in difficulties, and were able in a fairly formal office relationship to resolve their resistance in verbal ways. Some of our key social work concepts, such as the client's right to self-determination and the value of his participation, have been narrowly interpreted in terms of this ideal. Ego psychology and other theory now provide a scientific framework for application of these social work concepts. Cultural, physical, and personality factors each affect an individual's exercise of these rights. If we are to promote the client's exercise of these rights, we must assess each of these relevant factors and support the ego functions involved.

Fortunately, casework practice has in actual fact never fully incorporated idealized notions which ignore what occurs in the real world. In reality, concern for human need and for people who are suffering has never permitted repudiation of clients with impaired ego functions, even though in specific cases a reliance on incomplete conceptualization or intuition may not lead to the development of a constructive casework-client relationship or to agency policies which implement such a relationship.

Casework Intervention

The process of psychosocial diagnosis must be regarded not only as a definition of the kind of case and of the problems and needs of the client family, but also as the initial step, and an often repeated step, in treatment. As conceived of in casework, the diagnosis indicates the multidimensional problem and determines the direction and course of casework intervention.

Casework has used ego psychology most fully and systematically in developing concepts about treatment directed to individual clients' problems of adaptation, and more specifically to those adaptive problems related to, or caused by, underlying conflicts in the personality. The fact that in ego psychology concepts first were developed about ego functions related to the control of instinctual impulses and superego demands, such as defense mechanisms, is reflected in the classification of treatment which was formulated about the time of these theoretical developments.[18]

Ego psychology has now been extended to include a fuller range of concepts about the complexities of the reciprocal relationship between the individual and his environment. Several specific aspects of the adaptation deserve elaboration for casework purposes.

One significant aspect of adaptive capacity, as has been noted, is the presence of an autonomous ego which has functions under the control of the ego and relatively independent of instinctual conflicts or environmental pressures. Included here are conscious aims, activities, and interests. The autonomous ego functions are, in part, based upon an inherent capacity for maturation and for learning through experience. By definition, the conflict-free sphere at a given time is not involved in underlying conflicts. Through the assessment of these functions, casework treatment can direct itself to the adaptive potential within the individual. By casework methods and techniques, including education and manipulation, the client may be helped to make use of opportunities within the social environment for learning, for achievements, and for relationships which support a sense of self-esteem and identity with others. He may be helped to alter his physical or social environment; and, working together with other persons, he may achieve aims which benefit others as well as himself.

[18] Report of the Committee on Methods and Scope, Family Service Association of America, *Scope and Methods of the Family Service Agency* (New York: the Association, 1953), pp. 18–20.

Adaptive capacity is also dependent upon factors in the social environment which nourish and promote ego functions. These factors include, of course, basic requirements for physical health, for family life and other relationships, and for productive activity valued by others as well as by the individual. Alteration of these factors may have a reciprocal effect upon ego functions in everyday behavior and interpersonal relationships.

Modification of clients' everyday behavior, in ways which do not aggravate each individual's underlying conflict, are often of the utmost importance to family relationships as such, to the growth and development of children in the family, as well as to the more effective functioning of the parents in relation to their children.

Caseworkers have begun to report the application of some of these new concepts in individual cases. New approaches or variations in techniques and procedures have specifically promoted or supported certain ego functions for clients requiring this during the course of treatment. For example, the process of formulating an accurate psychosocial diagnosis is of therapeutic benefit to the client. During the mutual process of study, the caseworker's correct understanding of the meaning to the client of his circumstances and relationships not only supports the client in further elaboration of significant events and attitudes, but also, in some instances, appears to result in the client's increased perception of his real world, some modifications in daily behavior, or increased efforts to master some part of his problem. Although the central problem has not been touched, a client often reports an immediate sense of comfort or increased self-esteem. Although denial and other defensive operations are often thus manifested, an accurate diagnostic process enables the client to undertake further work with the caseworker.

Many clients who come to casework agencies have marked

impairment in ego functions, and whatever help is provided through the network of community services often consists of a series of fairly brief contacts to meet emergencies due to illness, unemployment, or some crises brought about because some family member is not doing what he ought to do. These clients often lack a sense of belonging anywhere. They have only limited interpersonal relationships, which fail to promote a sense of self-esteem and support achievements in reality; chronic unresolved conflicts involve much of their personalities. The psychosocial diagnosis in such cases indicates a multiplicity of causative factors and demonstrates the need to strengthen the network of community services. Only in such fashion can one provide a consistent focus for the casework in all the agencies involved, and achieve optimum support designed to stabilize the family and to anticipate and prevent further difficulties.

In such cases, there are various pressure points of significance in the family's problem toward which casework efforts are being directed at one and the same time. These may include: financial problems; the illness of one family member; another member's emotional conflict, reactivated by the situation; specific difficulties occurring every day between members of the family or between family members and others in the environment. Many such families initially cannot use individually centered casework treatment. They seem only able to sustain brief relationships for the alleviation of crises which occur with painful frequency but which are not anticipated or perceived realistically.

In some instances interviews are held with the entire family when individual interviews are too anxiety-provoking. For some clients other variations are required throughout treatment, such as interviews in the home rather than in the office, active intervention in working out more comfortable aspects of everyday living, or measures designed to improve one client's perception of reality and to promote another's use of intellec-tualization, rationalization, denial, or other defense mecha-nisms. It should be noted that concepts have not yet been fully developed about when to use a specific combination of such techniques and what results can be predicted.

In a given case, measures directed to different aspects of the family problem may be introduced simultaneously, such as the mobilization of resources to modify the reality situation, and the increase of gratifying relationships and experiences. Dur-ing the course of treatment of an individual client, modifica-tion of situational pressures, measures to promote ego func-tions, and clarification to stimulate some understanding of circumscribed aspects of his problem may be used in a design which follows no static progression but furthers the client's mastery of the tasks he has, and stimulates his capacities for self-perception. The closer to the client's core conflicts is the casework focus, the more essential are measures designed to be supportive and to reduce external overwhelming stress.

The course of casework treatment may be designed to deal with different aspects of a problem on different levels. For example, a discussion on the client's terms and in his language of something as specific as a family's weekly food budget may help a mother manage her household affairs more realistically, may ensure more pleasant mealtime experiences for the fam-ily, may better meet the children's nutritional needs, and may ensure the family's having a better credit rating with their grocer. This same discussion may help the mother gain in-creased self-esteem in her ability to produce a meal she is pleased with, and may also provide emotional gratifications because the caseworker is giving to her and helping her, or because she feels some identification with the caseworker. At the same time, this may be the means whereby a client is en-abled to put into words past events and feelings which she associates with this activity and this role. Such repeated dis-

cussions may indirectly focus, therefore, upon this client's underlying, disturbed feminine identification or her masochistic
behavior pattern which is heavily reinforced by her culture
and by her identification with her own mother, or other
models. Thus, such repeated work may provide reeducation
and also go far toward reversing the reciprocally frustrating
relationship between mother and children or between husband
and wife. It may substantially strengthen the client's perception of her reality situation and her own feelings and ways of
dealing with her family, even though she may not achieve
intellectual understanding of her emotional problems and instinctual conflicts.

Unresolved problems in diagnostic formulations continue to
plague casework practice despite the successful application
of certain concepts and the use of new approaches. When
theory is not systematized into a framework and specific concepts about how to apply the theory in practice have not been
developed, the caseworker who is not primarily a theoretician
has difficulty in making use of it in particular cases. A caseworker properly may ask: "Now that I understand the case by
using theory about unconscious conflicts, ego functions, physical handicaps, social roles, family organization, and cultural
factors, what should I do? Where should I intervene? What
action should I take in this case that is different from what I
would do in another case?" A psychosocial diagnosis can guide
the caseworker in answering these basic questions only if the
necessary concepts relating to procedure in the intervention
are developed in casework practice itself. Only from practice
can we, in fact, secure answers sufficiently specific to be useful
guides as to what the central focus of intervention should be
and what results can be expected from a strategy or treatment
method focused upon certain aspects of the problem.

It is now possible to develop further formulations about
casework methods, using current experience in practice and

the now available concepts of ego psychology and related theory. First, it seems possible to define more precisely casework aims and methods directed to the promotion of individual adaptation. Also, we appear ready to develop concepts about other types of casework intervention, focusing upon: the social, economic, and physical milieu; family organization and functioning; and interpersonal relationships, per se, such as the interaction between siblings, husband and wife, or parent and child.

While major conceptual tasks remain, the essential vitality and flexibility of casework practice stand out; efforts are constantly made to safeguard quality of treatment, to avoid "second-best" measures, and to respond helpfully to troubled people who are coping with the new dimensions of the present-day world which neither they nor we understand very well. This commitment to service continues to move the practitioner to action. Casework practice today is also adding a new dimension, namely, the responsibility for further clarification and formulation of the aims, the methods, indeed the theory, of casework treatment from work with real life cases and careful conceptual analysis. It should not be a matter of concern that this new responsibility is not immediately translated into fruitful action on the part of everyone, or that results in the form of final answers or even accurate modest hypotheses are not quickly forthcoming. The process of identifying diagnostic questions worthy of more systematic study and casework treatment measures worthy of more general trial is a slow one, although a productive one. From such a course of action we will become "educated borrowers" of theory, who apply it rather than absorb it passively, and who understand it more accurately because of a parallel development in the body of casework knowledge.

GROUP WORK AND THE
SOCIAL SCENE

WILLIAM SCHWARTZ

In the decades immediately following the Civil War, a re-united America gave itself over to the development of its vast economic and industrial potential. As the country set out to fill its territories and exploit its unlimited physical and human resources, there was a surging sense of power, emerging from the promise of man's ingenuity and technical genius.

Mark Twain called that period the Gilded Age. It was an era of frontiers, and the frontier spirit was individualistic, bold, adventurous, and competitive. And since the open frontiers were everywhere—geographic, social, industrial—the heroes of the time were the pioneers, the empire-builders, and the self-made men.

The philosophical mood was expansive, materialistic, and dynamic; "utility" and "change" were the bywords, and Herbert Spencer's doctrine of the inevitability of progress caught the imagination of Americans. Freedom and the machine were to go hand in hand as a prosperous people took increasing control over its political power. The ability of the machine to do the work of society would soon create a new element in life, which was leisure. Already, all things seemed possible for those with talent, resourcefulness, and the middle-class virtues.

For the mass of the people, converging on the new centers of industrial development, the prospect was somewhat grimmer:

. . . this picturesque America with its heritage of crude energy—greedy, lawless, capable—was to be transformed into a vast uniform middle-class land, dedicated to capitalism and creating the greatest machine-order known to history. A scattered agricultural people, steeped in particularistic jealousies and suspicious of centralization, was to be transformed into an urbanized factory people, rootless, migratory, drawn to the job as by a magnet.[1]

With the growth of large, sprawling cities and the concentration of the labor force, grinding poverty was out in the open for all to see. The scale of expansive creation and construction was soon matched by a similar scale of deterioration in conditions of urban life. As the nation grew richer, a large proportion of its people grew poorer, with families broken by want, children working in mines and factories, and gathered together in slums that perpetuated their own evils.

Moreover, the industrial system brought with it difficulties that transcended the purely economic. Factory work was stereotyped and oppressive, as Chaplin later illustrated so vividly in his film "Modern Times." Urban life was a complicated network of human relationships, and those who failed to meet its demands experienced the new phenomenon of loneliness in the midst of crowded cities. As the organization of society grew more complex, it became increasingly difficult to retain a sense of control over one's own destiny.

Since it was this element of control that constituted for many the central concept of a democracy, there was a growing concern—barely heard at the outset but swelling into an insistent clamor toward the turn of the century—that we were moving further from the democratic vision rather than closer to it. This fear was accentuated by rapidly increasing concentration of power and wealth in the hands of the few.

The social Darwinism of Spencer and William Graham Sumner provided the intellectual undergirding for the new competitive and individualistic order. The philosophy of the

[1] Vernon Louis Parrington, *Main Currents in American Thought* (New York: Harcourt, Brace, 1927), III, 26.

"survival of the fittest," applied to the facts of social and economic existence, offered a strong rationale for those who might have moral problems to solve as they surveyed the American scene:

In the Spencerian intellectual atmosphere of the 1870's and 1880's it was natural for conservatives to see the economic contest in competitive society as a reflection of the struggle in the animal world. It was easy to argue by analogy from natural selection to social selection of fitter men, from organic forms with superior adaptability to citizens with a greater store of economic virtues. The competitive order was now supplied with a cosmic rationale. Competition was glorious. Just as survival was the result of strength, success was the reward of virtue.[2]

But, in the words of Tawney, "there is no touchstone . . . which reveals the true character of a social philosophy more clearly than the spirit in which it regards the misfortunes of those of its members who fall by the way." Further, it was not possible "to consign to collective perdition almost the whole of the wage-earning population."[3] The disillusionment rode on the heels of two depressions, the agitations of labor, and the political unrest of the 1890s. The voices of protest insisted that a true democratic freedom could not be built on the hopes of a propertied elite and the promise of a static evolutionism. And they proceeded to reinterpret the evolutionary theme in a manner that was perhaps less strange to Darwin himself than it was to some of his prophets.[4]

If man was an animal, he was at least a new kind of animal, one who could by his wits and collective power control the

[2] Richard Hofstadter, *Social Darwinism in American Thought* (rev. ed.; Boston: Beacon Press, 1955), p. 57.

[3] R. H. Tawney, *Religion and the Rise of Capitalism* (New York: Penguin Books, 1947; originally published in 1926, Harcourt, Brace), p. 222.

[4] Hofstadter, *op. cit.*, p. 201.

forces of nature rather than submit himself docilely to its inexorable laws of survival and selection. Society was not a jungle, in which life for one meant death for another, but a system of cooperative and interdependent relationships designed to raise the level of existence for all men. Cooperation, it was shown, was at least as much a law of nature as competition; people were responsible to each other and government was their instrument of action. Social reform, far from being an unwarranted intrusion upon nature's laws, was man's way of adapting those laws to his own needs and conditions.

The philosophical voice of the new progressivism made itself heard through an organized labor movement, an aroused clergy, and the new relativistic thinking of economists, sociologists, and social philosophers. The pragmatism of William James and the instrumentalism of John Dewey were potent tools in the hands of those who saw democratic freedom as a social development rather than as a prerequisite of rugged and powerful individuals:

The pragmatists' most vital contribution to the general background of social thought was to encourage a belief in the effectiveness of ideas and the possibility of novelties—a position necessary to any philosophically consistent theory of social reform. As Spencer had stood for determinism and the control of man by the environment, the pragmatists stood for freedom and control of the environment by man.[5]

Agency Beginnings

These developments fashioned the social context in which the first leisure-time community agencies assumed their form and took on their function in American society. In their inception, they were native adaptations of services brought

[5] *Ibid.*, p. 125.

about by earlier and similar developments in the industrialization and urbanization of the English economy. The sectarian "Y" 's appeared first, just after the turn of the mid-century; the settlements followed, in the 1880s and 1890s; and the first two decades of the twentieth century saw the beginnings of the national youth-serving organizations and the recreation movement.

In many respects, the agencies were protective associations against the problems created by city life in a rising industrial society. They ranged themselves against the mobility and rootlessness, the stultifying, noncreative work, the rising rates of delinquency and crime, the patterns of neighborhood segregation, and, pervading all, the inability of transient and disorganized populations to pool their interests and take action in their own behalf.

To counter these forces, the agencies projected themselves as the protagonists of social responsibility in a competitive order and of individual and cultural identity in a faceless crowd. They stressed the need for individualizing, for a kind of collective security, and for the equalization of political and economic power. They stressed, too, the rehabilitating force of play and recreation and they made a key issue of the relationship between responsible citizenship and the creative use of leisure time. "In the play group (i.e., the free-time group)," wrote Mary Simkhovitch in her later account of the values of group living, "may be seen the happy exercise of power unrelated to oppression, the use of energy that brings no reward but the satisfaction of capabilities, and a sense of comity that enriches the spirit and is symbolic of a kind of society the world has not yet known." [6]

Above all, there were two common emphases which, taken together, constituted perhaps the community agencies' out-

* Mary K. Simkhovitch, *Group Life* (New York: Association Press, 1940), p. 34.

standing contribution to the American scene. One was their shared belief in the salutary social and personal effects of group association; the other was a tested conviction that the development of sound leadership was a central problem and a special task in the mobilization of group life in a democracy. In their preoccupation with human association, they created a great laboratory of group experience, in which attention was called to some of the major hypotheses later to be elaborated and tested by the social scientists: people in groups were more teachable, more reachable, and more susceptible to change; small groups in particular were crucibles of attitude and value formation; people together tended to solve problems more efficiently, since "group work" is more lasting and more accurate than individual work. Further, in acting together people could exert greater impact on their environment, and the group thus became the symbol and the instrument of the democratic ideal. A democratic society is one that acts through a multiplicity of active groups, trained in their own broadly conceived self-interest. As a further development of this idea, the group itself must be democratically evolved, structured, and oriented —a prototype, or special instance, of the democratic system in action.

In a similar way, the early work of the agencies served to dramatize the nature of influence within the structure of group experience. The fact that people seemed more amenable to the ideas of others directly involved in their activity than to ideas in the abstract brought with it a searching concern with the attributes of leadership and with its importance as an instrument of agency purpose. Although the first conceptions differed among agencies, they held certain important notions in common: "leadership" was seen as a fixed personality characteristic, distinguishing those who "lead" from those who "follow"; the term itself was used to describe the personal influence of group members and agency workers alike, without differentiating their separate functions within the group experience; and the exercise of influence, since it was a natural concomitant of personal strength and character, was essentially an intuitive process rather than a planned and conscious method of intervention in group life. The later efforts to identify leadership as a process rather than a trait, to distinguish peer influence from professional guidance, and to design a planned and teachable methodology of intervention were to constitute the first significant steps toward the development of modern group work practice.

Taken together, the agencies projected a strange and varied assortment of aspirations and functions: they were established to educate and to reform, to serve youth, to mobilize neighborhoods, to perpetuate religious and cultural identities, to preserve ethical (largely middle-class) values, and to exert a benevolent moral pressure on those whose low position in society rendered them especially susceptible to the confusions and temptations of the time. Some were specifically concerned with the vast throngs of immigrants from abroad and with the streams of young people moving from their homes on the farm in search of city opportunities. Thus, when Margaretta Williamson studied the job definitions of workers in leisure-time agencies in the late 1920s, she reported that:

The objectives of these various agencies would at first thought seem so divergent as to make it impossible to treat the duties and responsibilities of their workers in the same analysis. The evangelical motive, so strong a feature in certain of the agencies, is entirely lacking in others; some are concerned with group experience and leisure-time activities for the average everyday person of any walk of life, others for the so-called "underprivileged" person; neighborhood relationships, community organization, education, concern for the young man or woman away from home, or appreciation of out-of-door life, may loom large in the program of a particular agency. Upon closer scrutiny, however, and after acquaintance with methods and procedure, it becomes apparent that along with other motives and interests peculiar to the particular agency, they all have a common desire so to guide the leisure-time activities of the individual, through group experience and education, that he may develop an integrated personality with the capacity for living a full life, and accustom himself to the give and take of group life as an introduction to social responsibility. Quite apart, moreover, from the purposes of these organizations, it is certain that group activity has commended itself as a medium of work to a variety of agencies pursuing a variety of aims.[7]

In function and philosophy, the agencies combined the scientific, pragmatic, and materialist outlook of the new society with its equally characteristic heritage of puritanism and moral absolutism. Drawing their inspiration and sponsorship from middle-class philanthropy and from radical social protest, from religious idealism and from the scientific spirit of the progressive era, they both reflected and rejected the social Darwinism against which, collectively, they had set their faces. Emerging from both the revolutionary and the conservative spirit of the age, group work was born as a true child of its time.

The Search for a Reference Group

Those who began to gather around the discussion tables in the 1920s and 1930s to explore the problems of working with people in groups represented a wide variety of identifications and interests. They were educators and psychologists, settlement workers, church workers and social workers, recreationists, anthropologists, sociologists and social philosophers.[8] It was an unprecedented working collaboration of practitioners, philosophers, and social scientists; it was also short-lived, lasting only until academic and professional loyalties began to

[7] Margaretta Williamson, *The Social Worker in Group Work* (New York and London: Harper, 1929), p. 17.

[8] See, for example, list of contributors to Joshua Lieberman, ed., *New Trends in Group Work* (New York: Association Press, 1939).

harden and the separate fields and disciplines began to move off along their own lines of emphasis.

The substance of their communication was centered in three major areas of concern. They shared the results yielded up by the newly developing social sciences, finding both verification and inspiration in the emerging emphasis on the laws of change, the dynamics of interaction, the social determinants of attitude and value, and the motivational basis of learning. Said a psychologist:

If you believed in the constancy of temperament, personality, intelligence, etc., your groups could promise to be of little or no therapeutic value in these directions. Basic tenets of group work such as education and re-education would remain Utopian ideas. But there is already implicit in group work a dynamic approach. There is already present at least the hope of effecting change. It is on this ground that the new psychology and the new group work must meet.[9]

Second, they sought to develop a guiding ethical system and to specify the objectives of group education—both formal and informal—in a democratic society. They translated the philosophy of James and Dewey into the specific meanings of democracy in action; [10] inspired by the optimism of Mary Follett and Eduard Lindeman, their statements reflected a strong conviction about the perfectibility of human nature and the connection between self-interest and the social good. They stressed the existence of benevolent and creative forces in people, forces which needed only to be liberated by circumstances to enable individuals to act together in the interests of all. The connection between the *one* and the *many* was, in fact, so clear and obvious that it was not yet considered necessary to

[9] Dan L. Adler, "Contributions of Psychology to Social Group Work," in *Group Work 1939* (New York: American Association for the Study of Group Work, 1939), p. 8.

[10] Cf. Eduard C. Lindeman, "The Roots of Democratic Culture," in *ibid.*, p. 1.

describe the precise nature of the enabling process; the goals and values themselves, could they be clearly enough formulated, seemed powerful enough, in the hands of a mature, self-aware "leader," to produce alert, responsible citizens in socially active groups.

Finally, they attempted to define the "group work" entity itself, and to understand its scope and function, in a way that would provide an identification and a sense of direction for its practitioners and teachers. Group work, seeking a reference group, found itself bound by heritage and loyalty to a wide assortment of fields, agencies, social interests, and academic disciplines.

Our society has established certain institutions, beyond the family, which are designed to carry out its functions. Needing to transmit its accumulated heritage of knowledge, values, and skills to succeeding generations, it has institutionalized a system of education; seeking to provide means through which people can play, exercise, relax, and develop their cultural tastes, we have developed a field of recreation; to bring the sick back to health, a complex of therapeutic activity is organized; the field of social welfare functions to ensure its citizens against emotional and physical deprivation and to bring needs and resources into balance; and, to provide a climate and a machinery through which people may act to effect change and express protest, we have institutionalized structures through which people may exercise their right to influence social policy through social action.

To which of these systems did the developing entity of group work—or, as it was sometimes called, "social" group work—belong? In a real sense, it was all of these things, having brought together agencies, practitioners, and students of group phenomena in each of these areas of function. It was certainly, in its various aspects, a reform movement, a therapeutic tool, an educational method, a field of service, a small part of the recreational movement, and a moving spirit in the affairs of many social welfare agencies.[11]

There was another sense, however, in which group work was none of these, but something quite new, with an identity all its own. In this respect, it seemed to be developing as a unique and highly refined skill, limited primarily to functioning in small groups of people in intimate psychological interaction, and directed toward helping the group members to work together on their common goals and concerns, whatever these might be. A distinctive profession built around such an area of expertness could conceivably be utilized anywhere that people needed or wanted to be together, play together, work together, or even learn together. It could be used in industry, in social agencies, in education, in hospitals, and in other organizations and institutions.

There were, in fact, many who felt that this development was exactly what should happen and who pointed to the dangers of a premature or exclusive identification with one or another field of service. As late as 1939, Hugh Hartshorne, reporting as chairman of the Commission on the Objectives of Group Work of the American Association for the Study of Group Work (AASGW), said, "It is probably fortunate that the notion of group work has not yet settled down into a new educational stereotype." [12] And, after delineating the various kinds of tasks amenable to group work assistance, he continued:

Viewed in this way, group work has no objectives of its own, but represents, instead, the increasing sensitiveness of agencies to the conditions under which the social skills and attitudes needed in a democracy may be expected to develop. . . . the immense variety of objectives that have been proposed for group work is the con-

[11] Cf. Grace L. Coyle, "Social Group Work," in *Social Work Year Book 1937* (New York: Russell Sage Foundation, 1937), pp. 461–64.
[12] Hugh Hartshorne, "Objectives of Group Work" in *Group Work 1939*, p. 39.

sequence of this confusion between group work as an agency device and group work as an educational principle.[13]

In 1938, in a chapter entitled, "To What Profession Does Informal Education Belong?" Charles E. Hendry wrote:

It seems quite clear that we are not yet in a position to decide definitely on this question of the professional classification of informal and group education and recreation. Whether we have here an independent profession or a substantial segment of an existing profession remains to be determined. Just as a scientist would not want to restrict his participation to a single scientific society, so group educators, presumably, will not want to identify themselves solely with one professional organization or to isolate themselves from any professional organization that operates within the area of their social function.[14]

Thus, too, William Heard Kilpatrick, in his *Group Education for a Democracy*, published in 1940 under the auspices of the AASGW:

The author takes responsibility here for stating his personal opinion, assisted at points by publications of the Association, that group work is a highly worthy new interest, whether this go on in school classes or in recreation and other informal education. This group work is, however, not to be thought of as a separate field of work, but rather as a method to be used in all kinds of educational effort. "Group work" in this sense is just now more or less of a movement, and as such deserves support and success. But its success will be achieved when, and to the degree that, effective working in groups has established itself as an essential part of any adequate education of youth, however and wherever conducted.[15]

The reluctance to harden into a "field" persisted through the years, even as many of the agencies offering group work

[13] *Ibid.*

[14] Hedley S. Dimock, Charles E. Hendry, and Karl P. Zerfoss, *A Professional Outlook on Group Education* (New York: Association Press, 1938), p. 47.

[15] William Heard Kilpatrick, *Group Education for a Democracy* (New York: Association Press, 1940), p. vii.

services were being gradually but steadily drawn into the social work fold. The AASGW, started in 1936, did not become a professional association of group workers until 1946; until its amalgamation into the National Association of Social Workers ten years later, its membership was open to those with training and experience in public recreation, physical education, education, or social work. Even today, though the search for identity has slackened, it has not ceased. It has its present-day repercussions in the controversies on the psychiatric emphasis, the call for a revitalized program of social action, the attempt to distinguish the practice of "social group work" from that of "work with groups" [16] and, most recently, the proposals that group work withdraw completely from an educational to a therapeutic function.[17]

Group Work and Social Welfare

Despite the ebb and flow of other influences, the historical impetus of group workers and group-serving agencies was toward the identification with social work as a profession and with social welfare as a field of service. The roots of group work were in the activities of agencies reflecting concern with social conditions and their effects on people. Its origins lay in the general movement for social amelioration and social protest. Even as its workers drew inspiration from educational theory, psychiatric learnings, and small-group research, these developments were seen by many as instruments to be used in achieving social objectives. The ensuing efforts to build a scientific base and a unique methodology were undertaken not to replace the sense of mission, but to implement it.

[16] Gertrude Wilson, "Social Group Work Theory and Practice," in *The Social Welfare Forum, 1956* (New York: Columbia University Press, 1956), pp. 143–59.

[17] See, for example, letter to the editor by Max Doverman, *Social Work*, III, No. 2 (1958), 127, 128; see also reply by Mary Dot Monte and Rita Comarda, *Social Work*, III, No. 3 (1958), 126–27.

This tendency was expressed, on another level, in the fact that a substantial number of the group-serving agencies were sponsored and financed under the same auspices as the social casework programs and those devoted to social welfare organization and planning. The relationship among these various efforts took on new strength and meaning during the great depression of the 1930s; thrown together around common problems and a common clientele, caseworkers, group workers, and community organization workers came increasingly to regard themselves as partners in the same enterprise.

Social work, with its early emphasis on the individual in his environment, was a congenial host for those whose work lay at the very point of interaction between the two. Social work's concern with the total individual, the importance of community life, and the role of government in human affairs offered a comfortable resting place for group work's unique blend of scientific, humanitarian, and missionary zeal—more so than either education or recreation, each of which had for some time seemed to present a logical professional identification. The former was being increasingly torn by internecine conflict with regard to the most fundamental assumptions on the holistic nature of human psychology and human learning— many of which assumptions had been taught to group workers by the educators themselves. Recreation, slow to recognize the small-group potential, to individualize its clients, and to embrace the mental hygiene movement, became "merely" recreation and was relegated by many to a minor role in the field of human relations practice. It was a role, incidentally, somewhat similar to that assigned by caseworkers to the group workers themselves.

The identification had significant implications for both parties. It served to expand the scope of social work itself, bringing it back to earlier and broader conceptions of its function and responsibility at a time when these were being interpreted in ever narrowing terms. It brought fresh sociological thinking into a profession that was coming more and more to explain human behavior and social phenomena in biological and individualistic terms; it carried a renewed interest in social treatment, where the emphasis had been shifting almost entirely to individual therapy; the interest of the leisure-time agencies in prevention, in education, and in the broad range of human problems encountered in everyday living, made it necessary to extend concern to millions of new clients. The prospect of the "normal" client was completely antipathetic to the development of social work as a therapeutic profession, auxiliary to that of medicine in general and psychiatry in particular.

For group workers, the move lent strength and discipline where the need was greatly felt: it created a clearly marked professional identification, broader than that of a single agency or movement and hence more socially significant and status-giving; it gave promise of yielding a clearer and more distinct sense of function and focus, for which qualities many group workers hungered, and looked to casework for its skill and sophistication in these areas; it strengthened the movement toward developing a conscious method of working, supervising, and recording; and it stimulated awareness and understanding of some much-needed concepts regarding the psychodynamics of human behavior.

In its more negative aspects, the identification tended to bring about a gradual disengagement of group workers from some of their most fruitful professional and theoretical connections. The spirit of inquiry that had marked their early association with many sources of knowledge and insight gave way, in many quarters, to the prevailing uncritical acceptance of a single explanation of human behavior. Following casework, they embraced the Freudian system—part science, part doctrine—with characteristic missionary enthusiasm, weakening its essential contribution by holding it up as a theory that excluded all other theories and constituted a kind of loyalty test for any new ideas that might bear upon our understanding of people and society.

Over all, the alliance between group work and social work has been a dynamic one, strengthening both entities while posing significant problems of integration with which the field is still struggling.[18] These problems have been rendered more difficult, rather than less so, to the extent that group work has tended to follow the path of casework development rather than to identify and elaborate its own unique contribution to social work theory and practice. Wrote Clara Kaiser in 1957:

For better or for worse, social group work as it has been developed conceptually and as a field of practice is an aspect and method of the profession of social work. . . . Group workers often feel like "poor relations" in the family of social work practitioners, but instead of feeling resentment toward our sibling, casework, let us emulate her where this will deepen our insights and skills and let us develop the special methods which pertain to the helping process through the medium of group interaction and participation.[19]

And Louis Towley, summarizing the group work contribution, states:

Social group work has found a comfortable professional family in social work during the past thirty years—though who adopted whom is occasionally a question. The way has not been smooth. The younger member of the profession relied on social casework for many of its concepts. But the psychoanalytic view of the individual adapts poorly to the group, and its explanations by no means always consort with observed group facts. Then came a dynamic kind of sociology-anthropology: the concept of status, role, caste, and pattern, and the influence of the situation on conduct.

[18] See Harleigh B. Trecker, ed., *Group Work—Foundations and Frontiers* (New York: Whiteside and William Morrow, 1955), pp. 383–88, for examples of comments by social group workers on the group work–social work relationship.

[19] Clara Kaiser, "Characteristics of Social Group Work," in *The Social Welfare Forum, 1957* (New York: Columbia University Press, 1957), pp. 168–69.

Social group work responded to these sympathetic, explanatory, group-rooted ideas. Many workers shared [Nathan E.] Cohen's belief that the social group work field is closer to these developments than is casework and therefore should bring the ideas to social work as a whole.[20]

In the Current Scene

Any attempt to evaluate the present problems of social group work must begin with the effects upon its thought and work of our "age of anxiety"—to use Auden's phrase—fraught with doubts, pessimism, and the fear of imminent catastrophe. In a paper delivered at the National Conference of Social Work in 1955, Nathan E. Cohen traced the relationship between group work practice and the American scene and described the social climate in these terms:

Uncertainty, doubt, confusion and fear are the order of the day, intensified by an ever threatening international situation. The insecurities resulting from a structureless, and ofttimes contradictory climate add to the mental health problems of the nation. The reactionary political climate which is accompanying this period of change has brought an attack on our humanistic philosophy which has been the base of our more modern approach in family life, education and social welfare.[21]

In such a time, the group itself, regarded in a more optimistic era as a bulwark of democratic society, begins to take on sinister connotations. Against the faith in social action is counterposed the feeling that concerted movement is somehow dangerous, that all collectives are somehow tinged with

[20] Frank J. Bruno (with chapters by Louis Towley), *Trends in Social Work, 1874–1956* (New York: Columbia University Press, 1957), pp. 426–27.

[21] Nathan E. Cohen, "Implications of the Present Scene for Social Group Work Practice," in *The Social Welfare Forum, 1955* (New York: Columbia University Press, 1955), p. 49.

subversion, and that those who seek to assert their interests in this fashion are likely to be antidemocratic and revolutionary. The suspicion also takes a converse form, charging the group with creating inaction and conformity: against the vision of group relationships as a force which liberates creativity and individual power, there grows the fear of "group-think" and the "organization man"; and against the conviction that the group is an instrument for learning and change, there appears the fear that the changes are for the worst, toward the least common denominator, trampling on talent and individual creativity in the exalted name of the group product.[22]

Thus, as any anxiety creates both immobilization and the fear of it, so in the present climate the group experience stands accused of creating both conformity and rebellion. The call for a new individualism is an attempt to find a solution to the loss of human dignity; but in its plea for a new assertion of self, it proposes the one against the many and seeks the sources of freedom in man's liberation from his fellows rather than in the combined efforts of men to control their environment.

The theory and practice of social group work have been trapped, to an extent, by the pessimism of the time. Having developed their outlook on life in an age which had clearly identified the common interest of man and men, group workers built their practice on this insight and were certain, even in bad times, that worth-while ends could be achieved if men trusted the process by which, together, they could find the means. Today, many of their discussions reflect a pervasive anxiety lest social values be lost in the search for means by which to gain them. As one writer has put it, they "cannot be left to chance"; [23] the value system that is abstracted by the social group worker and designated as socially desirable, can-

[22] Cf. William H. Whyte, Jr., *The Organization Man* (Garden City, N.Y.: Doubleday and Co., Inc., 1956), pp. 57–59.

[23] Harold Arian, "Developing Positive Jewish Attitudes through Jewish Center Activities," *Jewish Social Service Quarterly*, XXX (1953), 160.

not be subjected to the trials and errors of the life process and the ways in which people use help to find their way toward what they need. A "positive methodology" [24] is one which produces the predetermined end.

Back in 1939, Eduard Lindeman had said:

The distinction between education and propaganda is simple: in the former there is visible a constant aim to formulate ends and then to invent means which are consonant with those ends; in the latter there is a constant tendency to utilize whatever means are available to achieve ends, already determined.[25]

And before that, in the 1920s, John Dewey's profound effect upon group work thought came through statements like the following:

To say that the welfare of others, like our own, consists in a widening and deepening of the perceptions that give activity its meaning, in an educative growth, is to set forth a proposition of political import. To "make others happy" except through liberating their powers and engaging them in activities that enlarge the meaning of life is to harm them and to indulge ourselves under cover of exercising a special virtue. . . . There is a sense in which to set up social welfare as an end of actions only promotes an offensive condescension, a harsh interference, or an oleaginous display of complacent kindliness. . . . To foster conditions that widen the horizon of others and give them command of their own powers, so that they can find their own happiness in their own fashion, is the way of "social" action. Otherwise the prayer of a freeman would be to be left alone, and to be delivered, above all, from "reformers" and "kind" people.[26]

Shaken from their own philosophical foundations and captured by the false dualisms of an anxious era, many have urged impossible choices between the "psychiatric" and the "social," means and ends, "process" and "content." The true

---

[24] *Ibid.*, p. 165.   [25] Lindeman, *op. cit.*, p. 5.
[26] John Dewey, *Human Nature and Conduct* (New York: Random House, 1922), pp. 293–94.

measure of an anxious conflict is in its grandiose visions of
outcomes and its accompanying distrust and fear of concen-
trating on hard, step-by-step methods of achieving them. So,
in social group work, the rejection of process goes hand-in-
hand with an obsessive formulation and reformulation of objectives. Ends without means must, in fact, have recourse to
magic, and there is a mystical, prayerful quality about these
exhortations to achieve something important without skill and
without method, but merely through the sheer power of intent.

Thus, while the preoccupation with social outcomes remains
a vital part of the group work inheritance, the conviction is
growing that the field of service must send its "humanitarian-
ism in search of a method" [27]—or court disillusionment with
the goals themselves, with the group work process, or with
both. At this moment of history, the concern with method,
far from representing an abandonment of larger aims, constitutes a high form of dedication to their achievement. Writing on the development of social work as a whole, Cohen
draws this connection between individual and social aspirations, and thence to the requirements of a professional method:

Better family life, improved schools, better housing, more understanding courts, more protected economic conditions, better relations between the various racial and religious groups, and more
adequate medical care will all help the individual in his adjustment
and development. On the other hand, the achievement of these
desirable conditions depends on the use the individual can make of
existing institutions and the resources he can mobilize both personally and in cooperation with other people . . .

. . . Integral to these objectives, however, is the method through
which we arrive at them. An approach which seems to accomplish
the goal but which, in the process, destroys the very values from
which it stems is a false accomplishment. On the other hand, without the security of an adequate standard of living, our "ideal" values
can be reduced to hollow and empty slogans. For social work, there-

[27] Nathan E. Cohen, *Social Work in the American Tradition* (New
York: Dryden Press, 1958), chap. i.

fore, both objectives must be pursued together through methods that reflect the "ideal" values from which they arise and grow.[28]

The problem of defining the nature of the helping process as it is carried out by social group workers has been rendered more difficult by the fact that it has been a "profession without professionals," depending on volunteers and unskilled personnel to document what actually happens in practice. Although this situation has changed somewhat with the advent of professionally educated practitioners into clinical and institutional settings, the picture remains much as Towley described it in 1957:

This specialized field is rich in democratic concepts; it has a wealth of examples; but in professionally unique concepts, "method theory," it has been curiously poor. . . . It is possible that no social or economic class in a community is beyond profiting from what goes under the name of a "group experience." But it is difficult for a social group worker to communicate how and why this near-miracle happens, except to another group worker.[29]

On Method

The historical tendency, culminating in the 1948 "Definition of the Function of the Group Worker," has been to define the function of the worker not by the nature of his acts, but by what he *knows,* what he *believes,* what he *is,* and what he *hopes to achieve.* Thus, it is stated that the group worker has knowledge of individual and group behavior, that he holds certain attitudes and beliefs about human dignity and the social good, that he is mature, aware of his own psychological needs and sensitive to others, and that he works in such a way that the group experience will produce individual growth and socially desirable goals.[30]

[28] *Ibid.,* pp. 8–9.   [29] Bruno, *op. cit.,* p. 422.
[30] Dorothea F. Sullivan, ed., *Readings in Group Work* (New York: Association Press, 1952), p. 422.

The qualities of knowing, believing, and aspiring, indispensable as they are to the practitioner, describe neither his function nor the nature of his skill but simply the equipment he needs in order to carry these out successfully. In a dynamic, interactional system,[31] the function of any of its actors can only be stated in dynamic terms, describing a moving part within a system of moving parts, and emphasizing the way it moves rather than what it looks like or what it may help—in a small way, for it is only a part of a relational system—to achieve. It would be as futile to say that the function of a carburetor is "to make the car go," or to act "in such a way that" the car does not stall, as it is to describe the function of the worker as enabling the group members "to use their capacities to the full and to create socially constructive group activities." [32] It is not that these things may not be true, but simply that such a description enlightens us only on ethics and intent rather than on the nature of the helping process.

In theorizing about the helping process, the initial emphasis on function emerges from the basic principle that what one does in any situation should express his purpose in being there. Thus, the establishment of a consistent and workable function for the group worker in the group situation should yield valuable clues as to the roles he must play in order to carry it out. In this context, the term "role" is used to designate the dynamic aspects of a function, or the active, implementing ways in which the worker proceeds to carry out his own unique *raison d'être* within the group system.

To return to our analogy, we may say that the function of the carburetor, within its own dynamic system, is to regulate

[31] See Talcott Parsons, *The Structure of Social Action* (Glencoe, Ill.: Free Press, 1949), pp. 30–38, for a discussion of the properties of organic systems. See also Lawrence K. Frank, "Research for What?" *Journal of Social Issues,* Supplement Series, No. 10 (1957), for discussion of systems of "organized complexity."

[32] Sullivan, *op. cit.,* p. 422.

the mixture of air and gasoline, and then proceed to describe the various kinds of acts it performs in order to fulfill this function. The acts thus described would have several characteristics: they would be appropriate to the ascribed function; they would be directed at tasks for which only this part is uniquely fitted, and which would remain undone if there were no carburetor, or substitute mechanism, in the system; they would express relatedness with other parts of the system, deriving much of their utility from them and being, in fact, inconceivable without them. What is perhaps most important is the fact that the results of its action are limited, and the sphere of its influence defined, by the number of factors over which it has some control.

The mechanical analogy is not meant to be carried to its extreme, but simply to provide a model for considering the relationship between function and movement in a system of reciprocal interaction. In describing the nature of the helping process it implies that: the description should begin with an assignment of function within the group process, and the assignment must be made in terms of concrete and immediate action rather than ultimate, hoped-for outcomes; the functional statement should then point the way toward the elaboration of certain roles, also expressed in the terminology of action, which are appropriate to the worker's function, unique and specialized within the system, and interrelated with the movements of the group members; and the roles themselves—which actually constitute categories or classifications of acts—should be amenable to further breakdown into discrete acts, which serve to illustrate the movements of the worker and the events of the helping process.

To see the process in these terms would make it difficult to project objectives and outcomes that go beyond the worker's actual sphere of influence. In this perspective, goals like "preventing juvenile delinquency," "enabling people to become mature," and "creating a healthy social climate" would be revealed as obviously unrealistic for a given worker or agency, or even for a single profession.

It should be mentioned at this point that such an effort would not represent an attempt to reduce the helping process itself to an automatic, "scientific" procedure, or to deny that professional ways of helping contain artistic components unique to the specific movements of each worker. The art of helping cannot be standardized without defeating its own purpose. But an art cannot become individualized and creative until it establishes its roots in science and in a discipline of knowledge and purpose. While techniques will, inevitably, vary with each worker, a theory of method must be formalized, transmissible, and amenable to interpretation to those in whose service it is pledged. Without a theoretical foundation for method, we have knowledge and cannot use it, or we have goals without a sense of how they can be reached. Both these conditions lead to systems of exhortation rather than of helping. Method, properly understood, is neither mystical nor mechanical.

Within this general frame of reference it is suggested that the history of social group work lends itself strongly to a conception of function in which the group worker assumes, as his area of responsibility, the task of searching out and clarifying the vital connection between the driving motives of the group member and the external requirements of his social situation. This connection becomes increasingly obscure as a society grows more complex; the function of the group worker emerges from his conviction that the normal biological and social development of individuals carries them toward and into the nurturing group. "It is only through social survival that the individual survives, but it is only through the survival of the individual and of some measure of his self-centered concerns and ambitions that society survives."[33] In Baldwin's words, written early in the history of modern sociology:

It is, to my mind, the most remarkable outcome of modern social theory—the recognition of the fact that the individual's normal growth lands him in essential solidarity with his fellows, while on the other hand the exercise of his social duties and privileges advances his highest and purest individuality.[34]

What Jessie Taft called the "living relationship"[35] between the individual and his significant milieu is essentially a compelling mutual attraction, a symbiosis which, however diffuse or obscure it may become in complex social situations, persists in the life process and offers the only ground on which help is given and received. It is only on this common ground that the worker can offer his skill and the group member can utilize it to help himself to learn and grow.

Representing as he does the mutual attraction between two dynamic, changing entities—the individual and his culture— the group worker finds it thus unnecessary to choose between them. He has no need to create impossible alternatives between goals and methods, process and content, but can assume full status as a helping person. He is, in fact, a third force, focusing his activity on the task of uncovering—where it is obscure—and clarifying—where it is confused and conflicted —the member's sense of identification with his own past and present. In the helping situation, he knows he cannot "meet the member's needs," but he attempts to help the member relate these needs to the tasks before him.

The worker is thus enabled to distinguish between present-

[33] Arthur T. Jersild, *Child Psychology* (3d ed.; New York: Prentice-Hall, 1942), p. 158.

[34] James Mark Baldwin, *The Individual and Society* (Boston: Richard G. Badger, the Gorham Press, 1911), p. 16.

[35] Jessie Taft, "The Relation of Function to Process in Social Case Work," in Virginia P. Robinson, ed., *Training for Skill in Social Work* (Philadelphia: University of Pennsylvania Press, 1942), p. 100.

ing a value—as a fact of the member's life—and sponsoring it. His lack of anxiety lest the value perish if he does not "sell" it is born of the knowledge that if it has no utility it cannot be sold, and if it has, it need not be sold, but only revealed and made accessible.

Such a statement of function, further elaborated and clarified, presents the group worker with working problems requiring the utmost in personal maturity, knowledge, and skill. In the roles which emerge, he must find ways of searching out the common ground where it is often hidden by overlays of bitterness and antagonism on both sides; he must help to clarify the nature of the obstacles between people and their immediate tasks; he must provide access to information and ideas they need as they pursue these tasks; he must reveal his own identity and his sense of function so that people may come to know him and be encouraged to use his help; and he must offer the function of the agency as an additional fact of life with which they must come to grips.

Closer analysis will reveal other roles which stem from the function designated above. The illustrative acts which dramatize these roles cannot be specified here for lack of space, but the records of group workers are rich with examples; often intuitive and unfocused, these instances nevertheless reflect Towley's judgment that:

Social work's secret tool is the infinite untapped, unused, unsuspected capacity for growth in the sovereign individual personality. . . . Of all types and breeds of social worker, the social group worker most consciously accepts this democratic premise in his work.[36]

The above is obviously only a brief attempt and a crude beginning in the process of building a functional theory of method which may serve ultimately to remove some of the mystery from the helping process in general, and from the

[36] Bruno, *op. cit.*, pp. 421–22.

group work process in particular. The studies of practice undertaken by the Council on Social Work Education, the National Association of Social Workers, and the Group Work Section of the NASW, indicate that important discoveries will soon be made in this area of concern.

Toward the Future

A transitional phase provides a difficult vantage point from which to see the future, and social group work is, in many ways, in transition to a new identity. It is, on the one hand, still preoccupied with many of the normal problems of a self-sufficient profession, with its own structure, its distinctive agencies, and its own clientele. In the pursuit of these problems, its practitioners are concerned with the interpretation of its function, with its public relations, with the economic status of its workers, with the effort to recruit personnel for the enormous number of job vacancies, and with the educational program for those who will carry on its service and tradition.[37]

Simultaneously, social group workers are working on the common social work task of welding the total profession into a unified entity, and contributing their share in the general effort to uncover its generic foundations. The repercussions of the generic hypothesis are being felt in many ways in the professional association, in the schools of social work, and in the functions of agencies. As professionals work together, as the schools learn how to teach social work rather than a particular method, and as the agencies become increasingly multifunctional, the common base for the profession may extend even further than has been envisioned in some quarters. Beyond a common ethic, common knowledge, and common aspirations for mankind, there are those who are convinced that the help-

[37] See Trecker, *op. cit.*, pp. 373–418, for comments by social group workers on an "agenda for the future."

ing process itself is essentially generic and that the time is not far off when a social work method can be developed and taught. Such a method would be abstracted from the accumulated skill and experience of caseworkers, group workers, and community organization workers over more than a century of practice.

Social group work's history of close association with people where they live, its continuing concern for collective action in the social interest, and its experience with the strength of people in action predispose it to make a significant contribution to a mature, full-bodied social work profession. The group will always be the most potent instrument of social change, and to work closely with people in groups is to become oneself an instrument through which people gain a more civilized condition of life.

REVERSING THE PROCESS OF SOCIAL DISORGANIZATION

NATHAN E. COHEN

It has been far more difficult to define community organization within the context of social work than to identify the essence of casework and group work. The problem has been accentuated in recent years as social work has placed its emphasis more on method and process in the adjustment of the individual and less on the improvement of the social institutions through which the individual functions. Helen Witmer, for example, draws a sharp distinction between social work and social welfare. According to her,

Social welfare is basically secured through the institutional organization of society. Social welfare activities are directed toward the improvement of that institutional organization; social work activities toward assisting in their use of it.[1]

Community organization for Witmer would be an ancillary or coordinate service in furthering the work with individuals by focusing on the coordination and planning between agencies rendering these services to individuals. In regard to broader concerns such as housing, social insurance, labor laws, unemployment, and so on, Witmer's view is that "to call planning involved in all these spheres a part of social work, and all the people who engage in these activities social workers, would deprive the terms of their specific meaning." [2]

[1] Helen Witmer, *Social Work: an Analysis of a Social Institution* (New York: Rinehart and Co., Inc., 1942), p. 39.
[2] *Ibid.*

Definitions of community organization in social work have varied in terms of their focus on method, process, activities, structure, and point of view.[3] In line with the historical development of the professional body of knowledge of social work, the efforts in the past fifteen years have given emphasis to formulations of community organization as a method and a process. The following definition by Ross is a good example:

Community organization, as the term is to be used in this book, is to mean a process by which a community identifies its needs or objectives, orders (or ranks) these needs or objectives, finds the resources (internal and/or external) to deal with these needs or objectives, takes action in respect to them, and in so doing extends and develops cooperative and collaborative attitudes and practices in the community.[4]

The concentration on community organization as a method and a process leads to the following theoretical formulations about objectives and methods: The objectives are a better adjustment between needs and resources as determined through community participation. An integral part of reaching the objectives is the method and process utilized. In other words, just as important as arriving at the objectives is how one gets there if the results are to be lasting and in line with democratic values. The methods include fact-finding, diagnosis, communication, social education, and action. Basic to these methods are such generic principles of social work as:

1. Help the individual, the group, or the community to help himself or itself.

2. Begin where the individual, the group, or the community is and move at a meaningful pace.

[3] See Robert P. Lane, "Report of Groups Studying the Community Organization Process," in *Proceedings of the National Conference of Social Work, 1940* (New York: Columbia University Press, 1940), p. 464.

[4] Murray Ross, *Community Organization, Theory and Principles* (New York: Harper, 1955), p. 39.

3. Focus on the individual, the group, or the community as well as on the problem.

4. Take into account the stage of development (for example, in the case of the community, physical and economic resources, morale, leadership, etc.).

5. Function with flexibility.

As in casework and group work, relationship becomes the kernel of the approach. The pattern of relationship in community organization, however, is different and determines the difference in method. For example, in community organization although one deals with individuals, it is primarily as representatives of groups or group interest. In the functioning of the representative group, there is a variety of patterns of relationship such as:

1. The relationship between the individuals in the representative group structure
2. The relationship of each individual to the group as a whole
3. The relationship of the individual to the group he represents
4. The relationship between the groups represented
5. The relationship of the worker to each individual, to the representative group as a whole, and to each group represented

Since the focus of the community organization worker is on the achievement of the social objective, he deals with the relationships described above within this context. Confusion arises, however, as to whether the objective is the specific goal under consideration (such as new housing, new agencies, legislative action, etc.) or the further development of "cooperative and collaborative attitudes," or both. In brief, the separation of *content* and *process* becomes a more glaring problem in community organization than might be true in casework. In group work, too, there is growing controversy about such separation, especially for those who are interested not only in treatment but also in the use of group work as a vehicle for training for citizenship in a democracy. The problem becomes most sharply defined, however, as one attempts to analyze the role of social work in helping to reverse the process of social disorganization.

The experience in community development in underdeveloped countries has pointed up this problem in bold relief. As outlined by Sanders, there are four ways of viewing community development, namely, as a process, a method, a program, and a movement. In the first, the emphasis is "upon what happens to people, socially and psychologically"; in the second, the "emphasis is upon some end"; in the third, the "emphasis is upon activities"; in the fourth, the emphasis is on promoting "the idea of community development as interpreted by its devotees." [5] These are not separate concerns but rather represent the why, the what, and the how of the community organization approach. To leave out the concern for economic ends and activities related to them in underdeveloped countries and to focus only on what happens to people socially and psychologically can result in a meaningless program. Better social relations experienced in a leisure-time program will not necessarily result in raising economic standards or in meeting the basic needs of food, clothing, and shelter.

The Concept of Causation

Implied in any attempt to reverse the process of social disorganization is an interest in prevention. A preventative approach, in turn, proceeds on the assumption that the cause of social disorganization is known and that it can be eliminated. It becomes obvious immediately that the principle of cause and effect when applied to the multidimensional nature of a social problem is not so simple and clear-cut as may seem to

[5] Irwin T. Sanders, "Theories of Community Development," *Community Development Review*, No. 9 (June, 1958), p. 31.

be true in the physical sciences. Social disorganization is, for example, a relative term whose evaluation may vary with one's value system. Thus, social disorganization exists in the South. For some the disorganization may be evaluated as a negative thing, but others see it positively. In brief, the same observable phenomena of social disorganization may be viewed from a number of perspectives, and there may consequently result a wide variety of theories to explain the causes and the possible solutions. Such theories may run the gamut from a concept of the problem as residing in the individual to a stress on the core as residing in the society, or in the political and religious design of life. Projected solutions to problems of social disorganization, therefore, vary in terms of their focus on changing and reforming the individual or the society, or on letting nature take its own course. Within the context of changing the individual or the society the method for achieving this goal may also vary.

For understandable reasons applied fields dealing with social disorganization have found one-dimensional answers easier to utilize. If one begins with the premise that either an economic, psychological, biological, or cultural factor is the cause, the pattern and methodology for solution can be built accordingly. Much has been learned from the intensive efforts along one-dimensional lines. It has become apparent, however, that the problems of social disorganization are of a multidimensional nature and demand a multidimensional approach in their solution.

A good example of the one-dimensional emphasis can be seen in the approach to prejudice. As pointed out by Allport,[6] there are the following six existing approaches: historical; socio-cultural; situational; individual personality; phenomenological; and stimulus object. There is a tendency for the proponents of each approach to see their particular emphasis as the one im-

[6] Gordon Allport, *The Nature of Prejudice* (Cambridge, Mass.: Addison-Wesley, 1954), pp. 206–8.

portant causal factor. Allport states that "there seems to be value in all of the six main approaches, and some truth in virtually all of the resulting theories. . . . There is no master key. Rather what we have at our disposal is a ring of keys, each of which opens one gate of understanding." [7] The challenge is to put our specialized pieces of knowledge into larger wholes "in the interests of a more adequate understanding of a concrete social problem." [8]

Causation in Social Work

Social work has been concerned with the problems of social disorganization throughout its entire history. It too has veered from emphasis on the individual to emphasis on the environment in seeking the cause and solution of social problems. [9] In recent years its absorption in treatment has been so pervasive that it has been accused of losing sight of its responsibility in helping to shape the course of welfare events. Hollis and Taylor warn of the effects of this trend:

The social work profession in the last quarter century has predominantly concerned itself with . . . the improvement of the quality of individualized services. Proportionately, less attention has been paid to . . . enriching and expanding social welfare programs. The profession has accepted too little of a unified responsibility for appraising and improving social welfare institutions. A continuation of the concern with improving the direct rendering of service to individuals and groups, to the neglect of a study of the causes of the individual and social maladjustment and the possibilities of broader programs of prevention, will seriously limit the expanding role of social work. [10]

---

[7] *Ibid.*, p. 208. [8] *Ibid.*, pp. 206–7.

[9] Nathan E. Cohen, *Social Work in the American Tradition* (New York: Dryden Press, 1958), chap. ix.

[10] Ernest V. Hollis and Alice L. Taylor, *Social Work Education in the United States* (New York: Columbia University Press, 1951), p. 142.

Thus, social work historically has developed a two-pronged approach: concern, on the one hand, for the adjustment and development of the individual toward more satisfying human relations and, on the other, for improving the social institutions within which the individual functions. These two facets should be interrelated but have tended to become separated. At times social work has been concerned with the individual; at other times, with the social institutions through which he functions. Not enough attention, however, has been given to the relationship between these two factors. Better family life, improved schools, better housing, more understanding courts, more protected economic conditions, better relations between the various racial and religious groups, and more adequate medical care will all help the individual in his adjustment and development. Yet, the achievement of these desirable conditions depends on the use the individual can make of existing institutions and the resources he can mobilize both personally and in cooperation with other people.

Process is a means of moving toward the two-pronged concerns described above. It has special meaning for furthering satisfying human relations. Human relations, however, do not take place in a vacuum, but rather around activities and content which have meaning for people. The emphasis on process as an end in itself, therefore, detached from goal attainment which has specific meaning for the life situation of the people involved, can result in reducing the social work approach to a narrow conception of adjustment in terms of the psychology of the individual. This approach fragments the multidimensional conception and leaves out the importance of social institutions and values and goals through which people function. It is a bit like reducing the problem to a single dimension about which we may have special knowledge rather than facing the problem in terms of all its variables. Furthermore, in so reducing the problem there is the danger of dealing with symptoms of the situation rather than with the real problem itself.

To focus on material goals alone without working in relation to attitudes and values of people can also represent fragmentation in dealing with social change. As pointed out by Alva Myrdal, it leads to the risk of "unbalanced development." Her major question in this connection is as follows:

Do the efforts so far undertaken aim as directly as they might toward increased social welfare, that is, human welfare? Are they not too optimistically directed toward an immediate increase of economic productivity, in the belief that such an increase would automatically ensure the welfare of the populations concerned? Are they not too little directed toward those factors which, in the special dynamics of any one country, could be considered as strategic for a long-term development that would both raise the level of production and of consumption and also assure the retention or recreation of indigenous values of culture and human rights? [11]

In brief, content and process are two sides of the same coin, bound together in terms of method, goals, and values. The substitution of one or the other for the whole, furthermore, can lead to the abstraction and fragmentation of the problem. In fact, process has one set of goals related to attitudes, human relationships, and group functioning which are as vital as the material goals—one dimension without the other is inadequate.

As indicated above, any attempt to help reverse the process of social disorganization involves a multidimensional approach. It will of necessity include not only the individual but also the institutions through which he functions and the goals and values of the society. In our approach toward a better equation of needs and resources there may be a tendency to forget that the society also has needs. It must help produce the type

[11] Alva Myrdal, "A Scientific Approach to International Welfare," in America's Role in International Welfare (New York: Columbia University Press, 1955), p. 8.

of individuals necessary for a continuation and expansion of its basic goals and values. In order to achieve this, any program of meeting human needs should take into account what the meeting of these needs will do to the basic social institutions. This means so ordering social institutions that both the needs of the individual and those of the society are being met at the same time.

For example, if social workers believe that one of our major concerns is to help develop a society devoid of group conflict, with freedom for personal development, and conducive to the perpetuation of political democracy, it will not be enough to deal with the victims of group conflict. An important aspect of tackling the problem would be also to help create the kind of economic and social environment offering the best conditions for this type of development. It took the great depression to make us realize that there was such a phenomenon as "structural unemployment" and that a solution to this problem of social disorganization involved working not only with the unemployed but also with the problem of unemployment itself.

Implications for Community Organization in Social Work

Recent trends in social work education reflect the growing interest in broadening as well as deepening its body of knowledge. The emphasis on a common core as a base for all social workers has forced a reexamination of what the caseworker, group worker, and community organizer need to know and be able to do to accomplish the purposes of social work, including reversing the process of social disorganization. This reexamination has involved not merely a reshuffling of the existing body of knowledge but also a look at the new dynamic concepts emerging from sociology, social psychology, cultural anthro-

pology, economics, and political science. The problem facing
the field is how to make this new knowledge usable and how
to integrate the knowledge of the individual with that of social
institutions and of goals and values.

If social work is to contribute to reversing the process of
social disorganization, the effort must pervade not only the
approach of the community organizer who has traditionally
dealt with the larger social problems, but also that of the caseworker and the group worker. Community organization, however, has the major role to play and the implications for it
should be quite evident. We are dealing with the question of
prevention in the full sense of the term. Location of the problem early enough to prevent it from becoming a larger problem
is important but not enough. The next step of utilizing our
knowledge to prevent a problem from coming into being is
essential. This means the willingness and the know-how to deal
with cause rather than symptoms. An analysis of community
organization within such a context might prove helpful.

1. How up to date are our knowledge and theory of community? Warren, in a challenging article on community, questions the validity and adequacy of existing theories and
develops a conceptual scheme of a horizontal and vertical axis
to analyze the structural-functional changes in a modern community. It is his thesis that modern conditions of societal interdependence, centralization, and specialization are changing the
role of the local association. For Warren,

[The] horizontal axis emphasizes locality. It involves the relationship of individual to individual or of group to group within the
locality. . . . Its principal task is coordinative, and its principal
leadership role is that of the "permissive community organizer".
. . . The vertical axis emphasizes specialized interest. It involves
the relationship of the individual to a local interest group and of
that local interest group to a regional, state, or national organization.

. . . Its principal task is accomplishing some specific achievement, and its principal leadership role is that of the "problem area specialist." [12]

A good example is the problem communities face in relation to the numerous national health appeals and programs, such as those for cancer, heart disease, and tuberculosis. The existing community organization structure which is predicated primarily on what Warren refers to as a "horizontal axis" is having difficulty in absorbing the special interest of these national programs. Policies have run the gamut from the "closed door" to the "screen door" to the "open door." Similar problems emerge in relation to state and Federal programs which affect the local community. How can these views best be reflected and represented in a community structure based on local organizations?

Whether or not one agrees with Warren's formulation, there is no question that the knowledge and skills necessary for community organization in a local community relatively free of the forces and pressures of the larger society are not adequate for the organizational demands of our present system. In the same way that there is danger in abstracting the individual from the life around him, so too one can make the mistake of abstracting the community from the surrounding society and culture of which it is a part.

2. How adequate is our ability to "case" a community? Since the community organizer never deals with the total community but only with representative segments, there is need for greater skill in "casing" a community. This involves knowledge of the demographic, ecological, governmental, associational, economic, ethnic, leadership, and power structures of the community. It also involves a greater knowledge of the interdependence of these various forces. In the last several

[12] Roland L. Warren, "Toward a Reformulation of Community," *Community Development Review*, No. 9 (June, 1958), p. 41.

decades the social sciences have moved toward a dynamic formulation which permits a fruitful exploration of these phenomena within the context of operational concepts. The increasing number of studies on caste and class, social roles, group processes, value orientations, value conflicts, reference group theory, social organization, and social control provides useful leads for the social worker. For example, Kurt Lewin's reformulation of groups as sociological wholes which can be defined operationally has led to an increased attention to such properties of the social group as its organization, its stability, its goals.[13] It is important for the community organizer to know that these properties are different from the organization, the stability, and the goals of the individual in it.

A former student visited me several years ago to obtain some help in understanding a "strange phenomenon" he had just experienced. He is the executive director of a Jewish community center in a small community. The center receives supplementary help from the Jewish Welfare Fund, whose primary function is to raise money for national and overseas causes. The board of his agency constitutes 90 percent of the board of the Welfare Fund. When his board, therefore, voted unanimously to ask the Welfare Fund for an additional $5,000 grant to the center for expansion of the staff, he felt sufficiently certain about the outcome to interview prospective personnel. When the board of the Welfare Fund met, however, they turned down the request. "How could this happen when I had 90 percent of the votes?" was his query. My first question to him concerned the attitude of the 10 percent toward the center. It seems they were not ideologically identified with the function and purpose. My second question dealt with the status of the 10 percent. It turned out that they were the high status group and the power structure in the community. My

[13] Kurt Lewin, *Resolving Social Conflicts* (New York: Harper, 1948), p. 73.

third question referred to the aspiration of the 90 percent. It was to be accepted by the 10 percent group. The board of the Welfare Fund was for all intent and purpose a new group whose organization, stability, and goals were different from those of the individuals in it. My former student had done no work with the 10 percent, counting on the strength of the 90 percent.

This is not an infrequent occurrence in the day-to-day operation of the community organizer. There are instances where community groups have engaged in a process around a particular problem for long periods of time without any resulting change except, perhaps, for some adult education experience. The reason for the lack of results frequently has been the absence of the power structure in support of the process. Although we are not too well versed in the ways of dealing with the power structure, its members do represent a reality in community life and cannot be ignored if the goal is social change affecting major social problems. In approaching this group we are on sounder ground if our knowledge of the problem has a valid factual underpinning. As stated by Gustafson:

In the final analysis, the planning group must enjoy the confidence of the various power interests in the community, its product must represent good workmanship, and its recommendations must have an influence on decisions made by those who establish policies and establish budgets for health, welfare, and recreation services.[14]

3. Have we given sufficient attention to research as a tool in social change? Research is an important tool for reversing the process of social disorganization. Social work in its attempt to draw a distinction between cause and function in its professional development has tended to forget fundamental prob-

[14] Howard F. Gustafson, "The Changing Functions of Community Welfare Councils and Their Research Programs," paper delivered at the National Workshop on Community Research Personnel (Indianapolis), November, 1957.

lems. Although there are "cause issues" which are outside the realm and power of social work, there is a larger area of "cause issues" where a sizable contribution can be made to the formulation of social policy which would help in a program of prevention. The method for achieving this type of social change involves a better research base as well as a knowledge of social action. The skills essential for evaluating existing social policy and helping to achieve new policies go beyond a knowledge of process. Process in bringing about change is essential, but greater knowledge of the economic, cultural, and human factors involved in major social policy issues represents the other side of the coin and is a *sine qua non* in trying to help reverse social disorganization.

Community welfare councils have not been too successful in moving beyond the level of coordination of existing services. Planned community change affecting large-scale social issues has been spotty at best. As Danstedt puts it:

Community action is the thread that runs through all council activities. Since the council possesses no coercive powers, it must depend upon the power of logic and public opinion as generated through social responsibility, effective participation by responsible groups, and publicity. The community improvement facet of council operation is by far the most difficult of its functions to carry through. In securing action on such large scale social issues as race relations, social security, health, housing, and substantial expansion of the tax-supported services, many interests are affected, and the reconciling of these interests—often bitterly antagonistic—is a task at which many councils labor with indifferent results.[15]

One would add to Danstedt's observation that the power of logic is strengthened if it rests on a case well documented through research.

4. Is our present structure for social welfare planning ade-

[15] Rudolph D. Danstedt, "Councils in Social Work," in *Social Work Year Book 1954* (New York: American Association of Social Workers, 1954), p. 144.

quate to meet the challenge of social change? The statement by Danstedt implies limitations. Structure is not an end in itself but a means to an end. It is important, therefore, to understand the forces which bring the structure into being and which constantly affect it. Even a democratically conceived structure can become a machinery for a small group with power to control large segments of social policy and to protect the status quo. As they face a growing number of social problems, communities are beginning to look more critically at the function of the council. Gustafson points out that:

Currently, a number of communities are taking a look at Council objectives. In general, these reviews have reaffirmed the long-standing objectives—of coordination among local services to improve quality and eliminate duplication; definition of community problems in health, welfare, and recreation; citizen study, planning, and action to prevent and remedy such problems; and general interpretation of social needs and services to the community.

But more significant, these reviews have emphasized:

1. That a high-level brand of planning on major social problems is a necessity. This is in contrast to the usual practice of coordination and planning among local health, welfare, and recreation agencies.

2. That policy decisions in community planning are primarily the responsibility of lay citizens.

3. That such planning should result in giving guidance and direction to the community as it makes policy and budget decisions affecting all health, welfare, and recreation services.[16]

The emphasis on a high-level citizens' group is important. This group should have the respect of the various power interests and yet be sufficiently above the din to utilize research results objectively and within a community-centered context.

The changes suggested are major and go beyond mere refinements of what we are now doing. For example, if the

[16] Gustafson, *op. cit.*

direction referred to by Gustafson is followed to its logical conclusion the present conception of the council may become a model of the past. The area of concern would be enlarged to include social welfare in the broadest sense with social planning based on research as a priority concern. Coordination of existing services would be important but only in relation to the social planning conception. The planning structure, furthermore, would include both the public and private efforts in a pattern different from what is true today.

For all intent and purpose the planning council is now looked upon by public authorities as a private voluntary organization. As pointed out by Davidson:

The public agency representative does not in many cases feel free to discuss new policies or plans or proposals (for which he is responsible to his ultimate superiors, the elected representatives) with groups of voluntary social service representatives having no statutory or elective relationships with the whole community, and working within the framework of a voluntary, nongovernmental, coordinating agency. . . . It may be necessary, in fact, to change the form or structure of our present coordinating agencies and to give them more official status in the community as agencies that are neither public nor purely voluntary (if that is possible), but agencies whose place is formally and officially recognized by the public authority as entitling them to exercise for public and for private agencies alike the appointed function of coordination.[17]

5. How adequate is our knowledge of communication in a society whose complexity is constantly increasing? This problem is related to that of structure. With industrialization and urbanization the local primary groups with their intensive face-to-face personal relations have given way in importance to organizations of a nonlocal and indirect character. These associations are more formal in structure and organized around

[17] George F. Davidson, "Responsibility to Meet Social Service Needs," in James Russell, ed., *National Policies for Education, Health and Social Services* (New York: Doubleday and Co., Inc., 1955), pp. 161–62.

special interests. Many of them are part of national structures. It is this development which has led Warren to his analysis of the local community in terms of a vertical as well as a horizontal axis. Not only have formal organizations increased, but they have grown in size and given rise to "foci of centralized control." Williams points out:

This centralization and bureaucratization of organized controls is not confined to the New Leviathan of modern government but is also characteristic of corporate business, of large labor unions and of many other associations. Thus, even at the level of the local community the ubiquitous Community Chest is one of the clearest homely examples of the degree to which the practices of large-scale formal organizations have permeated the voluntary private associations.[18]

The problems of communication become manifold both in terms of the "horizontal" and the "vertical" axes. It becomes more and more difficult to relate planning from the community, state, and national levels to the grass-roots. New ways will have to be experimented with to maintain the flow of ideas without fragmenting the planning process to the point of confusion and inaction.

6. Is our emphasis on self-determination a limitation in helping to reverse the process of social disorganization? The concept of self-determination finds its roots in philosophical idealism. In a sense, it was a protecting of the individual's right to do what he wanted to do, provided what he chose to do was right. As pointed out by Williams, "in an age of localism and small groups, the unforeseen consequences of organized actions had a limited impact on the wider society and often were in a sense self-corrective in the short-run because of the immediacy of the consequences." [19] As society has grown more

[18] Robin M. Williams, *American Society* (New York: Knopf, 1951), p. 473.
[19] *Ibid.*, pp. 447–48.

complex and interdependent, a conception of self-determination which does not take into account the ramification of such decisions on larger wholes results in an abstraction of the situation from the larger whole of which it is a part. For example, a study was made in a blighted area as to whether or not the people wanted public housing. The majority of the residents preferred their present dwellings. The larger community, however, favored a slum clearance project since they felt that the slum area was a focus of physical and social infection for the entire community. What is the unit of decision in this case? Is protection of the principle of self-determination for the immediate group more important than the consequences for the larger community? Can change be brought about without offending the limited conception of self-determination? Little Rock, Arkansas, is a good example of a situation which raises these questions.

7. Is our body of knowledge and skill adequate? If community organization is to help reverse the process of social disorganization, the community organizer must be trained for more than the process of adjustment in intergroup relations. This represents but one side of the coin. Even in this important area the body of knowledge, attitudes, and skills will have to come from sources beyond just those dealing with the individual. As indicated above, we will want to work more closely with other disciplines, such as economics, sociology, anthropology, political science, public health, and psychology, both to broaden and deepen our knowledge and jointly to help translate such knowledge into usable form. In the same way that knowledge for working with the individual has come from studies of the pathology of the individual, so too there is much to be gained for community organization in studies of intergroup pathology. Coleman's study, *Community Conflict*, is a good example. Through an analysis of a number of case studies of community controversy he noted that "the same pat-

terns appeared: the same kinds of feelings were generated between the participants; the same kinds of partisan activity occurred." [20] Although these controversies followed a similar pattern in the dynamics of development, the outcomes varied with the conditions available in the community for intensifying or reducing the tensions. The study provides leads for future research on the methodology for dealing with and preventing such controversies. As pointed out by Coleman:

It permits us ultimately to make general statements about the growth of community conflict, and about the factors in the community which affect this growth. Such generalizations make the study of community controversy per se a valuable implementation of our knowledge about community life.[21]

In order to move closer to a program of prevention we will have to learn more about the conditions under which groups will best cooperate with one another. From studies of the individual we know that cooperation takes place:

a) When groups are striving to reach the same or complementary goals that can be shared

b) When the effort is equally distributed

c) When individuals have relatively many psychological affiliative contacts with one another

d) When there is a discrepancy between the desired goal and the ability of any one of the individuals to achieve it alone; in other words, when they need each other

e) When the attitude toward cooperation overbalances possible conflicting attitudes toward potential cooperators and their general philosophy

f) When the rewards of reaching the goal will be judiciously distributed.[22]

[20] James S. Coleman, *Community Conflict* (Glencoe, Ill.: Free Press, 1957), p. 25.

[21] *Ibid.*

[22] Robin M. Williams, *The Reduction of Intergroup Tensions* (New York: Social Science Research Council, 1947), chap. iii.

Although there is a danger in utilizing with groups hypotheses gained from studies of individuals, these findings are suggestive for study and research. For example, in community organization the method of setting intermediate goals to help groups learn to know each other before they move on to long-range goals reflects recognition of the importance of many psychological affiliative contacts as a base for cooperation.

The emphasis on working with related disciplines has implications, too, for the future training of community organization workers in social work. It may be easier to begin experimentation in the advanced programs where the curriculum is more flexible. Thus, a plan has been proposed for several experimental training units sponsored jointly by planning councils and schools of social work. The students would be in the third year or advanced program. The training unit would also include students from related disciplines, such as public health, urban redevelopment, city planning, sociology, and economics. Field work would stress both research and community planning. Courses would be available in community organization method, research, and in the related fields referred to above. The plan of courses for each student might vary, depending on his previous educational background and experience. Through this type of experiment the base of the various disciplines might be broadened and the future community workers would have a direct experience in communication between the disciplines. This specific proposal may not prove to be a workable design, but new patterns should be tested out if better ways of accomplishing our goals are to be found.

In summary, if community organization is to help contribute toward reversing the process of social disorganization, several developments will be necessary. First, we should be clearer about the interweaving of content and process as two sides of the same coin. Relationships are important, but they cannot be regarded as an end in themselves. A better integration of economic, social, political, and human factors is essential. Secondly, our body of knowledge needs broadening and deepening and we require a better bridge to the social sciences and related disciplines. Thirdly, our methodology will have to be brought into line to reflect the new emphasis on goals and the new sources of knowledge. Fourthly, new structures should be developed for the high-level planning related to major social problems.

THE GENERIC-SPECIFIC CONCEPT
IN SOCIAL WORK EDUCATION
AND PRACTICE

HARRIETT M. BARTLETT

Social work has now arrived at a point as a unified profession where the relation between the whole and its parts can be understood clearly. It is timely to examine the concepts which have guided the development during the recent, formative years and to consider the directions of thinking likely to be most useful in the immediate period ahead.

We shall here examine that important and characteristic phase of social work thinking which is concerned with the generic and specific in education and practice. For the purposes of analysis it is helpful to think of it as an inclusive concept, composed of two subconcepts which are interdependent and complementary in meaning.

Ever since its appearance three decades ago, the generic-specific concept has dominated social work thinking. It has been valuable in moving the profession to its present stage. The concept has, however, been loosely employed, without careful definition. Educators have used it from one orientation and practitioners from another. Since the assumptions related to each of these orientations were not usually made explicit, educators and practitioners, although using the same words, were frequently not communicating with each other. The thinking never progressed to the point where an authoritative statement, acceptable and useful to the whole profession, was produced. A social work committee planning a research project could not find such a basic formulation in the literature, although many vigorous and stimulating statements were noted.

It is not the purpose of this paper to analyze the extensive literature in which this concept is used or to produce a new definition of "generic" and "specific" in social work. The aim is, first, to identify some of the major phases of professional thinking which have been furthered through this concept and, secondly, to consider some of the directions in which this thinking is now moving, in the light of better understanding of social work as a whole. Special effort will be made to keep the viewpoints of education and practice related in order to avoid the gap which has been a problem in the past. Furthermore, to prevent getting lost in a maze of terms, the actual trends, issues, and other phenomena in education and practice will be sought and identified, as far as possible. At this point in its evaluation, the profession's main concern must be, not to construct a terminology, but to identify the major phenomena which need to be conceptualized in order that social work may move forward into its next phase in an orderly manner.

Historical Development of the
Generic-specific Concept

Contrary to the pattern in most other professions, social work grew through practice in separate fields, which only gradually coalesced into a single profession. The generic-specific concept has been an important instrument in the process of unification. The concept was first clearly set forth in the Report of the Milford Conference, a voluntary committee of social workers who began meeting in 1923 because they felt that practice had outrun formulation and an orderly analysis was greatly needed. In spite of the tendency to create specialized forms of social casework under different agency auspices, "the outstanding fact," said the Report, "is that the problems of social case work and the equipment of the social case worker are fundamentally the same for all fields." The content of generic social casework was conceived as embodying such elements as: knowledge of norms and deviations of social life; methods of particularizing the human individual and using community resources in social treatment; the adaptation of scientific knowledge and formulations of experience to social casework; and a conscious philosophy.[1]

The final report of the committee, published in 1929, was entitled *Social Case Work, Generic and Specific*. The "application of the subject matter of generic social case work in a specific setting," it was stated, "means chiefly the adaptation of the various concepts, facts and methods which we have discussed as generic social case work to the requirements of the specific field."[2] In discussing education the Report assumed that the specific aspects of the field in which the student was training would be taught in the classroom and in the field work, but stressed the central importance of generic social casework. Because of the nebulous state of much of the subject matter of social casework at that time, it was considered that research was needed to answer the basic questions. The members of the Milford Conference regarded their formulation only as a beginning exploration, "in the hope that it may stimulate, guide and give coherence to the efforts of social workers throughout the country to study their own professional problems and equipment."[3]

Writing in 1938, Grace F. Marcus confirmed the thinking in the Milford Conference Report with the following statement of the generic-specific concept:

. . . the term generic does not apply to any actual, concrete practice of an agency or field but refers to an essential, common property of case work knowledge, ideas and skills which case workers of

[1] American Association of Social Workers, *Social Case Work, Generic and Specific* (New York: the Association, 1929), pp. 11, 15.
[2] *Ibid.*, p. 35. [3] *Ibid.*, p. 10.

every field must command if they are to perform adequately their specific jobs. As for our other troublemaking word, "specific," it refers to the form case work takes within the particular adminis-trative setting: it is the manifest use to which the generic store of knowledge has been put in meeting the particular purposes, prob-lems, and conditions of the agency and in dispensing its particular resources.[4]

The generic-specific concept thus emerged around one phase of social work—social casework—and was not extended to all social work until later. It referred to: (1) a body of common concepts and methods—the *generic* aspects of social casework; and (2) their application in practice, in a wide range of dif-ferent settings—the *specific* aspects of social casework. Clearly, these ideas were interdependent, and both were needed to describe social casework as a whole—its principles and prac-tice.

The generic-specific concept can be traced in the thinking of social work up to the present time. Because of lack of ade-quate communication between various segments of the profes-sion in the earlier decades, however, the original concept did not take firm hold through all of social work. As various groups tried to make use of it, they too frequently fragmented and distorted the concept. They did not push their thinking through far enough to formulate clear alternative concepts. Rather they tended to focus on that portion of the generic-specific concept most useful for their own orientation—sometimes the generic and sometimes the specific—with a vague acceptance of the remainder of the concept but failure to grasp or define its full implications. Terms were used without perceiving their differ-ent connotations within different frameworks of thinking. Thus "specific" and "specialized" were employed interchangeably,

[4] Grace F. Marcus, "The Generic and Specific in Social Case Work—Recent Developments in Our Thinking," *News-Letter*, American As-sociation of Psychiatric Social Workers, VIII (? 1938–39), 3–4.

the confusion in meaning not even being recognized. Further-more, the distinction between specialization in education, a concentration of courses, and specialization in practice, expert-ness in performance in a defined area, was not perceived. The historical account which follows shows the shifting emphases in the use and interpretation of the concept. (It seems appro-priate to put the words "specialized" and "specialization" in quotes whenever used in a manner which the writer considers inaccurate or vague.)

After the publication of the Milford Conference Report, the next major step in the development of the generic-specific con-cept took place in education. The early schools of social work had seen their purpose largely in terms of preparing workers for agency jobs. The first curriculum statement of the Amer-ican Association of Schools of Social Work, in 1932, went a step beyond vocational training. The growing recognition of common knowledge and principles, particularly the concept of generic social casework, stimulated movement toward profes-sional education. The second curriculum statement, in 1944, prescribed eight basic courses as the generic foundation for all professional practice. It recommended that so far as possible these subjects should be covered in the first year of profes-sional education.[5]

Concurrently, the fields of practice were emphasizing the importance of the specific, that is, that phase of the generic-specific concept which had to do with practice in specific settings. The two oldest membership organizations represent-ing "specialized" practice, the American Association of Medical Social Workers and the American Association of Psychiatric Social Workers, had included educational requirements in out-lining their eligibility criteria. Because of their concern for the

[5] Katherine A. Kendall, "A Conceptual Framework for the Social Work Curriculum of Tomorrow," *Social Service Review*, XXVII (1953), 15–17.

quality of practice, these associations had also offered consultation to schools of social work. In order to ensure that the
courses should meet an accepted standard, these two organizations started to review and approve them. Thus what began
as a concern for professional membership requirements became eventually a form of educational accrediting. The activity was not limited to "specialized" content, since assistance
was also offered to the schools in developing basic courses for
all students in "medical and psychiatric information," as it was
then called. Group workers and school social workers later defined the requirements for their particular areas of practice
but did not undertake approval of course sequences.

These concurrent trends in the thirties produced a curriculum which was divided in its emphasis between the generic
and the specific. The prevailing pattern in the early forties was
that of a generic first year and a second year organized almost
entirely along "specialized" lines. "Specializations" included
not only the above four fields but also such others as family
welfare, child welfare, public welfare, community organization, and research. Scholarships were most frequently offered
for the second year and tied to practice in a given field.

Soon it became evident, however, that the subject matter
essential for all students was growing so fast that it could no
longer be covered in a single year. The concept of an
integrated two-year curriculum gained rapid acceptance. In
1948 an important curriculum report was devoted to a discussion of the generic and specific in the teaching of social casework. The existing pattern, by which beginning casework had
been conceived as generic and advanced casework as specific,
was questioned. The idea of a sequence of generic casework
courses for all students, running through the two years in
orderly progression, was presented. It was suggested that the
application of social work to the administrative structure and
working relationships in specific settings was based on general

principles which could be taught as generic content in the schools.[6]

The courses in the second year had been described as "specialized sequences." With the expanding curriculum, the second year could no longer be so focused. There was increasing discussion of the need to relieve the curriculum of the problems of "specialization." From generic casework, the thinking broadened to cover other generic content running through the whole curriculum and, finally, the concept of a whole generic curriculum.

Meanwhile, the progress of thinking in social work practice was less orderly. The generic-specific concept advanced in the Milford Conference Report stimulated practice, but the results were uneven and uncoordinated, since there was no regular channel for examination of practice such as existed for the educational curriculum. The generic-specific concept was widely used in the literature. However, as was pointed out by Dora Goldstine and Roger W. Little,[7] social work literature has not in the past had that cumulative quality which is essential to the growth of professional and scientific thought. Writers customarily started from their own experience and discussed one limited phase of their own practice, with case illustration. They did not sufficiently indicate their assumptions or relate their use of terms to definitions by previous writers. As a result, the generic-specific concept, while valuable and stimulating as an idea, was used with widely differing meanings. Its extension from social casework to other areas, and to social work as a whole, raised a host of new problems in definition. Since the thinking in education was moving at a

[6] Florence R. Day, "Current Developments in the Graduate Curriculum," *Journal of Social Casework*, XXIX (1948), 337–42.

[7] Dora Goldstine, "The Literature of Medical Social Work, Review and Evaluation," *Social Service Review*, XXVII (1953), 316–28; Roger W. Little, "The Literature of Social Casework," *Social Casework*, XXXIII (1952), 287–91.

faster tempo and with greater clarity than in practice, the educational interpretation of generic-specific was applied in practice in undiscriminating fashion. Finally, since the Second World War had convinced social workers that they must have a unified profession, much activity was being devoted during the latter part of this period to the organization of a professional association. This trend reinforced the generic concept and gave the false impression that a common practice really existed and was understood. Thus the final outcome was a kind of fluid thinking about practice which had genuine vitality but was inconsistent and full of gaps because of the failure to come to grips with the problems involved in an orderly analysis of social work practice as a particular phenomenon.

The Milford Conference Report, which recommended a research program, was published by a practitioner organization, the American Association of Social Workers, but seems to have had no influence on its program. The urgent recommendation for research in social casework fell unheeded. Why this was so, is not clear. It is interesting to speculate how much further ahead the profession might be today if a continuing program of basic research had been instituted a quarter of a century ago. Identification of the common elements in social work would have been advanced by analysis of practice. Concepts could have been formulated and tested. The manner in which generic principles are applied in practice in various settings could have been studied, thus clarifying the relation between the generic and specific. The extension of the concept from social casework to social work as a whole could have been more soundly carried through. Many of the present confusions would have been avoided. Finally, the imbalance between education and practice would not have occurred, since the curriculum could have been built on disciplined analysis and description of practice from the beginning.

This did not take place; instead the most consistent stream

of thinking regarding practice during the thirties and early forties was to be found in the studies being undertaken by the "specialized" professional organizations. By this time considerable literature had been published, mainly directed toward definition of appropriate function.[8] No practice studies were focused on the common elements in social work because there was then no channel for a comprehensive approach. Since in describing their specific functions the various fields had to analyze the social work knowledge, skills, and values which they used, they also advanced the understanding of the generic elements at the same time, but too indirectly. New fields and new professional organizations continued to proliferate. Community organization workers formed an association in 1946, and research workers organized in 1950. Corrections and rehabilitation appeared as new areas for social work activity. The new fields joined the older ones in efforts to study and clarify their practice. Until the profession became united, however, these various efforts remained relatively separate and without significant impact upon social work as a whole.

In the late forties and early fifties there seemed to be a real gap between social work education and practice. They were moving along separate lines, each engrossed in working out its own problems and forming its own professional organization. Education was still far in advance in conceptual thinking. Several crucial events accelerated movement toward the generic in social work education. An accrediting crisis in the forties (when for a while there were two accrediting bodies in social work) led to the first comprehensive review of social

[8] Harriett M. Bartlett, *Some Aspects of Social Casework in a Medical Setting* (Chicago: American Association of Medical Social Workers, 1940); Tessie D. Berkman, *Practice of Social Workers in Psychiatric Hospitals and Clinics* (New York: American Association of Psychiatric Social Workers, 1953); Mildred Sikkema, *Report of a Study of School Social Work Practice in Twelve Communities* (New York: American Association of School Social Workers, 1953).

work education [9] and the formation of a national council more broadly based than the previous association of schools. During this period many searching questions as to the objectives and methods of social work education were raised. Immediately after the war the majority of the schools undertook analysis of their curricula and began experimenting with new patterns of teaching.

Finally, in 1952 a new curriculum policy statement called for a comprehensive, generic, two-year curriculum. It was stated in terms of educational objectives, not courses. The three areas of learning were identified as: (1) the social services; (2) human growth and behavior; and (3) social work practice. The statement made no reference to specialization.[10] With its broadened program and generic curriculum, social work education was now in a position to visualize its responsibilities as a whole.

The subsequent discussion and interpretation of the proposed curriculum showed that it was envisioned as a full professional curriculum. The objective would be to give students, not a mass of detailed information and techniques, but a broad foundation of knowledge, concepts, principles, values, and methods essential for all social workers, with some competence in one method. The product of such education should be a worker of professional stature, with capacity for continuing growth, disciplined thinking, initiative, and keen awareness of social responsibility.[11] Much time and effort would be needed to make this teaching a reality in the schools of social work. While regarded as generic, the curriculum

[9] Ernest V. Hollis and Alice L. Taylor, *Social Work Education in the United States* (New York: Columbia University Press, 1951).

[10] Kendall, *op. cit.*, pp. 19–25.

[11] Mildred Sikkema, "Some Aspects of Curriculum-building," *Social Service Review*, XXXII (1958), pp. 11–23; Charlotte Towle, *The Learner in Education for the Professions* (Chicago: University of Chicago Press, 1954).

would need to incorporate whatever of the specific is found to be important for all students. A rethinking of the generic and specific would thus be required.

The movement toward the generic curriculum had been rapid. While it was sound for the profession, it involved certain hazards. The attitude toward "specializations" had become increasingly negative in tone. Questions were increasing as to the validity of the criteria for "specialization." The early assumption had been that each field had certain unique features, because of the differences in the settings. For a while, family problems were regarded as "belonging" in the family field, teamwork was seen as characterizing medical and psychiatric social work, and problems of separation of children from parent figures were thought to be peculiar to adoption agencies. As knowledge flowed from one field to another, it was recognized that these concepts and methods were common to all social work and that the difference was only one of degree.[12] As a result of this thinking there was an increasing tendency to regard the "specializations" as unnecessary and to sweep them away without bothering further about the problem. Because of the confusion between "specialization" and "specific," some persons even began to see generic and specific as opposed and to ask whether there was room for both in social work thinking.

While the concept of the specific was thus becoming weakened and confused, the generic concept was expanding until it seemed on the way to cover all of social work. If the generic curriculum will prepare all social workers for practice, the thinking seemed to go, then this must be all that is important in social work. The generic *is* the whole. The fallacy of translating to practice concepts originally intended for education was not noted.

[12] Florence Hollis, "The Generic and Specific in Social Casework Reexamined," *Social Casework*, XXXVII (1956), 215–17.

Thus, having emerged from separate fields, social work was now moving toward an overemphasis on the generic. It was showing its pattern of swinging to one side or another of an issue, with danger of losing the gains of the past by premature rejection of the specific. This emphasis on the generic alone missed the essence of the complete generic-specific concept, which rested upon *both* elements as essential for description and analysis of social work. If these trends had persisted, the whole concept would have been destroyed.

During this period educational decisions having important implications for practice were being made, and education itself was moving ahead without sufficient awareness of its dependence upon practice. Fortunately, forces in both areas now began to bring these two parts of social work closer together.

When the "specializations" first crystallized, they appeared as two types: as fields within casework, such as medical, psychiatric, and school social work; and as social work methods, such as group work. Trends in practice, however, had been steadily widening this concept. Medical social workers, for years focused on casework in the hospital, were drawn into public health programs, where they became engaged in consultation and community activities. Psychiatric social workers were similarly drawn into mental health programs. Thus it became apparent that, far from being "narrow specialties," each field of practice actually needs and employs all the essential knowledge, skills, and values of social work. The *Social Work Year Book* of 1943 described medical and psychiatric social work as casework "specializations," but in 1945 the volume identified them more broadly as forms of social work. This is a markedly different picture from the original premise regarding "specializations" on which the generic social work curriculum was constructed.

In 1955 the organization of practice was accomplished through the formation of the National Association of Social

Workers. All the groups and segments which had formerly been thought of as "specializations," whether by setting or by method, came together to form a single profession. The establishment within the new association of a Commission on Social Work Practice offered for the first time in the history of the profession a channel through which consistent, comprehensive, and cumulative analysis of practice could be undertaken. In that same year the Council on Social Work Education had launched an important curriculum study, which aimed to move thinking ahead significantly in relation to overall educational objectives, as well as to analyze more fully the educational needs in some selected areas, such as public assistance.[13] The Commission on Social Work Practice was also moving toward a plan for analyzing and describing social work practice, including long-time basic research, but such a program would require time.[14] Thus education was still ahead of practice.

Another concurrent development was, however, diminishing the distance between education and practice. In 1952 the Council on Social Work Education had taken over the accrediting of the "specializations" from the separate organizations. In 1956 the decision was made that schools would be accredited only for their basic curriculum and that accrediting of "specializations" would be discontinued. In preparation for this change, the Accreditation Commission asked the major social work fields to analyze their practice in order to determine: (*a*) what particular content in terms of knowledge, skills, and attitudes is basic for all social workers; and (*b*) what particular content remains as essential for professionally qualified

[13] Werner W. Boehm, "The Curriculum Study: Its Relationship to Social Work Education and Social Work Practice," in *Education for Social Work* (New York: Council on Social Work Education, 1956), pp. 89–96.

[14] Harriett M. Bartlett, "Toward Clarification and Improvement of Social Work Practice," *Social Work*, III, No. 2 (1958), 3–9.

workers practicing in the field. The fields of practice from which these analyses were sought were: child welfare, corrections, family welfare, leisure-time activities, medical social work (including public health), psychiatric social work, public assistance, education, and community planning services.[15] This project, still current in 1958, brought practice and education together in exploration of common interests.

The Scope and Use of the Generic-specific Concept in Social Work

While it is not the intent of this paper to analyze the detailed content of the generic-specific concept, an effort will be made to gain some understanding of its range and of the problems involved in its use. During the early period when educational thinking was dominant, the educational interpretation of the concept was loosely extended to practice. At the time when the first year in schools of social work was generic while the second year was "specialized," agencies used for initial field work placements were described as "generic" agencies. Later, as the curriculum broadened, graduates who had not taken a "specialized" course were described as "generic" workers. The assumption was that they could, and would, move freely from one field of practice to another. Thus workers who did move from field to field were similarly described. A vague idea of "generic practice," as meaning broad, nonspecialized practice, began to take hold, in spite of the fact that careful thinkers kept asserting that "generic" referred only to conceptual thinking.

As applied originally in casework, the specific meant the application of generic knowledge and principles in specific settings. Gradually, however, it came to mean specific practice

[15] Ruth E. Smalley, *Specialization in Social Work Education* (New York: Council on Social Work Education, 1956), pp. 5–10.

itself. When extended to all social work, it necessarily covered all forms of "specialization," which were now following several patterns, partly by settings and partly by social work methods. This illogical situation resulted in many inconsistencies in thinking.

No comprehensive analysis of the generic-specific concept is available in the social work literature. Such an examination would require extensive research. In order to illustrate the variety of its use in social work education and practice, a few selected items will be presented.

Writing in 1949, Elizabeth P. Rice restated the generic-specific concept from the viewpoint of specific practice, clarifying the nature of the interrelation between the two component parts of the concept. She said:

The knowledge that may be considered essential for all social casework may be the basic casework that we have considered generic plus certain knowledge and skills developed in the specialized fields. This, then, means not an eradication of the special area but rather a strengthening of the common base from the experiences of persons within the specialized areas. It means also, and perhaps this is more important, the recognition of the fact that all persons practicing in whatever area of specialization must have a sound basic foundation in casework skill on which to develop the specialization.[16]

In 1948 the curriculum report of the American Association of Schools of Social Work advanced the following premise:

That the major element of difference which is imposed by the special setting is that of agency structure and program.[17]

In a report on one of its workshops the Association said in 1952:

[16] Elizabeth P. Rice, "Generic and Specific in Medical Social Work," *Journal of Social Casework*, XXX (1949), 131.

[17] American Association of Schools of Social Work, *Report of the Curriculum Planning Committee* (New York: the Association, 1947–48; mimeographed), p. 10.

During the past decade, there has been a steadily growing conviction that educational programs in social work must focus primarily on preparing competent professional personnel for the field as a whole and not for narrowly conceived specialties within the field.[18]

Speaking from the background of a particular field, Leon Lucas in that same year raised questions whether the specific was yet sufficiently understood:

Are the concepts which are generic perhaps confused with the principles of practice which are both generic and specific? Are the identical elements in various practices sufficiently alike that they can be taught through generalizations alone? Is enough of the content in various areas of specialized practice sufficiently well known to assume that no specialized content need be taught to students with specialized interests or goals? [19]

Katherine A. Kendall indicated some of the educational problems related to the generic-specific concept in 1955:

I believe we must face frankly that our classifications as to what is specialized and what generic are confused. Consider, for example, that we classify group work both as a specialization and as a process that runs parallel to case work in providing basic preparation for social work practice.[20]

Discussing "specialization" in 1956, a committee of the Council on Social Work Education said:

Any field of practice can use all of the social work processes. Any social work process can be used in any field of practice.[21]

In 1956 local chapters of the National Association of Social Workers asked the following questions regarding practice:

[18] American Association of Schools of Social Work, *Towards an Integrated Program of Professional Education for Social Work* (New York: the Association, 1952), p. 1.

[19] Leon Lucas, "Can We Reconcile Generic Education and Specialized Practice?" *Journal of Psychiatric Social Work,* XXIII (1954), 216.

[20] Kendall, *op. cit.,* pp. 25–26.   [21] Smalley, *op. cit.,* p. 6.

What are the common, basic elements in all social work practice?

What is the generic content in the social work specializations? Of what does specialization actually consist?

What criteria can guide in the identification of generic or specific practice?

What are the changing needs of workers moving from one field to another within the social work profession?

Why are social workers uncomfortable in relation to the dichotomy which appears to have arisen between generic and specific? [22]

It is evident that these practitioners found many problems unresolved in relation to the generic-specific concept.

In the past the concept was clearest when it was used to refer to generic concepts applied in specific settings. The wide range of other meanings and the inconsistency in the use of the concept are only too evident. At various times "generic" has been taken to mean elementary, nonspecialized, common, basic, core, fundamental, essential, comprehensive, and whole. Some of the meanings attached to "specific" have been specialized, different, particular, and unique. Thinking and doing, education and practice, have not been kept distinct. There has been no clarifying, authoritative interpretation which could provide the profession with a consensus and a stable frame of reference in the use of these terms.

Why have there been so many problems? In the first place, there was the difficulty of a two-term concept in which the terms were interdependent but were used within different frames of reference, "generic" usually referring to education and "specific" to practice. Furthermore, the first emphasized thinking, while the second emphasized doing. These transitions were not easy to make and led to endless confusion, as well as to fragmentation of the concept.

In the second place, the generic-specific concept has not

[22] National Association of Social Workers, *Chapter Reports* (New York: the Association, 1956; mimeographed).

been formulated by the profession in a disciplined manner. It would seem that greater clarity could have been attained in the course of three decades, but progress has been hampered by the very nature of social work thinking itself. Because concepts are greatly needed to illuminate teaching and practice, they are grasped at eagerly. There being no over-all stable conceptual framework within which to anchor any individual concept, it is given one meaning here and another there. Terms are thus bandied about until the term itself becomes the reality in the social worker's mind. Effort is expended in defining the term rather than in examining its relation to the actual phenomena of social work and its usefulness in explaining them. In any further thinking of this nature it is essential that social workers learn to fix their eyes firmly on the actual entity which is being conceptualized.

In the third place, social workers have used the generic-specific concept narrowly and without examination of its full implications. "Specific" was too often taken to mean "narrow specialization" in spite of the growing evidence that all the essential elements of social work were to be found in each specific field. "Generic" could have been applied to basic professional concepts, wherever they appeared, but was most frequently attached to education. This may be because so much of social work education derives from the knowledge of other disciplines and the teaching of skills and processes by social workers directly out of their practice, that a fairly well-rounded curriculum could be established on this base. Only recently has it come to be recognized that there is social work knowledge to be extracted from our own practice. The Hollis-Taylor report on social work education in 1951 showed convincingly that a valid educational curriculum could not be built until the profession had examined and defined more clearly its goals, values, knowledge, and methods.[23] For their

[23] Hollis and Taylor, *op. cit.*, pp. 220–26.

advancement both education and practice need to answer the same basic question: What knowledge, skills, and values are essential for competent practice in social work? It is encouraging to note that this key question was finally asked of practice by education, early in the 1955–58 curriculum study of the Council on Social Work Education, and that practice actually set out to find the answers, although with recognition that the road would be long and arduous.

New Directions in Thinking Regarding Education and Practice

If these are some of the problems in the use of the generic-specific concept, what can be learned from this past experience? In what directions should future thinking move? First, it is important to identify those entities in social work which must be conceptualized in order to provide an adequate and inclusive framework of thinking. The essential parts of a profession relevant to this discussion might be regarded as:

1. A body of integrated theory and values
2. A practice embodying the theory and values
3. An educational system embodying the theory and values.

A Body of Integrated Theory and Values. The body of theory on which a profession is based encompasses its generalizations and principles, derived from scientific knowledge and professional experience. The body of values encompasses its philosophy, attitudes, and ethics. At once it becomes apparent that social work, in using the generic-specific concept, has not sufficiently emphasized—in fact, has not clearly visualized as a separate entity—the body of theory and values which supports it. Because of the nature of social work as a helping service, values have been emphasized and considerable progress has been made toward their formulation. Theory, however, remains largely unexplicated.[24] There are fragments and islands of knowledge,[25] but an integrated system of theory is not yet visible. Possibly this failure to begin at the beginning explains the real difficulty in relation to the generic-specific concept and its limitations as a framework of thinking for the profession. There has been an indirect recognition that social work rests on a body of theory and values, but this is seen mainly as a concern of education and not distinguished as a separate entity.

It has been shown that during the period under discussion education has been continually in advance and has made an enormous contribution to social work. The question arises, however, whether the curriculum is being developed in too great isolation from the rest of the profession. How hazardous for the profession is this imbalance between its parts? Should education be recognizing more clearly its dependence upon better understanding of the fundamentals of practice and a more rapidly growing body of theory? No matter how excellent the curriculum procedures, a curriculum can be no better than the foundation of knowledge on which it rests. Is it being assumed that faculty can factor out the concepts to be taught and practitioners can analyze the essential elements in their fields, without more basic research? Educators are in a posi-

[24] Alfred J. Kahn, "The Nature of Social Work Knowledge," in Cora Kasius, ed., *New Directions in Social Work* (New York: Harper, 1954), pp. 204–5.

As used in this discussion, *theories* state the relationship between facts (and their component concepts). As a profession grows, theories are brought together into a body of theory. *Generalizations* express what is generally thought to be so, that is, verified or verifiable propositions. *Values* refer to what ought to be. *Concepts* are abstractions, logical constructs, which can be used (and are needed) in any area of thinking. *Principles,* as used in social work, represent guides to action, composed of knowledge and values in combination (see Kahn).

[25] Talcott Parsons, "The Prospects of Sociological Theory," *American Sociological Review,* XV (1950), 3.

tion to ask the questions and stimulate the rest of the profession toward strengthening the knowledge base. Their leadership in this direction is greatly needed. Meanwhile, practice is at last initiating a long-range research program, which should slowly but steadily enlarge the body of social work knowledge and principles. The delay has been long and serious. If the profession is to advance, educators, practitioners, and researchers must now prepare to work together within a more adequate conceptual framework than was provided by the generic-specific concept in the past.

A Practice Embodying the Theory and Values. A second major part of a profession is its practice. The inadequacies of the generic-specific concept as applied to practice have been shown. One source of difficulty lies in the lack of definitive statements regarding social work goals and functions, which greatly hampers efforts toward analysis and description of practice. Social workers tend to set expansive goals relating to broad social functioning and adjustment to the total environment, which are shared with other professions and impossible of attainment by a single profession. A responsible profession must identify and limit its area of competence. While it is true that there is hardly a life problem which is not at some time the concern of social work, the professional worker enters such a situation under a particular set of circumstances, namely, when there is some inability on the part of individuals or groups to function effectively with the resources at their command. Most often there is some actual or threatened stress or deprivation. The equally balanced emphasis on the psychological and environmental aspects seems to be a peculiar characteristic of social work and probably one of its major contributions, since other disciplines tend to emphasize one or the other approach. Out of its experience in working with social problems and social relationships, social work is increasingly able to emphasize prevention in social treatment and to offer a positive contribution to social policy and planning.

Since social workers are more interested in process, in *how* to do things, than in *what* they do, functions also remain undefined. Actually, the service and the process are at present imbedded in such terms as "casework" and "group work," as now used in social work. It is important that the *what* and *how* elements should be distinguished. In general, it can be said that social work has a right of entry into other people's lives because it brings a helping service which involves an increasingly skillful and disciplined intervention through two main channels: (1) a direct professional relationship with individuals and groups; and (2) collaborative processes (such as administration and consultation) with other interested workers, lay and professional.

The problem of crystallizing these fluid goals and activities into well-defined entities still lies ahead and is a considerable undertaking.[26]

Coming now to practice itself, an approach is greatly needed which will encompass all its major facets in clear and appropriate terms. Promising new orientations are now emerging.

As long as social work practice was carried on in separate fields, no unified concept was possible. When the profession came together, the practice could for the first time be seen as a whole. The center of gravity shifted from the parts to the whole, as was necessary for further progress. The question arose as to how this new and complex phenomenon could be suitably analyzed and described. Practice and education each has its own dimensions. What dimensions are suitable for analyzing practice? A beginning is to be found in the Working

[26] Grace L. Coyle, *Social Science in the Professional Education of Social Workers* (New York: Council on Social Work Education, 1958), chap. iii.

Definition of Social Work Practice of the Commission on Social Work Practice, National Association of Social Workers.[27] Faced with the necessity of developing a set of concepts on which to base its program and lacking an authoritative definition of social work, the Commission sought criteria through examining actual instances of practice. The tentative definition, still at an early stage, covers the dimensions of value, purpose, sanction, knowledge, and method in social work. The plan is that it shall be continually tested out against actual instances of practice until its eventual form and validity are established. The important gain here is the clear focus on practice in operation. The concepts and the criteria are to be derived from examination of what one social worker after another is doing in his work, using all forms of analysis from informal examination to disciplined research.

It is important to note that this definition is based on consideration of a constellation of interrelated factors. The effort to find single factors unique to social work is being abandoned. It is now clear that the description of social work practice will eventually emerge in the form of a configuration, a whole with interacting parts.

In its present early stage this practice definition naturally focuses upon the elements common to all social work practice. How can it also deal with that phase of practice known in the past as "specific"? The assumption is that the basic configuration (the common elements) must be found together in all areas of practice which can be regarded as professional social work. But in each segment of practice there will be differences in emphasis, extent, and use of the elements. In other words, the nine fields of practice identified by the Council on Social Work Education, as previously described, and any new fields, will embody the common elements, but each with its own spe-

[27] Bartlett, "Toward Clarification and Improvement of Social Work Practice," *op. cit.*, pp. 5–8.

cial emphasis and use. The fields will thus be distinguishable from each other but clearly recognizable as forms of social work practice.[28] It will be noted that this method of analyzing practice enables us to progress from what was thought of as the generic to the specific without any sharp division or dichotomy, through the use of a single concept appropriate to practice.

Examination of the fields of practice will show that they have grown up around distinct areas of human welfare and social interaction, such as family life, economic maintenance, health, recreation, and corrections. The idea that all the basic social work elements are to be found in each field, but differently manifested, eliminates the old problem of trying to define specialization through demonstration of uniqueness. Furthermore, such a constellation of factors offers a far more adequate framework than the old concept of "setting." Those social workers who practiced in the "specialized" fields became increasingly aware that the early definition of settings in terms of administrative structure and program [29] was not adequate for describing the complexities of a field of practice. There are other important differences in the nature of the human need to be met, the usual types of human behavior associated with this need, the specific body of scientific knowledge, the cultural attitudes and the emotional response of the worker. This constellation of factors is necessary to describe the characteristics of each field of practice.

This newer approach is well demonstrated in an exposition by Elliot Studt of the contribution of correctional practice to social work theory and education.[30] The title of her article

[28] *Ibid.*

[29] Helen Harris Perlman, "Generic Aspects of Specific Case-Work Settings," *Social Service Review,* XXIII (1949), 293–301.

[30] Elliot Studt, "The Contribution of Correctional Practice to Social Work Theory and Education," *Social Casework,* XXXVII (1956), 263–69.

recognizes clearly the interrelation of the three major parts of the profession—basic theory, practice, and education. She shows how the emergence of a new field need not result in a "narrow specialty." Now that we have a better framework within which to place our thinking, each new field can take its place smoothly as a form of social work practice, incorporating the common elements at the same time that it brings a contribution of new knowledge to professional theory and education.

There is one unresolved issue deriving from the generic-specific concept and relating to social work practice which greatly needs clarification. This concerns the relation between generic education and subsequent practice. According to current views, every school of social work graduate should have acquired the knowledge, skills, and values needed by all social workers, with some competence in one method, such as casework or group work. It is assumed that he will then be ready to enter practice in any field and to move from one field to another. This certainly implies nonspecialized practice, although not the broadest type of general practice seen in other professions. Many workers actually are moving about in this way at present. It is further possible that there is less difference between methods and fields in social work than in some other professions, as suggested by Charlotte Towle.[31] In this general line of thinking, however, the distinction has not been made between the practice of the individual worker and the development of the profession.

Consider the picture of a total profession in which all workers would be moving from field to field in this way. How would such a profession advance? How would workers gain that mastery of any one segment of practice which is necessary for advancement of knowledge and theory? It is true that

[31] Charlotte Towle, "The Distinctive Attributes of Education for Social Work," *Social Work Journal*, XXXIII (1952), 66.

such social workers would be learning more about human nature and the particular social work methods they are practicing. But since social work is a service to help people with problems of adjustment in all areas of social functioning, the profession must be continually deepening its knowledge and theory regarding the stresses and problems in all these areas of life, as represented by the fields of practice. This means that there must be a continually growing body of knowledge and theory regarding psychosocial implications of family instability, economic dependency, illness and handicap, delinquency, and other life situations. It also means theoretical understanding of the manner in which social work values, knowledge, and skills can best be applied in these areas. Without such ever growing knowledge, how can social work expect to make its contribution in a rapidly changing society and continue to practice in effective collaboration with other scientifically oriented professions?

This brings us to the question of specialization in social work. If we look at the other professions, we see that specialization implies mastery of one defined segment of theory or practice. In social work the idea has been confused with the taking of a few courses or practicing in a specific field. True specialization means continuous and disciplined effort in relation to some particular problem over many years. The specialist is the expert, who must often pass severe technical tests. In its further advance social work must give more thought to the nature and significance of specialization. Identification of the common elements is only the first step in building a body of theory. As Elliot Studt says, we must also understand "the *range of variations* possible for each of these common factors, the conditions under which variations occur, and the resulting variations in treatment." [32] The profession must see that a sufficient number of specialists are working on the key prob-

[32] Studt, *op. cit.*, p. 264.

lems, so that the body of knowledge and skills may be continually expanding.

An Educational System Embodying the Theory and Values. The dimensions by which education is analyzed and described differ from those of practice. Education and practice are both concerned with the same subject matter—knowledge, skills, and values—but from different orientations. Education is concerned with formulating suitable teaching objectives, in terms of the changes to be brought about in the students. Learning experiences appropriate for attainment of these objectives must be planned and organized into a curriculum. Social work education is today relatively clear as to its goals and well organized to move toward them in orderly fashion. A generic curriculum has been established and appropriately placed within the total framework of social work education, which includes undergraduate, graduate, and postgraduate education. There is agreement that the focus upon producing a well-rounded professional social worker in the graduate course is sound.

In the movement toward the generic there has been more success in identifying the common areas of knowledge and value than in dealing with the social work methods. There is still uncertainty as to whether social casework and group work (and perhaps the other social work methods) represent basic content in the curriculum or should be regarded as "specializations." With the recognition that all social work methods are needed and used in every field of practice, the distinction may become less important. What is increasingly evident is that every social worker has to do with individuals, groups, and the community. Whatever his primary method, he needs to draw on the other methods for selected knowledge and techniques. In other words, the methods are more frequently combined in practice, and there is more overlapping in their content than was originally supposed. The definition of "specialization" thus greatly needs rethinking and clarification in social work, with appropriate distinctions between education and practice. Observation of other professions suggests that social work has not placed sufficient emphasis on specialization in knowledge. However they emerge later, the social work specializations seem likely to encompass both knowledge and method, in varying combinations, in education and practice.

An unresolved educational issue which demands further consideration is how the specific content is to be taught now that we have a generic curriculum. According to present thinking, part of this content will go back into the generic curriculum. What happens to the residue—defined as essential for the specific field but not for all social workers—has not been faced. Educators seem to be saying that this additional content can be learned through field work and a few electives at the school, followed by supervised practice on the job. This assumption requires examination.

In the generic-specific concept, the specific was always considered to be the application of generic concepts in practice. The specific was regarded as the "doing" and not as involving additional concepts. The present idea that a field of practice is a constellation of essential social work factors, combined and used somewhat differently in each field, calls attention to the fact that there is also conceptual thinking at the specific level. The adaptation of the constellation of factors which is social work to a particular field of practice requires a considerable degree of theoretical understanding and intellectual discipline, both in relation to the total field and the practice of the individual worker. The experience of medical social work,[33] for instance, suggests that the integration of social work with medicine and public health is a relatively complex and demanding intellectual process, not effectively mastered by the graduate of a generic curriculum who receives only the customary orientation to the job. It is not just a matter of

[33] Harriett M. Bartlett, "Medical Social Work Today and Tomorrow," *Medical Social Work,* I (1951), 13–15.

adding to social work a certain amount of information regarding the medical setting and disease. If the social worker is to practice effectively with his professional peers and be genuinely helpful to patients, he must gain command of the developing theory relating to illness and its psychosocial aspects and must be continually integrating it with his own thinking and practice. As in any other field, a considerable body of new knowledge and theory regarding the central problem must be acquired and continually integrated with generic knowledge and skills. Thus a constellation of factors representing social work is being continually combined with another constellation of factors representing a particular area of human life and human need. In this process the wholes must be kept together. This activity seems to be peculiarly characteristic of social work as a profession yet was not clearly delineated in the past, since the concept of "specialized" practice in a specific setting did not reveal the activity in its full dimensions. It has only recently become recognized and may well have within it the seeds of a new basic concept.

The decision that "specializations" will not be taught in the schools thus raises some important questions. During this transitional phase there should be careful study of what is involved in the process of applying basic knowledge and skills in a particular field. Until more is known, adequate decisions cannot be made as to what can be taught in the school and what in practice. One question already stands out. According to current thinking, the material from the fields will continually flow back into the curriculum and will appear at various points in different courses, thus being fragmented. Students will nowhere grasp what is involved in relating social work theory and values as a whole to one field of practice as a whole. For adequate practice later, students need to acquire this concept in the school. They should also recognize the degree of intellectual effort required on their part if they are to become effectively functioning members of a field of practice. We do not have all of social work until the common elements are fully integrated in practice. The schools have responsibility to make sure that students master the complete conceptual framework of their profession in its major outlines.

This comprehensive concept has been taught in the seminars related to "specialized" fields but may be lost unless measures are taken for its inclusion in the generic curriculum. What is learned in field work can be only a beginning. What is learned in casework or group work classes is not broad enough. Students may still have to do this learning around one field. The difference will be, however, that the content of the field will not be taught as a "specialization." The school's responsibility will not be to prepare students for special fields but to ensure that all students grasp this basic conception regarding fields of practice as one essential part of their learning and are motivated to involve themselves in the disciplines necessary to prepare for adequate practice each time they enter a new field. This type of learning requires an abstract and theoretical approach characteristic of the academic setting. Practice will not be able to develop the necessary competence in workers unless education lays the groundwork.

Looking Ahead

An examination of the generic-specific concept and its use in social work has been attempted because this is a crucial time for the profession to assess its position and thinking. This concept, which first appeared three decades ago, was stretched to its limit to carry social work through a transitional period from practice in separate fields to the status of a united profession. The concept was never clearly defined and was used interchangeably between education and practice.

A more comprehensive and appropriate framework for thinking is now needed by the profession in its next phase. There is already evidence that the old concept may no longer be necessary, in the sense in which it was used. Caseworkers now recognize that social casework is a basic method which does not have to be designated as "generic." Other terms than "specific," which do not carry such a connotation of separateness, are appearing to describe social work practice. Some of the old distinctions appear less important, now that social workers have come together in one profession.

Some desirable qualifications of any new framework of thinking to be used by the profession, as indicated by the experience with the generic-specific concept in the past, are as follows:

1. The profession as a whole and its major parts—its theoretical base, its practice, and its educational system—should be clearly delineated and described.

2. The system of theory and values should be given its proper place as the foundation of both education and practice.

3. A more definitive statement of the goals and functions of social work is needed to indicate the scope and focus of the professional activity.

4. The new concepts should cover both the common elements in social work and the range of their variations.

5. In the conceptualization of social work and its major parts (theoretical base, practice, and education), dimensions appropriate to each part should be used. The relationship between the parts should be explicated. Thinking at one level or within one particular framework should not be confused with thinking at another level or within another framework. The transfer of concepts from one level or framework to another should be done with careful consideration as to their validity and meaning in the new context.

6. Constellations of factors should be kept together as wholes.

7. The characteristic pattern by which theory is integrated with practice should be shown.

In future, a more disciplined approach to conceptualization

will be required and will be possible because of new channels for consistent, cumulative thinking. Increased ability to view all parts of the profession in their proper relationships should minimize the tendency to swing from one extreme to another, which has too frequently characterized social work. While appropriately emphasizing its core strengths, social work cannot afford to discard prematurely the gains made in the past, and foreseen in the future, through its characteristic pattern of practice in a wide range of fields. Better understanding of the phenomena and operations of social work is needed before adequate concepts can be developed. Clear identification of the entities necessarily precedes formulation and definition.

There are many signs that social work is moving into a new phase in both thinking and doing. Assessment of past experience with the generic-specific concept will enable the profession to gain better control over its thought processes and thus to become more effective in action.

SHAPING AMERICA'S
SOCIAL WELFARE POLICY

BERTRAM M. BECK

Social work's central concern has long been the effort to enable each man to develop to the full extent of his potential.
From the very beginnings of the profession, social workers perceived the manner in which destitution, ill-health, poor housing, and the like could thwart growth. Early social work leaders not only enlisted in the ranks of those who fought such
evils but were in the vanguard of social reform. If the founders
of the social work profession had been content to dole out a
pittance without any effort to correct the underlying causes of
poverty, they might properly be accused of merely bolstering
up an evil situation. They most certainly could never have laid
the foundation of a profession with its growing ability to base
practice upon theory evolved in biological, behavioral, and
social sciences. It was the basic values of the social work
pioneers which led them to look beyond the handout and it
was the searching look into basic cause that made professional
development possible.

Social work faces a situation today similar to that faced by
its founding fathers. If it cannot influence the social policies
that create problems, it will merely give a handout of technical
help, ignoring the source of the infection. In time social work
will be wholly occupied in picking up the pieces of those who
break under the burdens of modern society, and it will itself
become an instrument seeking adjustment above all. If, on the

other hand, social work can not only give direct service to individuals and groups but learn from such activities, its knowledge in the light of the teaching of other disciplines, and act as an agent of social change, then social work will continue as a vital force.

There is no question, then, as to whether or not social work should continue with a social action program designed to shape social policy in America; nor is there any question as to whether or not social work has, in the past, had such a role. There is, however, real doubt as to social work's ability to discharge its policy function in the light of recent developments within the profession.

The question of ability to continue the social policy role is carefully examined in a thoughtful article by Herbert Bisno published in the journal of the National Association of Social Workers. Mr. Bisno points to the low status accorded social work by society and the evidence of the interest of many social workers in attaining improved status. Social action programs which have characterized social work in the past are seen as intimately related to the practitioner's identification with his disadvantaged clients. Bisno sees social work as currently preoccupied with method and techniques and with offering service to all classes within the community. He suggests that the motive force behind these directions is, in part at least, the quest for status. Should these trends continue, Mr. Bisno holds, it is likely that social work will de-emphasize controversial social action which has broad implications, and there will be a related lessening of attempts to influence social policy and the acceptance by social work of the role of technician–implementer.[1]

Such consequences as Mr. Bisno predicts would be disastrous for social work and, of course, harmful to the society in

[1] Herbert Bisno, "How Social Will Social Work Be?" *Social Work*, I, No. 2 (1956), 12–18.

which it functions. While one cannot deny the reality of the trends which are described, their consequences may be predicted in quite a different manner. In the course of this paper an effort will be made to demonstrate that the trends described by Mr. Bisno and others [2] are not such as will vitiate social work's role as a determinant of social policy; but rather they are such as will strengthen and define that role. These trends have the potential, at least, of allowing social work, not to make so vigorous a contribution as was made by the early pioneers but certainly to make a unique one, and one rooted in a refined and strengthened practice. Social work's future need not be, and in all probability will not be, a sharp break with its social action-oriented past but rather a logical continuation from the past gaining vitality—and not repeating old errors.

Social Action in the Past

Although social work lacks a definitive history, several excellent volumes have sketched its past, particularly in reference to social action.[3] Sometime around the end of the nineteenth century social work in America began to develop a consciousness of itself, not perhaps as a profession, but certainly as a social force. Social agencies and the persons who were employed by them were just as interested in social action to remove or temper the causes of human distress as in ministering to the needs of the families they served. Out of the interest in social reform which characterized social work up until the First World War came notable advance in court

[2] Nathan E. Cohen, *Social Work in the American Tradition* (New York: Dryden Press, 1958), p. 346; Eveline M. Burns, "Social Welfare Is Our Commitment," *The Social Welfare Forum, 1958* (New York: Columbia University Press, 1958), pp. 3–19.

[3] Cohen, *op. cit.;* Elizabeth G. Meier, *A History of the New York School of Social Work* (New York: Columbia University Press, 1954).

reform, improved housing, recreation facilities, and measures designed to protect and better public health. As might be expected, the curriculum of the early schools of social work were as much concerned with providing students with a base for the understanding of social and economic problems as they were with furnishing a base for work with individuals and their families. Early in the history of one of the first schools there was difference of opinion as to the degree to which the school would prepare students for their day-to-day work with clients as opposed to preparation for the understanding of broad social forces. The conflict was resolved in terms of the needs of the agencies, but this merely meant a more balanced curriculum relating the study of social problems to the helping task; it did not mean an abandonment of social policy tasks.[4]

It would appear, therefore, that the problem social work faces today as a profession concerned with affecting the nature of society and also dealing with the impact of society on groups, individuals, and communities is as old as the profession. Because of its persistency one may fairly conclude that the problem is inherent in social work's unique task. Reviewing the important analyses of the problem made in the course of social work's history, it appears that neither the advocates of "methods and techniques" nor the advocates of "social action" deny the dual responsibility of social work; they merely seek a proper balance and functional relationship between the parts.[5] As the scientific base of social work develops and the society in which it functions changes, the balance and relationship must shift. The examination of the problem is, there-

[4] Meier, *op. cit.*, p. 8.

[5] This emphasis is found in Cohen, *op. cit.*, who says function (a mode of action in which purpose is fulfilled) exists within the social reform approach and social objectives are inherent in the practice of social work (p. 315). Also see the writings of Porter Lee as quoted in Meier, *op. cit.*, pp. 77–78, 83–89; and Kenneth L. M. Pray, "Social Work in a Revolutionary Age," *Proceedings of the National Conference of Social Work* (New York: Columbia University Press, 1947), pp. 3–17.

fore, a task which must be tackled anew by succeeding generations of social workers, not with a view to disentangling the necessary organic unity of cause and function in social work, but with a view to finding the appropriate balance and relationship for the particular generation.

One of the first efforts to achieve the necessary balance was the development around the second decade of the twentieth century of a differentiation in training for those social workers who worked with individuals and those who worked to bring about social change affecting the mass of people.[6] Between 1917 and 1929 the growth and elaboration of social work practice dealing with work with individuals far exceeded that dealing with social change. During this period evolved the definition and refinement of the many special applications of skill in helping individuals which came to be known as medical social work, psychiatric social work, child welfare, and family service. Most important, methods of helping were revolutionized by the infusion into social work thought of psychoanalytical theory. By the time of the depression social work had refined its methods of helping and had demonstrated its usefulness in a variety of settings in addition to its home base—the social agency.

Equivalent progress was not made by that branch of social work concerned with social change. Community organization became the field of study and action designed to carry forward the social reform aspect. The effort was made to shift emphasis in community organization from ends to means and to perceive the relationship between ends and means—thereby paralleling the shift in casework thinking. There was, however, a persistent failure to clearly distinguish between the social worker as an advocate of social reform and the social worker as a practitioner who sought to aid community groups in finding their own solutions.

According to Elizabeth G. Meier, the community organizer

[6] Meier, *op. cit.*, p. 66.

no longer exhorted "reform" but attempted to help the community evaluate its own needs and formulate its own objectives. This did not prevent the community worker from gathering data as effectively as possible, presenting it in ways and to the persons and groups upon which it would have the most effect, and *judiciously stimulating* these groups to take appropriate action in order to achieve socially desirable goals.[7]

In cruder words, the goals were those deemed socially desirable by the worker, but he no longer exhorted those who listen to pursue those goals. Instead, he gathered data to prove his point, used it with people in positions of power, and in a quiet way tried to get things accomplished.

Miss Meier suggests too that "possibly the same use of psychological knowledge which taught the caseworker that knowledge cannot be imposed from the outside in behalf of an individual but that he must be 'helped to help himself' also influenced the community organizer. . . ." This is undoubtedly true, but, unfortunately, psychoanalytical theory derived from the treatment of neurotic individuals could not readily be transposed to the field of social change. The effort to do so resulted in muting and masking the social reform component in social work and making the process of community organization a process of hidden manipulation.

Nathan E. Cohen, in accounting for the decline of the social reform component between the First World War and the depression, suggests that "the point of view in social work reflected that of the general society, namely, the sharp diving from the era of social reform at the turn of the century to the search for a return to 'normalcy' after the war." [8] Bruno sees the failure to maintain the social reform aspect as a result of social work's reaction to Dr. Abraham Flexner's paper denying that social work was a profession. Bruno holds that Flexner's challenge caused social workers to set about "defining and

[7] *Ibid.*, p. 67 (italics are mine).   [8] Cohen, *op. cit.*, p. 138.

perfecting their methods with a singleness of purpose that has all but blinded them to the fact that method is only one test" of a profession.[9] Both Bruno and Cohen seek explanations for the decline in social action by focusing on what social workers did not do, when at least part of the explanation may be found by viewing what they did do. Social workers during this period were, of course, dealing with the impact of psychoanalytical theory on practice. This should not be underestimated as a kind of faddism; for an enormous amount of courage, imagination, and intellectual integrity was required in order to assimilate this radically different way of viewing the nature of human beings.

Prior to the advent of the new psychology, it had been generally assumed that social reform could remove the major environmental handicaps placed in the path of man and that casework could by education, persuasion, and guidance aid the individual man to make the most of his environment. Psychoanalytical theory exploded all that. Man was revealed as motivated in large measure by unconscious forces not susceptible to the persuasive methods of the caseworker and, by definition, not accessible to the simple will of man himself. Such problems as alcoholism were seen as unyielding to simple measures of social reform, but deeply ingrained in a complex personality structure, functioning in a specific social environment. The interaction of personality and culture was made explicit and immeasurably heightened the complexity of the tasks social work had set for itself.

Americans were initially as resistive to psychoanalytical theory as were people everywhere.[10] The nature of resistance suggests that it was not merely a dispassionate difference

[9] Frank J. Bruno (with chapters by Louis Towley), *Trends in Social Work 1874–1956* (New York: Columbia University Press, 1957), p. 141.

[10] Frederick J. Hoffman, *Freudianism and the Literary Mind* (Baton Rouge, La.: Louisiana State University Press, 1945), pp. 58–94.

of opinion but rather the psychological resistance which springs from the difficulty of facing unpleasant truths about ourselves. There was nothing about social workers that made it easier for them to accept the shocking suppositions about human nature emanating from Vienna except their dedication to basic social work values. They perceived in the new psychology useful explanations for phenomena that they had daily encountered in their work, and they had the moral fiber to welcome and assimilate these new teachings into their process.

Granting the organic unity of cause and function in social work, it is not surprising that the incorporation of psychoanalytical theory in function would influence the pursuit of cause. The dire results of the effort to apply the new psychological knowledge to social reform have already been noted. It may be posited, however, that if there had been a body of theory pertaining to social change, and equivalent in utility value to psychoanalytical theory as it applies to individual change, social change theory would have been incorporated into the social reform process with a consequent growth of both cause and function in social work. The failure to accomplish this was not for want of trying, but for want of a theoretical base to nourish the effort.

In the wake of the new psychological knowledge came a concentration on the use of self in social work process. Since an understanding and use of the nature of relationship was a key to helping, it was necessary that the practitioner develop an acute self-awareness as well as an awareness of others and of the dynamic quality of relationships. This stress affected the nature of those coming into the profession and probably reduced the number of people coming into social work who could readily take the role of ardent advocate of social reform. While it is, of course, possible to find an individual who can be both a skilled social work practitioner and a social reformer, it is an unusual combination. Porter Lee described zeal as the most conspicuous trait in the advocates of a cause and intelligence as most necessary to those who administer a function. He called for devoted sacrifice and flaming spirit for the cause and fidelity, standards, and methods for the function.[11] Since the combination of qualities desired is so rarely found, it is not strange that those preoccupied with social reform came quite understandably to lament the absence in social work of the pioneer type of leader that characterized the early years. Moreover, the pioneer leaders who had come into social work as reformers and were not personally affected by the impact of theoretical knowledge on practice became increasingly restive with their colleagues and disparaging of the developments which de-emphasized reform as they had known it.

Despite these marked changes in the form and structure of social work, the adherence of social workers to a basic set of humanistic and democratic values made them ever responsive to human need. When the great depression struck, social work was able to demonstrate that nothing had transpired to alter the basic ability of social work to serve on a broad front, although its role as an instigator of social policy had been greatly diminished. Even as severe a critic of social work's alleged failure to discharge its broader responsibilities as Eveline Burns acknowledges that

at the time of the depression of the 1930s and the creation of the Federal Emergency Relief Administration, it was the social workers who brought the intensity of need to the attention of the nation and its lawmakers and who influenced the content of the developing program. For this they can never have too much honor.[12]

Dr. Burns goes on to say, however, that when social insurance was suggested as a new and more efficacious way of dealing

[11] Porter R. Lee, "Social Work as Cause and Function," *Social Work as Cause and Function and Other Papers* (New York: Columbia University Press, 1937), pp. 1–25, quoted by Meier, *op. cit.*, p. 78.

[12] Burns, *op. cit.*, pp. 7–8.

with poverty social workers, with very few exceptions, were not prominent among those developing and crusading for the new method. Again, when the Second World War followed the depression years,

> social work showed great ability and flexibility in mobilizing its resources to help defeat axis powers . . . social work began to pull itself together internally. It also expanded its activities on the international scene, and into new fields. . . . The war experience also necessitated new approaches which, in turn, brought new insights and skills.[13]

But in spite of—or perhaps because of—this sharpened ability to meet emergency and large-scale needs, social work's contribution remained limited as it pertained to questions of broad policy in the development of social services to meet the needs of a nation at war.[14] Thus the years between the onset of the depression and the close of the Second World War demonstrated that nothing had happened to social work to lessen its social concern and much had happened to make possible more effective and skilled services than ever before, despite the limited contribution to the development of social policy.

Acknowledging these gains, the friendly critics of the profession still called for the kind of social action which had characterized the years prior to the First World War, and while, in some instances at least, appreciating the discipline that limited social work's concern to content it had mastered, these critics called upon the profession to develop the balance between cause and function. Marion Hathway asked that the schools produce students equipped with knowledge of the political and economic framework in which social work func-

[13] Cohen, *op. cit.*, p. 249.
[14] Marion Hathway, "Social Action and Professional Education," in *Proceedings of the National Conference of Social Work, 1945* (New York: Columbia University Press, 1945), p. 89.

tions, a conviction to face its implications, and skill to move ahead.[15]

In the decade following the end of the Second World War, the schools were not able to meet this goal nor was social work able to attain the role in social policy many of its leaders wished for. There was instead a renewed consideration of the methods of social work with particular gains being made in the development of social work research, the infusion of theoretical knowledge from the physical, behavioral, biological, and social sciences into the stream of social work practice, and a beginning of systematic consideration of the nature of social work practice.

Social Work Practice and Social Change

Although social work's critics reviewing the development of social work have freely attributed to social workers a lack of interest in broad social policy,[16] there is little evidence to support the charge of lack of interest, and it seems probable that lack of effectiveness would be a more accurate allegation. If the Proceedings of the National Conference on Social Welfare reflect social workers' interest, there does not seem ever to have been a lack of persons to call attention to the social reform function. While concerns certainly shifted from the broad, idealistic, self-confident approach that marked early conferences, the Proceedings for practically every year are replete with accounts of solid gains made in terms of more adequate social provisions.[17]

In a similar sense, those who speak of social work's lagging interest in social policy would be hard pressed to account for the development of social policy programs in the professional

[15] *Ibid.*
[16] Ernest V. Hollis and Alice L. Taylor, *Social Work Education in the United States* (New York: Columbia University Press, 1951), p. 141.
[17] Bruno, *op. cit.*, pp. 370–408, 414.

associations. During the Second World War when social work was, according to some, retreating into introspection, social work's only sizable professional membership association—the American Association of Social Workers (AASW)—was voting to raise its dues in order to support a legislative representative in Washington. When the AASW joined with six smaller professional membership organizations in 1955 to form the National Association of Social Workers, one of the first acts of the Board of Directors was to rank social policy with social work practice as top priority and to establish a legislative representative in Washington. While some held that within the new association dominance was likely to be exercised by those with the greatest allegiance to casework theory, a survey of activities among local chapters in 1958 showed that 78 percent had chapter committees on social policy, and only 35 percent had chapter committees on social work practice.[18] Available evidence, therefore, suggests that social workers do not need their interest in social policy stimulated, but they do need help in translating that interest into action most effectively and in developing and maintaining an interest in perfecting their practice as keen as their interest in social action.

One way in which both these ends may be achieved is by highlighting for the social worker and those interested in social work the relation between social work practice and social change. Those interested in social work's role in social policy need to recognize that social change is not something that takes place mainly when a law is passed or a social institution altered. It is a constant phenomenon that grows out of the clash of ideas.

Modern sociology has been greatly concerned with the development of theory to aid in understanding social change, but not until comparatively recent times were formulations pro-

[18] *Study of Chapter Program and Finance* (New York: National Association of Social Workers, 1957; mimeographed).

duced to which social work practice might be related and from which there might, in the future, be derived a theoretical base for "social action practice" in social work.

Up until only twenty-five or thirty years ago sociology's efforts to explain social change lacked a scientific base. Schools of sociology which sought to throw light on this all-important problem based their analyses on philosophical assumptions or postulates concerning the history of man which had little relationship to recorded history. It was not until the 1920s with the development of the Realist school represented by Pitirim A. Sorokin and Arnold Toynbee and others that there emerged a sociology of social change based on actual history and attempting to use empirical and logical methods to wring from history some clues concerning the principles governing social change.

Although the views of the Realist historical sociologists diverge widely they can be reconciled. It is, of course, not social work's task to accomplish such reconciliation, nor is it social work's task to take major responsibility for further development of the theoretical formulations at hand. Knowledge concerning the nature of social change, however, will one day aid man, and social work as an instrument of man, in controlling change. Such knowledge as is available today will aid us in seeing the contribution of all social work processes to social change.

Toynbee, for example, finds that all through the life cycle of a civilization there is a constant process of challenge and response: [19]

[19] Toynbee's theories are utilized in order to provide an example of the manner in which sociological theory aids in defining social work's contribution to social change, and therefore no effort is made to present alternate theories of social change or to summarize criticisms of Toynbee's work. Those interested in such a summary may consult Nicholas S. Timasheff, *Sociological Theory: Its Nature and Growth* (Garden City, N.Y.: Doubleday and Co., Inc., 1955), pp. 268–71.

The challenge idea is used essentially by Toynbee to mean two things. First there are the challenges in the environment, such as climate or warlike neighbors which, if successfully met, make for the initial emergence of a civilization. Once the civilization is underway, its major challenge is largely from a difference in ideology between the proletariat or masses and the elite or creative minority. These differ as to the responses to be given to a situation. As long as the elite have the better answers and can carry the masses with them the civilization prospers.

When the élite become demoralized or are incapable of leadership, the internal proletariat are alienated from their leaders and join forces with the external proletariat or barbarians. The weight of these two groups together enable the masses to destroy the civilization simply—to put it in non-Toynbean words—because they live illogically for the moment and do not have the foresight to see the long time implications of their acts.[20]

Such hope as Toynbee holds for our present civilization is through the development of religious values. Although the values of social work are essentially humanistic, they are the values stressed in the great religions. Seen in the light of Toynbee's formulation, social work's unique role in social change might be not simply to advance measures of social reform which embody those values—for there are many who will do this—but through the application of social work methods to check forces of barbarism in individual, group, and community. In this respect it is worthy of note that in the Working Definition of Social Work Practice [21] adopted by the National Association of Social Workers (NASW) the values of social work are not seen merely as a creed to which social work subscribes, but rather as inherent and presumably detectable in every "piece" of social work practice.

[20] Carle C. Zimmerman, *Patterns of Social Change* (Washington, D.C.: Public Affairs Press, 1956), p. 37.

[21] "Working Definition of Social Work Practice," *Social Work*, III, No. 2 (1958), 5–8.

Viewed within the context of Toynbee's formulation the social work process contributes to constructive social change in two important ways—leaving aside for the moment social work as an ardent advocate of a particular change. Toynbee states that one of the conditions which determine the ability of a civilization to advance is the capacity of leadership to supply workable answers to the problems that beset masses of people. Deeply embedded in the democratic philosophy is the premise that no one man or group of men have a monopoly on "good ideas." The potential contribution of each man must be nourished, for each contributes to the development of workable ideas. Nobody can predict from what man may come the brilliant synthesis that constitutes a major advance in civilization. Because social work sees in every man a potential contributor to the achievement of mankind's goal, social work practice is directed against the personal and social forces which limit the contribution of any man.

Toynbee sees as a second condition of civilization's survival the ability of the masses of people to accept the "better answers" evolved by leadership. The social worker influences the manner in which those with whom he works will respond to proposed solutions to the challenges posed a civilization, at the same time as he enhances the capacity of a society to find solutions. Social work methods are essentially socializing processes. As a result of their application man is better able to relate to his fellow men. Hostility and hate, having a base in neurosis or in social anxiety, are diminished with a concomitant growth of the capacity to care and the development of personal values as social values. Individual maturation, signified in part by an ability to withstand immediate frustration in pursuit of long-term goals, is accompanied by a social maturation which makes the individual and the group less vulnerable to the seduction of the leader of barbaric forces.

The practitioner of social work methods thereby influences

the system of beliefs in a way limited because of the limited number of practitioners and the limited scope of practice, but of fundamental importance because of the relationship of ideas and systems of belief to social change. Both Toynbee and Sorokin implicitly point to this relationship. Hogan and Ianni write:

We seem to be on firm ground when we assert that ideas and systems of belief determine human action, not to the exclusion of other factors such as heredity and role experiences, but above their influence. Of far greater consequence for action than other factors are the beliefs which direct efforts and give them a sense of rightness. Leighton confidently asserts that human groups cannot effectively carry out acts for which they do not have a system of belief. Lewin establishes our basic postulate in the following statement: "Since action is ruled by perception, a change in conduct presupposes that new facts and values are perceived." Let us agree that it is systems of belief with which we must deal if we are to explain changes in action.[22]

Seen in the light of this analysis, the practitioner is no mere "technician implementer" but is a potent instrument shaping social policy. The caseworker is not merely a passive aide to the troubled individual but an active ally of the creative ego in his client, aiding the ego to gain ascendancy and control of barbaric forces. To the degree that the casework process is helpful, the client is helped not only to solve the immediate problem at hand but also, as a result of the casework experience, to make the fullest social contribution of which he is capable.

In a similar sense, the group worker, in contradistinction to the recreational aide, is not focusing on activities as ends in themselves, but on individual development through group experience; so that individuals can fully participate in man's

[22] Joseph D. Hogan and Francis A. J. Ianni, *American Social Legislation* (New York: Harper, 1956), p. 25.

struggle to fulfill himself. The socializing aspect of group work is even more apparent than that of casework. When group work is used with therapeutic intent, the individual members of the group are helped to personal and hence social maturity. This is accomplished through the medium of relationship within the group. When group work is provided as an important life experience for individuals without particular problems, those individuals gain a sense of identity within the group and an ability to maintain that identity while relating constructively to others. In this process there also comes growth to greater personal and social maturity.

The contribution of the community organization practitioner to social change has the same elements as the contribution of the caseworker and group worker, but quite a different emphasis. Unlike his colleagues, the community organizer does not work with people with the articulated purpose of serving their personal needs; rather he works with people on the basis of their concern about the needs of the community.[23]

The community organizer is in the front lines of the social change process. He actually assists groups of citizens to assess, in Toynbee's terms, various responses to challenges posed, to select what appears to be the workable response, and to make the response selected manifest in social policy. To the degree that the community is a microcosm of society, the community organization practitioner is actually teaching methods of survival. Like all good teachers, however, he is not seeking to attain his ends by simply telling those with whom he works

[23] It is recognized, of course, that perception of, and interest in, social needs is related to personal needs. More important, however, is the as yet almost unexplored contribution of the community organization experience to the citizen-participants in terms of their personal and social growth. Murray Ross in *Case Histories in Community Organization* (New York: Harper, 1958), pp. 3–33, emphasizes community organization as a social work method and refers to the contribution of the method to the achievement of a social identity by the participants.

what must be done. He is helping them do it. This point is of particular importance because of the continued confusion between the early role of the community organizer as an ardent advocate of social reform and his much more important role today as a practitioner of a social work method inducing, not directing, constructive social change.

These roles are mutually exclusive. Social work methods aim to strengthen individuals and groups so that they can make their own choices. The caseworker does not press upon the client a particular solution to the client's problem. His aim is to help the client make a free choice within the realm of possible alternatives. He seeks to create ability within the client to solve his own problems. The group worker does not himself assume executive leadership and advocate a program. His goal is to build participation and leadership within the group. In a similar sense, the community organizer cannot define a solution and "sell" it or pull the strings of power to "get things done," for his role is to increase the community's capacity to deal with its own problems.[24]

The increase of the community's capacity to deal with its own problems as a part of social work's function is a necessary partner to the social reform program. One of the limitations of social reforms gained by the vigor and dedication of the social pioneer is that often they are achieved by acts of executive leadership which gain consent but not conviction. As such they

[24] To say that the practitioner of these social work methods does not aim to superimpose his judgments does not, of course, mean that he has no opinions or that he never expresses them. It means that his major emphasis and goal are to increase the inner-directedness of the individual, group, or community. Nor does the failure of the practitioner to superimpose judgment mean that he is a party to any direction defined by those with whom he works. The community organizer would not ardently advocate a specific solution to juvenile delinquency, but neither would he serve a group of individuals concerned with stimulating delinquency. Social work methods are always allied with the goals and values of the profession.

are vulnerable to attack by equally vigorous leaders of reaction.

Speaking in 1917 at the National Conference of Social Work, Dr. Edward Devine, one of social work's great pioneers, suggested that:

perhaps, appropriations wrested from reluctant legislators do not represent real social progress. If social gains are to remain steady, the slower methods of educating the public are needed to insure such gains becoming a vital part of the standard of well-being which the community is ready to support.[25]

More recently, Eveline Burns, writing on the need for social reform in social work, noted that "our consternation when the Federal confidentiality standard was relaxed was our own recognition that an imposed policy might not have secured a wide base of support . . ." Dr. Burns goes on to suggest that "we may soon be paying a stiffer price for our neglect of [social] action on the state level." [26]

Actually, the neglect of which Dr. Burns complains may well be neglect of a strengthening and expanded practice of community organization. Through such a process communities will gain conviction concerning high standards. Through such a process Federal aid will be drawn down into local communities by a knowledgeable citizenry rather than pushed down mainly as the result of the skill of the social actionist.

Not only does community organization practice directed at increasing community capacity to solve problems induce constructive social change as casework and group work induce personal change, but, like casework and group work, it implants in the participants a sense of their ability to command

[25] Edward T. Devine, "Social Problems of the War—Committee Report," in Proceedings of the National Conference of Social Work, 1917 (Chicago: the Conference, 1917), p. 49, quoted by Meier, op. cit., p. 55.

[26] Burns, op. cit., p. 16.

their own destiny. It relieves the participants from the sense of being helpless and hapless victims of personal or social forces of irrationality. It reinforces the sense of personal and social responsibility for events, and the sense of personal and social ability to shape events.

Today's Issues

This contribution to man's sense of personal and social identity which can be made through the application of social work methods, as well as through social work's social action program, is probably the most important contribution social work can make to the solution of modern social problems. To accomplish this not only does the social change function have to be seen as part of the totality of social work, but social change must be sought in a direction appropriate for the times.

Dr. Burns, in her 1958 presidential address to the National Conference on Social Welfare, lists a series of crucial issues which require social action by social workers.[27] Of fourteen issues named, ten have a major focus on economic and social security; important as these issues are, the question may well be posed as to whether they are the issues to which today's generation of social workers must give first priority.

Edward T. Devine, in setting goals for social work at the turn of the century, said:

Other tasks for other ages. This be the glory of ours, that social causes of dependence shall be destroyed. . . . This be the chosen field of philanthropy, that relief shall come at last to those who in the very nature of the case—the child, the sick, the weak— cannot help themselves.[28]

[27] *Ibid.,* pp. 3–19.
[28] Edward T. Devine, *The Spirit of Social Work* (New York: Charities Publication Committee, 1911), p. 194, quoted by Harold L. Wilensky and Charles N. Lebeaux, *Industrialization and Social Welfare* (New York: Russell Sage Foundation, 1955), p. 195.

Since Devine wrote, enormous progress has been made in conquering the problems of dependency. Modern technology has doubled productivity in the United States between 1900 and 1950, half of this increase occurring after 1940, so that the prospect is that the rate will be even greater in the second half of the century. As a result of this great rise in productivity, both personal and family income have greatly increased and although population is growing rapidly, productivity is growing faster.[29] Such sociologists as Jessie Bernard see the social problems of our time as concerning role, status, and stress in a context of abundance,[30] and this judgment is supported not only by the professional literature of sociology but by the intuitive perceptions of modern literature.[31]

While not for a moment suggesting that social work ignore the problems Dr. Burns cites, it seems plain that if social work is to give leadership to solving the key issues of our time, it must give first priority to the problems which have followed in the wake of advancing material welfare. The symptoms of these problems are seen not in material want but in the rising rate of personality breakdown, of misdirected rebellious behavior, and in the trend to faceless conformity. Less tangibly, the problems are reflected in a loss of a meaningful sense of personal and social identity, defined as *anomie*.[32] "Never before," writes Lloyd Ohlin, "have we faced such a steady and

[29] Jessie Bernard, *Social Problems at Mid-Century* (New York: Dryden Press, 1957), pp. 10–11.

[30] *Ibid.*, Preface.

[31] William H. Whyte, Jr., *The Organization Man* (Garden City, N.Y.: Doubleday Anchor Books, 1957); David Riesman, Nathan Glazer, and Reuel Denney, *The Lonely Crowd* (Garden City, N.Y.: Doubleday Anchor Books, 1955); and the literature of the "beat generation" such as Jack Kerouac, *On the Road* (New York: Viking Press, 1957), and James Braine, *Room at the Top* (New York: Houghton Mifflin, 1957).

[32] Robert K. Merton, *Social Theory and Social Structure* (Glencoe, Ill.: Free Press, 1957), pp. 131–49.

consistent pressure toward ideological conformity in our po-litical, social, and economic lives."[33] Those who yield sacri-fice personal development, creativity, and social growth. All too often those who resist manifest their resistance through deviant behavior that is personally or socially destructive.

The wellsprings of the drive to conformity have been defined as the growth of giant organizational forms which regiment and ultimately diminish man's control over his destiny.[34] These organizational forms are but one result of the technological revolution. Bigness is necessary for survival and success. Once created, these organizational forms are themselves subjected to the conditions of rapid social change, and successful or-ganizational adjustment generates new pressure toward ide-ological conformity.

Whenever rapid social change occurs, existing organizational ar-rangements are in some measure disrupted. Discrepancies occur between the aspirations of people to achieve success and the op-portunities which the structure provides for them to succeed. Rapid social change, by generating these discrepancies between aspira-tions and access to success goals, contains a tendency toward *anomie* or normlessness.[35]

In view of what is almost universally defined as the basic social problem of this generation, social work cannot appro-priately make economic security the cornerstone of the social reform program, even though it cannot and should not divest itself of continued responsibility for those in need. If social work continues to see its major social action goal as building services at a state and Federal level without regard for the impact of social organization on man, it may inadvertently add to the structuring of society characterized by greater material

[33] Lloyd Ohlin, "Conformity in American Society," *Social Work*, III, No. 2 (1958), 58.

[34] C. Wright Mills, *The Power Elite* (New York: Oxford University Press, 1956).

[35] Ohlin, *op. cit.*, p. 63.

wealth and a poverty of spirit. In such a society the forces of barbarism can easily take root and grow. When cause in social work is not attuned to the nature of the times, function may well be perverted and social work methods may become instruments of a sick society emphasizing adjustment when constructive self-expression is the end which must be sought.

Social work must through social action advance workable solutions to concrete problems of medical care, mental health, economic security, and the like; but such solutions must embody means of organization and administration which are geared to lessen, not increase, the dead weight of the pressure to conform on modern man. A beginning has been made in the definition of such means.[36]

Social Action Methodology and Personnel

The response which social work advocates to the challenges of our times must be derived from the experience of social work in working with individuals, groups, and communities. The methods and techniques of advocacy need to be based on theoretical formulations drawn from basic sciences concerning the nature of social change. These methods and techniques should bear an implicit relationship to other social work methods. It should be possible to embrace the method of advocacy within the Working Definition of Social Work Practice. Social leadership must be taught in schools of social work as, of course, it is not today taught.

Social work is not now ready to discharge its social action function in the manner described, but it is closer to readiness than at any other point in its history. Until it is ready it will continue to influence social policy, as in the past, through the social policy program of the professional association, through social work organizations devoted to social action, and through

[36] *Ibid.*, pp. 64–66.

local, state, and national agencies acting together and separately on social issues.

One indication of social work's increasing ability to refine and develop the social action function is the degree to which a beginning has been made in the definition of a method to collect and translate data from practice into social policy. In Washington, D.C., a NASW committee headed by Dr. Raymond F. Gould has embarked on this task, not by the type of abstract discussion which might have characterized such an effort a decade ago, but by the isolation of certain trends and then interviews with practitioners to determine the impact of the trend on families served as evidenced in case material. The method will eventually be applied on a national scale with NASW chapters all over the country participating.[37]

It is significant that leadership for the above-discussed undertaking is being offered by a social worker who also has training in sociology and who is one of a growing number of persons with similar background who have come into social work in recent years and who are helping to develop research methodology appropriate to social work's particular problems.

It is also significant that such a project was launched under the auspices of the newly formed single professional association.[38] In the past, when social action in social work has been discussed, the vehicle through which this responsibility was to be discharged has not been clearly defined. Certainly the individual social worker may as a citizen be a social reformer but, as Louis Towley has pointed out, "when this status is the basis of his community activity, he acts with all the rights and

[37] Raymond Gould, *Tentative Plans for Trend Study by D.C. Chapter* (New York: National Association of Social Workers, 1958; mimeographed).

[38] Prior to October, 1955, there were seven separate professional membership organizations in social work. Four were concerned with particular fields of practice, two with particular social work methods, and one with the over-all needs of the profession. In 1955 all seven were deactivated and in their stead a single organization was created.

privileges thereof and not as a professional, however much his equipment may accompany him." [39] Or, the social agency might have been looked upon as the vehicle, and, indeed, the agencies have increasingly carried responsibility, but "social agency" cannot be equated with "social work profession." However influential the leadership of professional social workers may be, it is the citizen board of directors or the responsible elected official who must have the final say concerning the social policy function of the social agency. Actually, it is only through the professional membership association with its combined concern for cause and function that the profession can speak to social issues. This being the case, obviously the development of a single professional association is a major step forward in the development of social work's social policy program.

It is, as a matter of fact, the very professionalization of social work, which some have seen as a retreat from social action, which is setting the stage for social action. The growth of social work skills so that workers practice under a wide variety of auspices, with some offering service directly to the consumer of services; the growth of fees for social work services; and the development of services adapted to meet the special needs of severely disadvantaged clients mean that social workers today, more than ever before, are coming in contact with clients from all strata of society. With the development of a means for translating data from practice into social policy, social work will be able to address itself to social problems and not merely to the problems of a single group. The analysis of the key problems of society today, which have already been summarized, suggests that unless social work does concern itself with all people—not the poor alone—it cannot effectively serve in advancing a democratic society. There are many types of disadvantages other than economic to which attention must be paid.

The growing professionalization of social work will also

[39] Bruno, *op. cit.*, p. 414.

serve the social action program by giving the practitioner a firm base in practice. The rise and fall of social work's contribution to social policy can be seen, in part at least, not as a function of developments within the profession, but as a product of the society within which the profession is based. While social work as a social institution can never escape the impact of society, it must itself be a social force and not merely the mirror in which the world in which it operates is reflected. If social work cannot make its own invigorating contribution from the hard inner core that is uniquely its own, then it will tend to reflect in its own apparatus the sickness of society. Unless the practitioner operates from a firm base, he is liable to seek social change by following a demagogue advocating ideas unrelated to the social worker's competence and leading not to social reform but to social disaster.

Lastly, social work's awareness of itself as a profession may contribute to the evolvement of the social action program by making possible the training of social workers for social leadership. At the present time, with social work finally moving toward the definition of a coherent program of education built around the basic methods of group work, casework, and community organization, it is hard to see how the schools could extend themselves to the training of the kind of leadership social work requires. However, out of the studies of practice launched by the professional association may come the knowledge which will make possible the definition of varying levels of practice requiring varying levels of competence. Once there is precise data concerning the nature of the tasks now being performed by social workers, it may well be that a whole series of jobs can be described as requiring preprofessional training only, and even possibly a series requiring one year of graduate education and a series requiring two years. With such reorganization one might envision the transformation of the present third year of training into an opportunity for those preparing for positions of social leadership in social work to receive the necessary education. Such a program would be geared to the development of certain skills, knowledge, and abilities over and above those embodied in the two-year program. As has already been suggested, the basic theoretical foundation would derive from theories of social change and students would be prepared to take positions of leadership in education, administration, and the development and implementation of social policy.

The definition of varying levels of practice will not create a hierarchy since the hierarchy is already with us. When the new professional membership association was founded, a master's degree in social work was set as the requirement for membership.[40] The majority of persons in social work positions were thereby shut out of membership. The definition of varying levels of practice will merely induce sense and order into a chaotic situation. With such a definition there may come into being a national organization for persons who do not have what is now considered full professional training but who have social welfare interests. Such a National League for Social Welfare might parallel the NASW and grow out of the local social workers' clubs or possibly be based on the state conferences of social welfare. The NASW and the National League could work side by side on issues of common concern but with each having its special concerns and homogeneous membership base.

It is quite possible that none of these developments can or should come to fruition. This should not, however, stop us from thinking imaginatively of ways and means by which social work can fulfill its appropriate social policy function. The real danger in the current growth of professionalism in social work is not that it will stifle social action but that it will

[40] Of the seven predecessor organizations only two required a master's degree. Some had no specific educational requirement.

freeze social work's program of practice and policy where it is today. There is always the danger of mistaking "what is" for "what should be." We must not, by defining the function of social work in society today, set limits on growth and development to meet changing needs. In this paper there has been a denial that social work has lost its interest in shaping social policy or is likely to lose that interest. The problem has been seen as translating that interest into effective program. The characteristics of an appropriate and necessary role for social work as an instrument of social change have been suggested. The fact that it is not possible to define with precision the ways and means by which social work can fulfill this role is not material. In order that social work may change as change is necessary to meet evolving needs, goals must be defined before we know how they may be attained. With such goals in mind, all avenues of possible attainment warrant exploration with the conviction that a dynamic social work with a hard inner core of substance will change in form to meet evolving needs.

THE FUTURE FOR VOLUNTARYISM
IN AMERICAN SOCIAL WELFARE

SAMUEL MENCHER

Few aspects of social work during this century have been the source of as much concern and controversy as the organization and function of voluntary social service. The role of voluntary activity has been intimately connected with two major developments of the twentieth century: the rise of governmental responsibility for social welfare and the growth of social work as a profession. However influential these factors have been in shaping its course, voluntaryism cannot be viewed solely in relation to the practice of social work or the field of social welfare. For voluntary activity, its nature and scope, broadly affects the structure of society and the relationship of its members to each other and to society as a whole.

Though much consideration has been given to voluntary activity in social work and social welfare generally, attention has been focused primarily on problems arising out of immediate needs and conflicts rather than on the formulation of the fundamental issues affecting the nature of voluntary service. The purpose of this paper is to examine some of these issues and their significance for the function and organization of voluntary activity. In this examination it will be advisable to put aside, at least for the moment, assumptions as to the values or vices of voluntary service—not because these assumptions are necessarily untrue, but because there is little evidence for their acceptance, and their establishment as premises can only limit free examination.

An analysis of the connotation of the word "voluntary" has indicated that, like other value-laden terms exploited frequently and in a variety of ways, it has become "worn out" and may, in fact, invoke unfavorable responses to programs connected with it. "*Voluntary* has been used too frequently to sugar-coat programs which are far from voluntary." [1]

In the field of welfare the term "voluntary" has generally been applied either to actions "performed or done of . . . free will, impulse, or choice" or to organizations "maintained or supported solely or largely by the free will offerings or contributions of members or subscribers and free from State interference or control." [2] There has been some tendency, however, to equate voluntaryism with this last characteristic, freedom from State control. In view of the close relationship of voluntary and governmental activities in welfare and the difficulty, at times, of discerning the relatively greater degree of "free will, impulse, or choice" in so-called "voluntary" organizations, relating voluntaryism to any particular institution or auspices merely serves to confuse rather than clarify. The emphasis here will be on the first component of the definition—actions "performed or done of . . . free will, impulse, or choice"—and the concepts of private and public organizations will be employed to differentiate two types of structures within which voluntaryism may be provided opportunities for expression. While the term "voluntaryism," as discussed here, will be applied only to formally organized bodies, this is not meant to minimize the significance of informal activities, such as neighborly help, whose development may be one of the most important goals and accomplishments of organized service.[3]

---

[1] James M. Vicary, "Worn-out Words," *Bulletin* of the American Association of Fund-Raising Counsel, III (November 1, 1957), 3.

[2] James A. H. Murray, ed., *A New English Dictionary* (Oxford: Clarendon Press, 1928), X, Part II, 302–3.

[3] See "Self-Help in Social Welfare," in *Proceedings of the Seventh International Conference of Social Work, Toronto 1954* (Bombay,

A Perspective on Voluntaryism

The nature of voluntaryism today has been influenced, in large measure, by the growth of professionalism in social work and the expansion of governmental responsibility for welfare services. These trends, reflecting and related to major social changes at the close of the nineteenth century, are relevant to the understanding of current voluntaryism as well as to the planning for future voluntary effort.

The growth of professionalism [4] in social work may be identified with the rise of the charity organization movement and the beginnings of scientific casework in the last two decades of the nineteenth century. Professionalism was a response to the general acceptance of the scientific approach to problem-solving as it permeated the social sciences and to the increasing expectation of the public in a democratic society that service be rendered in a spirit of "justice" and "impartiality." "Modern man," as Karl Mannheim has remarked, "prefers to have his rights and duties clearly defined, rather than to receive a personal favor"; he prefers that his "personal affairs should be treated impersonally." [5] These needs could only be fulfilled by

India: South-East Asia Regional Office, International Conference of Social Work, 1955).

[4] The term "professionalism" is used here broadly in contrast to "amateurism" and is not related to considerations of whether or not social work is a profession.

[5] Karl Mannheim, *Man and Society in an Age of Reconstruction* (London: Kegan Paul, Trench, Trubner and Co., 1946), p. 322. Mannheim significantly points out that the implications of this approach are not "necessarily . . . as at first sight it appeared, that human relationships must become impersonal and unemotional. The new conception of objective justice can be developed in such a way that the emotion becomes attached to the handling of the case and not to the individual who is helped." A description of this trend may be found in Robert H. Bremner, *From the Depths* (New York: New

a professional worker, a worker identified with a definite way of service.

In a field heretofore marked by voluntary effort, this combination of technical competence and objective service resulted in significant changes in organization and administration, and consequently in the nature of voluntaryism. The distinction between the paid worker and the voluntary participant was no longer merely one of social class or vocation. The paid worker became a highly trained and disciplined person whose role could no longer be fluidly interchanged with that of the volunteer. Even with training (and emphasis on training for the volunteer has kept pace with professionalization), the volunteer could not be expected to have the professional discipline required of the paid worker.

In the early years of the Charity Organization Society, the separation of voluntary and professional roles was symbolized by the removal of the volunteer from any connection with the administration of material assistance. Assistance became solely the responsibility of the paid worker. In contrast to the policy of earlier social work, the paid worker became the focal person in the provision of service, and as the concept of his role was clarified and enlarged the function of the volunteer decreased proportionately. By 1905 Mary Richmond observed:

During this last decade more especially, our national habit of thought has exalted the expert and the professional at the expense of the volunteer. By those who hold the extreme of this view, it is assumed that only officials should be permitted to be charitable.[6]

However, as already indicated, it was not only the greater knowledge or skill of the paid worker but also his disciplined

---

York University Press, 1956), particularly chap. viii, "The New View of Poverty."

See also the comment on efforts to conceptualize social work method as problem-solving, by Alfred J. Kahn in the first paper in this work.

[6] Mary Richmond, "The Retail Method of Reform," in *The Long View* (New York: Russell Sage Foundation, 1930), p. 220.

adherence to a formalized, bureaucratic structure for administering welfare which distinguished him from the volunteer. The bureaucratic structure responded to and encouraged the desire for objective and impartial service, and the growth of a professional group administering this service, in turn, effected greater cohesiveness within this structure.[7] The voluntary person, whatever his function, was a stranger to this structure, and his participation created problems indigenous to the conflict between the nature of bureaucratic organization and the nature of voluntary activity.[8]

In effect, the place of voluntary participation in organizations previously controlled and manned by voluntary persons was essentially similar to that in public bodies. The particular factors affecting voluntary participation might differ, but the result was much the same. The more complex structure and political environment of the governmental agencies was balanced by the more stringent professional practices and loyalties of the private bodies. Actually, at the turn of the century, volunteers were engaged in public welfare as much as they were in private organizations. In some cases they were the very same individuals and had been trained by the private charities. Aside from what other values the proponents of voluntary participation might have suggested, the cost of welfare services administered wholly by paid personnel was, at that time, considered prohibitive, and the volunteer filled a real economic need.[9]

The second major influence on voluntaryism was the expansion of public welfare services. Although public welfare had a long tradition rooted in the colonial period, public

[7] Mannheim, loc. cit.

[8] See Bernard Barber, "Bureaucratic Organization and the Volunteer," in Herman D. Stein and Richard A. Cloward, eds., Social Perspectives on Behavior: a Reader in Social Science for Social Work and Related Professions (Glencoe, Ill.: Free Press, 1958), pp. 606–9.

[9] Amos G. Warner, American Charities (3d ed. rev.; New York: Thomas Y. Crowell Co., 1919), pp. 371–72.

agencies generally had not taken leadership in the welfare field. However, the end of the nineteenth century saw a growing recognition of public responsibility and the development of administrative machinery, particularly in the state governments, to facilitate the increase of public activity. While there was no marked shift in public responsibility in the United States at the beginning of the twentieth century, as there was, for example, in England, there were definite signs of greater governmental interest—culminating in the New Deal programs and the social security legislation of the 1930s.

The growing activity and effectiveness of governmental bodies in the field of welfare could not but influence other types of organizations providing similar services. Some reassessment of both structure and function was necessary in light of the changing nature of welfare service. What should be the function of private organizations? How should they be organized to administer these functions? What should be the relationship of private to public welfare? These became and have continued to be pressing questions during an era in which the solid foundation of public welfare has been laid. While private agencies have not always responded with alacrity to the changes around them, the need remains for more than makeshift solutions to the questions posed above if private or nongovernmental organizations are to make a sound contribution to the public they serve, the groups who support them, and society as a whole.

Developments during the past half century have thus resulted in two major problems for voluntaryism in social welfare: (1) the role of the voluntary participant; and (2) the function of the organizations which originated largely from voluntary initiative and continue to derive much of their support from voluntary sources. These two problems tend to coalesce as they affect the scope and nature of voluntary action. For the role of the voluntary participant is greatly influenced by the kinds of functions performed by private agencies and by the way in which these bodies are organized to administer their functions. Though, as already suggested, the field of voluntary action is not totally dependent on non-governmental bodies, these organizations have been traditionally identified with voluntaryism and continue to be looked upon as important channels for voluntary effort.

The "new" philosophy of governmental responsibility for public welfare and the growth of the public services have had important implications for private agencies. True, private agencies could have a vested interest in the status quo; they could struggle to maintain their functions against the rising tide of public programs; they could resist the consolidation of the public system by pressing for private control of strategic functions within the framework of the public services. They could establish new footholds by filling in the temporary vacuums left in the frequently haphazard development of the public program. They could constantly adjust their functions and maintain themselves at the periphery of public advance.

All these solutions are possible and have, at times, been tried. For each there could always be found some justification. However, none has entailed a searching analysis of the appropriate role of the private agency, unless that role is reflected in an effort, whether competitive or cooperative, to share with the public agencies responsibility for the basic pattern of community welfare services. But reliance on this function fails to take account of the essential changes brought about by the introduction of an effective public program and the potentialities for creative contribution of the private agencies. For the demand for impartial and impersonal service finds its ultimate fulfillment in a democratic society through the public services. Though the private bodies were instrumental in setting the tone for such service, their identification with particular elements or interests in the community prevents them from meeting the final requirement of "classless justice." [10] Only the State which could subsume and conciliate the diverse elements of society could approximate this end. Only the State could provide the sense of mutual aid in those services where the condition of need and its satisfaction precluded any but equal treatment. As A. Delafield Smith has so cogently stated,

There is only one proved method of avoiding the growth of the sense of dependency in company with any increased reliance upon proffered services. That method is to make him who is dependent the legal master of that on which he depends.[11]

Thus the provision of services essential to the well-being of citizens has come to fall within the public sphere, and the definition of this sphere has greatly broadened as the understanding of what constitutes well-being has deepened. To the extent that the responsibility for providing efficient service— impersonal, impartial, and technically competent—to the population as a whole is a public function, to that extent the private agencies are freed from this task.

If the emphasis of the public program is on efficient service, can the private agency satisfy other needs of society, where efficiency of service to the client is not the primary end? We have seen that the demand for efficiency was related to the growth of bureaucracy and resulted in a highly professionalized service emphasizing the needs of the client as against the partial and personal motivations of the voluntary participant. Efficient service became to a great degree synonymous with disciplining and even eradicating the impulse and spirit of voluntary charity. These qualities came more and more to be viewed with suspicion and derision.[12] At the beginning of pro-

[10] Mannheim, *loc. cit.*

[11] A. Delafield Smith, *The Right to Life* (Chapel Hill, N.C.: University of North Carolina Press, 1955), p. 3.

[12] It is interesting to note that so acid a critic of upper-class mores as Thorstein Veblen found that charitable activity represented one of the constructive outlets for the "leisure class": "The tendency to some

fessionalization, the "benevolent" influences of the "better classes" was still considered of value if properly guided by the professional. The obvious clash with democratic values and the expansion of the professional role, however, made any type of direct voluntary service open to question. While Mary Richmond in 1905 could see "signs of a healthy reaction" against the monopoly of charity by "officials," [13] eight years later she did not seem so sanguine when she warned:

Against a certain opinionated and self-righteous attitude in some of the trained social workers themselves we have to be especially on our guard. This world is not a stage upon which we professional workers are to exercise our talents, while the volunteers do nothing but furnish the gate-receipts and an open-mouthed admiration of our performances.[14]

Miss Richmond was struggling, however, against overwhelming odds in a period when the knowledge gained from the Freudian psychology and the pressures toward professionalism made service by the volunteer almost anachronistic. The volunteer, if he were to be accepted at all, would be so as the helper of the professional. He would either be assigned tasks onerous to the professional or, where he showed promise, be permitted to assist in minor ways so that the professional could make maximum use of his own capacities. Since these roles could hardly be expected in themselves to appeal to the voluntary participant, great efforts were expended to make the volunteer an "organization man." Recruitment, orientation, training, incentives, and rewards, were emphasized. If the volunteer were no longer to find satisfaction in his assigned

---

other than an invidious purpose in life has worked out in a multitude of organizations, the purpose of which is some work of charity or of social amelioration." *Theory of the Leisure Class* (New York: Modern Library, 1934), p. 339, also pp. 332 ff.

[13] Richmond, *loc. cit.*

[14] Mary Richmond, "The Case for the Volunteer," in *The Long View*, p. 345.

tasks, he would at least be motivated by the same system of artificial stimuli which he encountered as a member of other institutions of society.

It is true that this approach did not pervade every aspect of social work. The settlements continued to provide a directly satisfying experience for many voluntary participants. Sometimes, too, the pattern has been reversed, and the most influential and responsible voluntary roles in private agencies, such as board membership, have been free of the controls and accountability normally expected of such positions.[15] On the whole, however, the volunteer has been caught up in the pressure for organizational efficiency. Where his interests had been predominant prior to the close of the nineteenth century, they are now considered, if at all, only in relation to the agency and its professional needs.[16]

The process of subordinating voluntary participation to bureaucratic control is probably most clearly illustrated by the growth of the community chest and the united fund. These represent the final phase of divorcing voluntaryism from private social welfare. The role of voluntaryism has changed from doing to giving, and, as one perceptive analysis has suggested, there has been a full swing from earlier philanthropy marked by "passivity in the receiver and activity in the giver"

[15] John R. Seeley *et al.*, *Community Chest, a Case Study in Philanthropy* (Toronto: University of Toronto Press, 1957), pp. 435–36. The authors contrast the relatively "irresponsible" behavior of voluntary leadership with the behavior of these same individuals in the bureaucratic roles of everyday business life.

[16] The literature of social work has abundant examples of this approach. For two illustrations spanning some forty years of social work practice the reader is referred to: Karl de Schweinitz, "Avocational Guidance," in *Proceedings of the National Conference of Social Work, 1917* (Chicago: the Conference, 1917), pp. 118–25; and Marjorie A. Collins, "The Volunteer's Role in Rendering Services to Individuals," in *Casework Papers, 1957* (New York: Family Service Association of America, 1957), pp. 59–72.

to "activity in the fundraiser and passivity in the giver." [17]

Through the chest or fund the private social agency removed itself from dependence on any specific public and made itself the anonymous recipient of an anonymous public. The private agency prided itself that the public had no longer any need for identification with specific causes, but was educated to the bureaucratic ideal of impartial and impersonal service, i.e., the general welfare. In effect, this approach represented the ultimate for bureaucratic freedom. True, the chests and funds have had their own problems in the competitive struggle to share community resources, but these problems are, in reality, as related to voluntaryism as the control of any large corporation is related to the great mass of common stockholders.

The ultimate implications of the united fund are the negation of the values of voluntaryism. More active participation than giving and collecting donations is discouraged both by the complex and impersonal nature of the structure and by the siphoning off of voluntary energies into these functions. The approved roles for voluntary participation, as defined by the fund and its member agencies, are almost entirely enveloped in fund-raising. Vicarious participation has become the goal where once "buying one's way" in lieu of performing actual deeds was viewed somewhat dubiously. A community's voluntaryism is measured by the success of its fund-raising campaigns, and the pressures for conformity are so great as to warrant the comment which Reisman has made of voluntary associations generally: they "are not voluntary enough to do the job" and they only increase the individual's sense of "helplessness." [18]

Apart from the conflict between the business of large-scale

[17] Seeley et al., op. cit., p. 37.
[18] David Riesman, "The Saving Remnant," in Individualism Reconsidered (Glencoe, Ill.: Free Press, 1954), p. 114.

fund-raising and voluntaryism, the efforts of the united funds to develop a theoretically unified community cut across the real differences and interests in community life which provide the setting for voluntary participation. Voluntary activity provides the opportunity for expression of goals meaningful to individuals and groups. Its function is not the achievement of a commonly acceptable program through eliminating, accommodating, or surmounting underlying divisions as is the case in governmental institutions.[19] The establishment of a supra-organization paralleling the community's political structure is neither realistic nor desirable in view of voluntary interests and needs.

The development of complex welfare organizations thus creates another obstacle to freedom of action and discourages tendencies toward "looseness" and "diversity" valuable in an already highly organized society.[20] Finally, the value, to which Mannheim alludes, of some institutions supported by "small groups" bearing the "risks and responsibilities" of proving the "necessity of their existence" is removed as private welfare becomes a more centralized and bureaucratic monopoly.[21]

The transformation of voluntary social work into a highly organized system with few surviving elements of voluntaryism has been sketched. However, while these changes were taking place, developments both within and outside the field of welfare greatly lessened the need for this kind of approach to private social work. The growth of the public services, as already indicated, removed from the private agency much of its responsibility as provider of service. The pressure of rigidly

---

[19] For an interesting discussion of this point see H. L. Lurie, "The Approach and Philosophy of Jewish Social Welfare," *Jewish Social Service Quarterly,* XXIX (1953), 255–63.

[20] There are many examples of the exclusion of "unpopular" organizations from chests and councils, such as the pressure against the National Urban League in community chests of Southern cities.

[21] Mannheim, *op. cit.,* p. 380.

advancing professionalism was lightened by the general acceptance of the professional ethic of service. The fear of the paternalism of earlier philanthropy was reduced by many influences, including changing class relationships, professional interpretation, and the growth of a sense of social responsibility. Thus, it would seem appropriate for private agencies to reassess their function and consider the value of returning to, and extending the principles of, voluntaryism upon which they were founded.

In Both Private and Public Programs

Now that measures have been taken to place service to the client on a proper footing, can a greater component of voluntaryism become one of the major goals of private effort? Can the private agencies afford the "looseness" that such an approach entails? Is it possible to distinguish goals for voluntary action unfettered by professional and bureaucratic demands? The solution does not necessarily require the loss of professional effectiveness, but rather different objectives with emphasis on opportunities for voluntary action.[22]

Hesitation in reorienting their functions toward the goals of voluntaryism is to be expected of private agencies. The flexibility usually ascribed to private agencies is a quality more rightly associated with their earlier voluntaryism than with their present professionalism. The private agency may validly ask: "Why should we assume the responsibility for supporting voluntaryism? Have we a greater obligation toward voluntary-

[22] Peter M. Blau, in *Bureaucracy in Modern Society* (New York: Random House, 1956), analyzes the problem of incorporating democratic procedures—citizen participation—in organizations which have "the double purpose of deciding on common objectives, on the one hand, and of carrying the decisions out, on the other." The tendency, as he sees it, has been for the latter function (as has occurred in social work) to overshadow the former. See particularly pp. 105 ff.

ism than other institutions of society?" Obviously, there is no clear-cut answer. While broadening the base of democratic participation in all institutions may be a generally accepted value, welfare, both public and private, has been considered particularly responsive to citizen participation. Other institutions too have evolved from informal and voluntary ventures into specialized and organized bodies. However, welfare is perhaps the only function of society in which the value for the individual of giving service has been maintained. Whatever the causes, secular or sacred, there has been less willingness to delegate this responsibility to formal institutions. And the organizations which act as the focus of this desire to be of service have an especial obligation to provide constructive and satisfying channels for its fulfillment.

This unique role for social work has been reflected in the development of a relatively new field of specialization, community organization. One of its major purposes is to enable "citizen groups to work out problems" related to community needs and services.[23] Other professions have emphasized citizen participation, but none has taken so great a responsibility for its implementation. However, as has been noted, social work institutions themselves have not always been the most avid consumers of their own doctrine.

Voluntaryism, however, is by no means the exclusive concern of nongovernmental bodies. The acceptance by government of the responsibility for social welfare has made the social services a matter of public policy. Following the depression of the 1930s, the function of government clearly changed from a residual responsibility for special groups, or for the general welfare in times of crisis, to a continuing and constructive role in maintaining a healthy society. As in other countries

[23] Campbell G. Murphy, "Community Organization for Social Welfare," in Russell H. Kurtz, ed., *Social Work Year Book, 1957* (New York: National Association of Social Workers, 1957), pp. 179–85.

with a tradition of voluntary action the expanding role of government, however, does not signify the elimination of voluntaryism. Though government may be the source of all major welfare services, it does not necessarily become the sole supplier. There is room for voluntary participation both within and outside the governmental structure. In effect, one of the most important issues of social policy is the incorporation of voluntary effort in public welfare planning; for the values inherent in voluntary action are too essential to be left to the haphazard discretion of public or private bodies.

The provision of "free zones" for autonomous voluntary activity and for voluntary participation within government basically involves public planning where the principles of public responsibility and voluntary effort are present in society. The free zones, while capable of making a valuable contribution, must be encouraged to assume appropriate functions and discouraged from obstructing the interests of the general welfare and dissipating voluntary resources. In a complex society the free zones cannot be expected to undertake this function either independently or in cooperation. As Karl Mannheim has so cogently stated (and as the history of the chest and council movement in social work has so clearly demonstrated), "freedom cannot consist in the mutual control of individual institutions, for this can never lead to planned cooperation." [24] This does not mean that voluntary functions are to be rigidly defined or limited; it means that the zones for voluntary initi-

[24] Mannheim, *op. cit.*, p. 378. George F. Davidson suggests another approach—the development of community coordinating structures with some "official status in the community as agencies that are neither public nor purely voluntary (if that is possible), but agencies whose place is formally and officially recognized by the public authority as entitling them to exercise for public and private agencies alike the appointed function of coordination." "Responsibility to Meet Social Service Needs," in James E. Russell, ed., *National Policies for Education, Health and Social Services* (New York: Doubleday and Co., Inc., 1955), p. 162.

ative will be considered with regard to the total pattern of welfare services. For the continuance of voluntary activity in welfare as in other fields will, in the long run, depend on its acceptance as reflected in the decisions of the political bodies of society.

Many aspects of social welfare have illustrated the conflict between the interests of the community or society as a whole and those of particular groups. Vested interests in the children's and health services, for example, have frequently limited the efforts of society to plan effectively and rationally for the common welfare. Sectarian groups in the children's services have often placed their own needs above the community's interest in the welfare of its children.[25] While there is room within the free zones for voluntary activity indicative of many kinds of child care philosophy, it is not the function of the free zones to define the nature or extent of public responsibility. Rather, public responsibility in the field of welfare must be clearly established without regard to the presence or absence of other resources. While the administration of this responsibility may vary, the goals of the community for its members must be guaranteed. In child welfare, for example, the standards set by the legal institutions must affect the welfare of every child; this responsibility cannot be delegated. However, the community may plan to enrich these standards by the appropriate use of voluntary resources.

The role of independent voluntary activity has been emphasized up to this point. However, the field of public administration offers many opportunities for the incorporation of voluntary effort within its own structure. Voluntaryism permeates the administration of public welfare, from boards and committees to direct service to clients of public agencies.[26]

[25] See Don J. Hager, "Religion, Delinquency, and Society," *Social Work*, II, No. 3 (1957), 16–21.

[26] U.S. Department of Health, Education, and Welfare, *Citizen Participation in Public Welfare Programs* (Washington, D.C.: U.S. Government Printing Office, 1957).

The relationship of voluntaryism to the public agency is, however, restricted by the nature of public institutions. While the public agency has much to contribute to, and gain from, voluntary effort, its accountability to the whole community complicates any role for voluntaryism which may result in the modification of public policy. A major and unique consideration for the public agency generally is the extent to which it may share its administration with individuals or organizations removed from the normal channels of public accountability. Insulation from political control is by no means always a drawback, and the effective use of voluntary effort in the public service is dependent on selecting for voluntary action those functions which have most to gain from its participation.

The social policy of maintaining a planned balance between public and voluntary effort is exemplified in the development of the British social services. From the time of the Elizabethan Poor Law, accompanied by the Statute of Charitable Uses (ensuring the proper employment of voluntary resources), to the extensive series of public services established after the Second World War, public responsibility has always included as a parallel consideration the appropriate role for voluntary action. On the contemporary welfare scene the partnership between public and voluntary service takes many forms: Voluntary bodies may be responsible for a total service or part of a total service sponsored by the public authorities. Frequently, these are services which would otherwise be undertaken by public agencies, but sometimes they are services outside the legal authority of the public body or not feasible for public administration. Voluntary bodies supplement the public program, both qualitatively and quantitatively, when there are insufficient public resources. Voluntary organizations supplement public services for the purpose of increasing the flexibility or reducing the cost of the public program. Voluntary societies may act as coordinating bodies, bringing together voluntary and public services in specialized fields. Voluntary organizations may be responsible for setting standards and establishing training programs for public personnel. Voluntary personnel and funds may be applied directly to strengthen the public service. Finally, voluntary individuals and organizations influence public policy-making directly through accepting membership on public committees and indirectly through giving testimony at public hearings, undertaking research, preparing reports, providing citizen leadership, and even acting as a channel for the expression of opinion by public officials.

A few illustrations from British welfare programs may further an understanding of the way in which these functions are integrated into public policy. Each of the major British postwar acts provided for voluntary participation and together they offered a variety of patterns for integrating voluntary effort into public services. The National Assistance Act permitted the local authorities to undertake a program of community services for the aged, but only under the auspices of voluntary bodies. The National Health Service Act established an elaborate system of voluntary boards and committees to share in the administration of the program. The Children Act permitted the use of voluntary child care services and at the same time established standards and methods of supervision for the voluntary bodies.

All these acts indicate specific principles in public planning for voluntary effort. In community services for the aged, the government sought to encourage an already established pattern of local clubs and services sponsored by voluntary groups and by the aged themselves. Looseness and diversity and avoidance of political involvement in services for a group of the population relatively capable of looking out for their own needs justified the government's dependence on voluntary cooperation. In the hospital service, experiences throughout this century and particularly during the war led to the decision that a service so vital and so badly needed must be undertaken directly by government. However, within this system ample opportunity was provided for voluntary representation. Finally, in the children's services, while the existence of two systems was possible, recognition of the importance of child care to the national welfare resulted in the establishment of a thorough and sound public program. However, continued opportunities for voluntary action were acknowledged, as they were not in the hospital service, and measures were adopted to ensure appropriate controls. For the acceptance of voluntary action did not diminish public responsibility for the welfare of all children. It is interesting to note that Lord Beveridge, one of the strongest supporters of voluntary effort, was also the strongest advocate of guaranteeing the child in voluntary care the standards fixed for public agencies.

This brief analysis of some aspects of governmental and voluntary cooperation in the British social services emphasizes only one aspect of the partnership: voluntary participation in governmental activities. There is, as well, governmental participation in voluntary activities. Aside from subsidies and the formal controls for assuring responsible voluntary action, many other approaches, both formal and informal, exist for governmental involvement in voluntary effort. In fact, in some programs and in some areas, it is the government official who is most conscious of the value of the voluntary contribution and who is most active in stimulating voluntary effort. From the British experience, there seems little evidence for the conclusion that the expansion of governmental activity necessarily results in diminution of voluntary participation.[27] Frequently,

[27] The Women's Voluntary Services is a unique example of governmental participation in voluntary activity. Organized for the purpose of mobilizing women's voluntary activity during the Second World War, the WVS has continued to receive government support and now serves locally and nationally as a source of voluntary activity in practically every sphere of welfare. Almost totally subsidized by government, the WVS has no need for fund-raising and is free to use its vast voluntary

the officials most conscious of their legal responsibilities are those who are also most diligent in encouraging voluntary activities. In fact, there is good reason to suggest that the present level of voluntaryism in England could not have been maintained without governmental interest and cooperation. Finally, it should also be noted that any static or traditional concept of structure or function for the voluntary services, or of their relationship with the public services, has been an obstacle to the fullest development of the voluntary potential.

Citizen Volunteers in a Democracy

The complex nature of social welfare underlies any analysis of trends in voluntaryism. The provision of social services is not a simple equation involving only worker and client. There are at least seven identifiable factors in the social welfare equation: (1) those who are served; (2) the profession of social work; (3) social welfare agencies; (4) those who support services, financially or otherwise; (5) the field of social welfare; (6) those who are desirous of participating in service; and (7) the community or society generally. At present, the first three factors have been emphasized most heavily, some-

---

membership for service alone. While its major responsibility is to cooperate with local and national governmental programs, this function is sufficiently broad to allow for much initiative in planning on the part of the many units of the organization.

In discussing the British program, the term "voluntary" has been used to include all nongovernmental activities. On the whole, British nongovernmental organizations conform more closely to "voluntary" than to "private" effort. Professionalism and bureaucracy have not made the same impress as on the American scene. In fact, there is a tendency to question voluntary organizations which have high budgets for administrative purposes. The volunteer remains much more the main resource for many organizations. "Giving" has not replaced "doing," and the measure of the potential of an organization is often the amount of voluntary service it commands. It is also noteworthy that the chest or fund concept has not yet taken root in Britain.

times almost exclusively, in the functioning of private social work. A broader definition of social policy would result in increased concentration on objectives that would permit the other factors in the equation to achieve an equitable balance. As can readily be seen, these factors are by no means inconsequential for the general advancement of welfare. With specific regard to voluntaryism attention needs to be given to: (1) the types of structures most effective for voluntary action; (2) the role of the professional; and (3) the goals for voluntaryism.

The preceding analysis has suggested that voluntaryism is not the unique attribute of any one type of social welfare organization; it may be incorporated in both public and private bodies. However, while voluntaryism may be included in large and highly organized structures, the more complex the structure and the more intangible the ends, the more likely that voluntary activity becomes automatous rather than meaningful to the participant. There is much room for exploration of the kinds of organizations in which voluntaryism may flourish. Perhaps there has been too much concentration on formal social work bodies. There are many existing institutions in the community, such as churches, schools, and unions, which may more feasibly supply the base for voluntary social service.[28] Organizations for mutual aid, such as parents' associations or societies interested in the promotion of community service, generally offer other possibilities for voluntary activity.[29] In a

[28] See Bertha L. Reynolds, *Social Work and Social Living* (New York: Citadel Press, 1951).

[29] In an interesting description of the use of community resources by a public agency, Nelson W. Stephenson, of the North Carolina State Board of Public Welfare, states: "If the welfare agency can become familiar enough with these [voluntary] groups to work with them on their own terms so to speak, and yet be able to help focus their efforts in relation to the agency program, maximum benefits in terms of service to people will result." "Resources Are Where You Find Them," *Public Welfare*, XII (1954), 61.

society suffering from "specialized" and "devitalized" social groupings, social work can often make a more significant contribution to itself and to the community by strengthening existing organizations than by draining their resources for specialized social work bodies.[30]

The professional worker in organizations stressing voluntary activity serves more in a "staff" than a "line" capacity. His major functions are to help the voluntary participants obtain maximum satisfaction and results from their efforts and to act as liaison for closer coordination of existing services.[31] While both functions entail leadership, the professional should recognize that his role is an enabling one and that voluntary leadership is the primary aim.

Finally, the goals for voluntaryism must take into consideration the interests of the individuals participating, the field of social welfare, and society as a whole. These are, of course, interrelated elements, and in many respects it is the kind of society we want which will determine our goals for voluntaryism and their effect on individual participation and the field of social welfare. If we want a "liberal" society with the rationality and security of social planning and yet with the values of individual initiative in decision-making and social action, if we want a pluralistic rather than a monolithic society, then one of the ways to achieve this is to strengthen voluntary participation in our social welfare institutions.

Through encouraging voluntaryism, opportunities will be provided for satisfying and creative individual action and for a real contribution to the field of social welfare. "What we need in our lay leadership," as Nathan Cohen has stated, "are not amateur social workers with an amateur knowledge of

[30] See Charles Frankel, *The Case for Modern Man* (New York: Harper, 1955), pp. 201 ff.

[31] Alan Moncrief, "The Meaning of Self-Help in Social Welfare," in *Proceedings of the Seventh International Conference of Social Work,* pp. 13–23.

methods and techniques, but rather citizen volunteers who understand the place of social welfare in a democracy." [32] In an era when there is greater leisure than ever before and commensurate concern for its use, it is strange that the field of social welfare has not moved toward enriching rather than restricting the possibilities for voluntary effort. A brief glance into history will indicate the worthwhileness of the investment in voluntary leadership. Such people as Herbert Lehman, Frances Perkins, Charles Beard, and Sidney Hillman were part of a voluntary tradition which contributed to social welfare and society generally in a way that cannot be duplicated or compensated for, no matter what may be the advances in professional know-how and organization.[33]

[32] Nathan E. Cohen, "Desegregation—a Challenge to the Place of Moral Values in Social Work Education," in *Education for Social Work;* 1955 Proceedings of Third Annual Program Meeting (New York: Council on Social Work Education, 1955), p. 22.

[33] See Arthur M. Schlesinger, Jr., *The Crisis of the Old Order* (Boston: Houghton Mifflin, 1957), especially chap. iii.

THE SOCIAL STRUCTURE OF SERVICE

ROBERT D. VINTER

What factors facilitate effective team relationships? How do clients' feelings about an agency influence their use of its services? What are the alternatives to close supervision for experienced professionals? What conditions foster personnel dissatisfaction and turnover? What is the optimum size for a department, work unit, client group?

These questions are among the many that social workers ask themselves as they seek to improve professional practice. They refer essentially to patterns of agency operation and can be distinguished from other familiar questions focused on practitioner skills, the development of pathology, and the origins of social problems. Questions such as these arise from the distinctively organizational context of social work practice. The agency is the locus of practice, and professional services are almost wholly provided within and through these administrative structures. Organizational conditions have a greater relevance for the social worker than for the physician or lawyer. Proportionately, many more members of these older professions continue to practice independently, outside bureaucratic structures. The social worker, in contrast, is a sophisticated and accomplished "organization man." Yet frequently he seems unaware of the paradox presented by the agency: it is something more and something less than an expedient means for transacting welfare services. As a means for serving human need, the agency generates its own requirements and deeply conditions the nature of the services rendered.

The American social welfare system has attained a scope and complexity which would strain the credulity of bygone humanitarians. New services constantly emerge, and existing agencies continue to expand. Aid and succor once available only from kin, friend, or neighbor are now routinely "administered" according to "policies and procedures" as part of a "coordinated plan" (with appropriate "recording and review"). Recognition of today's immensely different modes of service does not imply any nostalgia for the past, with its simpler—and less adequate—patterns of help. But acceleration of the trend toward large welfare bureaucracies impels examination of their distinctive features and of the dilemmas they present. Several broad areas merit our study: the relation of the social welfare system to other community institutions; the relations among organizations within the welfare system; and the internal structure and functioning of the agency as an organization. Only the last area can be included within the scope of this paper.

Dilemmas of agency operation have been perceived and studied from various perspectives. Most familiar are administrative studies, typically addressed to specific operating problems. These have been useful for illuminating problematic aspects of current procedures; they customarily assess performance in the light of authoritative judgments and standards. The knowledge derived from such studies is, however, limited and fragmentary. Comparisons between agencies are seldom possible, and a more general understanding of agency structure is not achieved. Another perspective has been that stressing the importance of human relations in management. Emphasis is given to the nature of interaction patterns among agency personnel, particularly those which generate tensions and threaten internal harmony and cohesion. This approach has also led to improved practices but has been limited in its conception of organizational problems. The approach which applies psychological perspectives to agency functioning is widely used for purposes of understanding, if not for study. Insights and knowledge pertinent for comprehending the individual and his behavior are employed to interpret patterns of agency operation. However, the agency is not an individual personality, and principles relevant to worker-client or worker-group relationships provide few solutions when generalized to the level of agency organization.[1]

The perspective of "organizational analysis" differs from the foregoing and will be used here as a basis for inquiry into the structure of social service. Sociological in nature, this approach conceives the agency as internally organized, having a distinctive structure with interdependent components and functioning in a social environment. Like the human personality, the agency must adapt to its environment, and may develop "pathologies" in the course of doing so. Unlike the individual person, the agency organization is deliberately created as an instrument to serve designated ends. All features of its structure and action may be evaluated as they contribute to stated goals, and efficiency is the major criterion. Agencies are designed as rational administrative systems; personnel are assigned to positions with specified tasks, each to be performed in accordance with prescribed policies and rules. The totality of positions, tasks, and rules constitutes the formal or administrative structure of an agency. Yet these official designs cannot govern all behavior within the agency. Individuals perform somewhat differently in comparable positions, rules can never anticipate every eventuality, and relations of friendship or rivalry develop among staff members. The unplanned patterns of behavior that emerge and persist constitute an organization's informal structure; they may largely complement and reinforce official designs, or they may subvert and conflict with formal norms and requirements. And finally, diverse

[1] See Talcott Parsons, "Psychoanalysis and the Social Structure," in *Essays in Sociological Theory; Pure and Applied* (rev. ed.; Glencoe, Ill.: Free Press, 1954), pp. 336–48.

consequences flow from specific administrative actions, only some of which are either known or intended. Thus, an administrative decision to institute a particular form of intake procedure may have far-reaching implications for clients, for staff members, and for other agency practices. Not all the ramifications of any decision can be anticipated in advance, or observed thereafter. The consequences of changing intake procedures may be advantageous for clients, but may also create strains by placing unforeseen demands on secretarial or professional staff.

The aims of organizational analysis are to understand the agency as a functioning system, and to develop general knowledge of the consequences of purposive social action (e.g., administrative behavior).[2] Only recently have organizations providing health and welfare services been examined from this perspective: the mental hospital,[3] general hospital,[4] prison,[5] public employment service,[6] national voluntary health organization,[7] and community welfare financing body.[8] Wilensky

[2] Formal statements of this approach to the study of organizations are available in the literature of sociology. See Chester I. Barnard, *The Functions of the Executive* (Cambridge, Mass.: Harvard University Press, 1938); Herbert A. Simon, *Administrative Behavior* (rev. ed.; New York: Macmillan, 1957); Robert K. Merton, *et al.*, eds., *Reader in Bureaucracy* (Glencoe, Ill.: Free Press, 1952); Max Weber, *The Theory of Social and Economic Organization*, trans. A. M. Henderson and Talcott Parsons; Talcott Parsons, ed. (London: Oxford University Press, 1947).

[3] Alfred H. Stanton and Morris S. Schwartz, *The Mental Hospital* (New York: Basic Books, 1954).

[4] Leo W. Simmons and Harold G. Wolff, *Social Science in Medicine* (New York: Russell Sage Foundation, 1954); see especially chap. vi.

[5] Lloyd E. Ohlin, *Sociology and the Field of Corrections* (New York: Russell Sage Foundation, 1956).

[6] Roy G. Francis and Robert C. Stone, *Service and Procedure in Bureaucracy* (Minneapolis: University of Minnesota Press, 1956).

[7] David L. Sills, *The Volunteers: Means and Ends in a National Organization* (Glencoe, Ill.: Free Press, 1957).

[8] John R. Seeley *et al.*, *Community Chest: a Case Study in Philanthropy* (Toronto: University of Toronto Press, 1957).

and Lebeaux have employed a similar approach in their analysis of the social agency,[9] as has Cloward in discussing certain problems encountered by group work agencies.[10]

Because the latter two writings present excellent analyses of agency structure, a comprehensive restatement need not be attempted here. Instead, attention will be directed at certain issues posed by the transaction of welfare services through administrative organizations. It is maintained that commitment to the agency as *the* means for providing health and welfare services has had significant consequences for professional social workers, for the social goals embodied in the services, and for the clients to whom the services are directed.[11] Some of these consequences have been recognized, although the terms of reference may be different from those used here; about some only speculation is possible due to the lack of previous study. Emphasis is given to dilemmas and events that are salient for social workers, but this is not to suggest that all organizational effects are problematic. These dilemmas and conditions are discussed under three major headings: bureaucratic structure and professional culture; organizational size; and the structure of authority. Such interrelated topics can be separated only arbitrarily for purposes of analysis.

The extremely broad range of organizational types in the social welfare field presents difficulties in any discussion of agency structure. Social welfare agencies may be national in scope, or limited to a small community; they may be governmental units or voluntary associations. Some are direct-service

[9] Harold L. Wilensky and Charles N. Lebeaux, *Industrial Society and Social Welfare* (New York: Russell Sage Foundation, 1958). See chap. x.

[10] Richard A. Cloward, "Agency Structure as a Variable in Service to Groups," in *Group Work and Community Organization, 1956* (New York: Columbia University Press, 1956).

[11] This conception follows the formulation presented by Philip Selznick, "A Theory of Organizational Commitments," in *Merton, et al., op. cit.,* pp. 194–202.

agencies, others are engaged in planning, coordinating, or forum activities. Furthermore, certain agencies have existed over several generations and some are oriented toward sectarian values. These wide variations are directly pertinent to organizational patterns, yet make it almost impossible to speak of *the* social agency. Attention is directed in this chapter to relatively common features of social welfare agencies, but with particular reference to those providing services directly to clientele.

Bureaucratic Structure and Professional Culture

Bureaucracies and the professions are consequences of similar forces in Western society. Both are expressions of general trends toward division of labor and specialization that characterize complex and highly technological societies. Yet not all bureaucracies are professionalized (e.g., the post office); that is, staffed by independently trained professional personnel. Nor are all professions bureaucratized (e.g., lawyers); that is, conducting most specialized effort through administrative structures. Bureaucratization has advanced further in the social welfare system than has professionalization, although the orientations of the trained career professionals are widely diffused, and this group maintains a dominant position. Stated differently, all social work is provided through bureaucratic organizations, although not all social welfare agencies are wholly or even largely staffed by professional social workers.[12]

The fact that not all professions are committed to adminis-

[12] Data presented by Wilensky and Lebeaux, based on the Bureau of Labor Statistics study, *Social Workers in 1950*, show that only 16 percent of all social work personnel held professional degrees. Percentages by fields of service ranged from 4 (public assistance) to 83 (clinic psychiatric social work). There is no reason to believe substantial differences exist today. Wilensky and Lebeaux, *op. cit.*, p. 292.

trative structures leads us to inquire into the nature and effects of the association between agencies and social work profession. It seems that the ideology and standards of the profession are generally compatible with the requirements of the agency as an administrative organization. For example, the norm of "professional discipline" (affective neutrality toward the client or client group) is largely consistent with the tendency toward impersonality found in administrative bureaucracies. The staff member is thus enjoined by profession and agency to regard clients with a certain detachment and without injecting his personal feelings into the service relationship. Similarly, the social worker's preference for discharging his professional function through a definite and circumscribed role complements the organization's assignment of activities among personnel as official duties. Agency goals and professional service aims are derived from the same overarching humanitarian value system. Many of the specific tasks agency workers perform are therefore perceived as contributing to attainment of ends sanctioned by their professional reference group. These and other convergences between the agency and the profession facilitate practitioners' harmonious functioning within welfare organizations.

Not all features of profession and agency are complementary, however, and several major sources of strain may be identified. It should be recognized that quite different organizing principles underlie agency and profession, although both are consequences of similar historical trends. The bureaucratic principle of efficiency impels agencies toward the best possible use of resources (including personnel) in attainment of their goals. The highest values of the profession incline practitioners toward mastery of technical skills and dedicated, selfless service. Limits of these orientations for the professional are stated in terms of competence and ethical commitments. But limitations on service imposed by the agency are of a different order, introducing administrative considerations of policy, rules, budget, and so forth. What constitutes the "best possible use" of resources for an agency in pursuit of its proximate goals is often at variance with orientations toward skill and selfless service. That professionals are generally able to work effectively in administrative structures attests to both the flexibility of these structures and the adaptability of professionals. Strains are usually manifested as role conflicts when the imperatives and constraints of profession and agency are not congruent.[13]

A pervasive type of role conflict arises from discrepancies between agencies' limited service goals (the "function" of each agency) and the profession's relatively unlimited commitments. As an agency employee, the social worker must often refuse service because the prospective client's needs do not assume the form appropriate to a given agency; he is deemed "ineligible." Such conflict can be especially acute as the practitioner becomes immediately aware, in the process of determining eligibility, of individuals' pressing (but inappropriate) needs, and as he must himself be the agent of refusal. Some of this conflict is expressed as staff dissatisfaction with "restrictive" agency policies, and is partially relieved by heavy emphasis on referrals and by attempts to expand the service jurisdictions of agencies. It seems probable that continuous growth of the social welfare services assuages some of the frustration of professionals, as they are inclined toward the optimistic belief that if people cannot obtain all the help they need here and now, they may there or later.

A second type of role conflict is generated by discrepancies between specific agency goals or practices and professional values. Social workers tend to concentrate in agencies whose means and ends are most compatible with the profession's codes and standards, and to avoid those where major incon-

---

[13] A similar analysis is offered by Wilensky and Lebeaux, *op. cit.*, pp. 245–46, 319–21.

gruities are perceived. Thus, disproportionate numbers of the professionally trained are found in all types of psychiatric settings and family service agencies, but very few in correctional and public assistance agencies.[14] Workers are sometimes required to perform tasks not perceived as commensurate with their training and professional images; they may experience constraints in the full utilization of core technical skills, or find little organizational support for their distinctive values and practices. These conditions may exist in any agency at a given time, but are believed to be more prevalent in certain sectors of the field not yet fully "professionalized." Ohlin has documented the processes by which value differences induce stress and high turnover of social work personnel in correctional settings.[15]

One approach to reduction in this type of conflict has been to redefine the situation so that the agency and professional value systems may be perceived as congruent. This can be achieved in part by stressing the compatible elements in both systems. For example, recent statements have presented assertions that professional aims are germane to correctional services, and that "use of authority" by the professional probation or parole officer need not contravene social work values.[16] Similarly, it is maintained that the determination of eligibility and giving of funds in public assistance require the exercise of professional skills consonant with social work principles.[17]

[14] *Ibid.*, p. 292; David G. French and Alex Rosen, *Personnel Entering Social Work Employment from Schools of Social Work* (New York: Council on Social Work Education, 1957; mimeographed), p. 11.

[15] Lloyd E. Ohlin, Herman Piven, and Donnell M. Pappenfort, "Major Dilemmas of the Social Worker in Probation and Parole," *National Probation and Parole Association Journal,* II (1956), 211–26.

[16] Committee on Corrections, *Working Paper on the Nature of Social Work Practice in Corrections* (New York: Council on Social Work Education, 1958; mimeographed); see especially pp. 10–17.

[17] Jeanette R. Grafstrom, "Casework in Public Assistance—Myth, Frill or Goal," in *Selected Papers in Casework* (Raleigh, N.C.: Health Publications Institute, 1953), pp. 52–66.

Another approach has been to introduce enough professional personnel to secure modifications in the practices and climate of agencies. Perhaps the most promising solution is to attempt modification of certain features of professional culture which are especially discrepant with organizational realities. For example, declining emphases on professional subspecializations (e.g., psychiatric social work) will serve to lessen status problems and strictures on practitioner roles to which these distinctions have contributed among agency personnel. The same trend toward generic preparation of professionals will permit a more flexible and extended utilization of practitioners in accordance with agency necessities. Agency field training as an integral part of professional preparation serves both to ameliorate and to increase the practitioner's role conflict. The graduate student in social work becomes acquainted with agency structure primarily by direct experience in it as a student worker. Accommodations to the agency as the context for practice are probably achieved at an early career point. On the other hand, most students are assigned to agencies largely permeated by the professional culture, while academic study emphasizes organizational features that are compatible with professional norms and values. Strain between profession and agency is thus accentuated for novice practitioners first employed in agencies whose characteristics are less than ideal. However, an essential point to be made is that orientations of the profession do not necessarily ensure more effective service to clients than do the patterns of specific agency structures.

Another type of conflict between professional and agency role demands is that arising from inherent differences between the administrative structure and the professional culture. The profession values skill rather than procedure, and service rather than routines. The agency, in contrast, interposes a variety of requirements relevant to the operation of a complex organization. Records must be written, files maintained, requisitions prepared and routed, directives adhered to, and so on. Furthermore, the worker must participate in a more or less elaborate system of informal relationships; he must "get along" with colleagues and be a good member of the "team." Some of these operational realities provide satisfactions; for example, case conferences frequently offer gratifying opportunities for the symbolic exercise of professional skills. Some provide frustrations; for example, the status problems experienced in teamwork with psychiatrists.[18] These events are intrinsic to the operation of the agency as an organization. When the net balance of satisfaction-dissatisfaction from such sources becomes adverse, workers tend to depart.[19] Continuity of service to clients is thus enhanced or diminished by the organizational circumstances of professional practice.

Organizational Size

Size is a characteristic of agency structure which merits particular attention. Questions often arise about the most desirable size for client groups, departments, staff committees, boards, and even whole agencies. There is general awareness that various effects depend upon the number of personnel grouped together in work units, but more precise knowledge is lacking. Although size has been an important consideration in administrative designs, relatively little empirical study has been given to it. Some knowledge of the effects of size is available from small group studies, however, and can be briefly reviewed. It has been found that an increase in group size is accompanied by lessening of member participation and satisfaction; con-

[18] Alvin Zander, Arthur R. Cohen, and Ezra Stotland, *Role Relations in the Mental Health Professions* (Ann Arbor, Mich.: Institute for Social Research, University of Michigan, 1957), see chap. iv.

[19] Most studies of personnel turnover have indicated the significance of administrative conditions for professional morale. See, for example the author's "Report of the Personnel Turnover Study," *The Round Table* (New York: National Federation of Settlements), XXI (1957), 2 and 5.

sensus among members also decreases, while leadership requirements increase. There is a tendency toward specialization of functions and roles within groups as they become larger and endure over periods of time. The number of potential relationships among members increases rapidly with increments in group size, yet the intimacy of relations among all members is reduced and factionalism emerges. Larger groups are able to undertake tasks impossible for smaller groups, but efficiency and size are not invariably associated; optimum group size depends partly on the type of task at hand.

These generalizations about the effects of size are substantiated by a number of studies,[20] but caution must be exercised in applying them directly to organizations. Most of these findings are derived from studies of small independent problem-solving groups, created for brief experimental periods, and lacking administrative structure. They are, however, suggestive of effects to be anticipated with variations in the size of organizations or their subunits. These findings also suggest that there is no ideal group size. Instead, differences in group size are accompanied by particular effects, some of which may be desired, such as greater efficiency or specialization. Other effects may be undesirable, such as reduction of participation. The administrative problem is one of determining what size achieves a net balance of desired effects.

The significance of size for administrative structures can be most clearly seen by examining the effects of increasing the number of personnel. Enlarging the size of the staff generally presents greater requirements for coordination and control. More supervisors are needed with added workers; at some point it becomes necessary to introduce a division head or "supervisor of supervisors." Direct positive relationships have

[20] For example, see Dorwin Cartwright and Alvin Zander, *Group Dynamics: Research and Theory* (Evanston, Ill., and White Plains, N.Y.: Row, Peterson and Co., 1953); and Theodore Caplow, "Organizational Size," *Administrative Science Quarterly*, I (1957), 484–506.

been found between the number of employees and the number of vertical ranks in comparable welfare units.[21] Extension of the vertical chain of command is not the only impact of size on the structure of coordination, however. Activities that are broadly distributed among personnel in smaller units become segregated in the large agency and are assigned to specialized roles: accounting, consulting, statistical control, and so on. Greater efficiency is obtained for the total work unit when such specialization occurs "on the line" (e.g., intake interviewers, program specialists, home-finders). And tasks impossible for the smaller, less specialized agency can be accomplished. But increments in number of personnel and the degree of specialization require that larger proportions of organizational resources be devoted to central administrative tasks.[22] This phenomenon is commonly referred to as increased "overhead costs."

Communication problems are another consequence of larger size. In a small office or agency workers usually have direct access to each other and to the executive. Problems can be explored and decisions shared by word of mouth. Conformity to policy and standards of performance are readily apparent, and can be reinforced by direct friendly relations among all personnel. In the larger agency, with many workers and several administrative levels, interaction among personnel takes on a more formal quality. Communication by memorandum and directive supplants contact between executive and practitioner. The larger number of people, who cannot all be known intimately, and the elaboration of the agency formal structure also contribute to greater social distance among personnel. The executive becomes a remote figure, contacts among workers at different levels or from different sections assume a more

[21] Edwin J. Thomas, "Role Conceptions and Organizational Size," *American Sociological Review*, XXIV (1959), 30–37.

[22] Frederick W. Terrien and Donald L. Mills, "The Effect of Changing Size upon the Internal Structure of Organizations," *American Sociological Review*, XX (1955), 11.

"businesslike" and reserved character, and many co-workers remain relative strangers. Under these circumstances intimacy and informality may continue to characterize relations among workers in the same subunit, but factionalism and interunit rivalry often develop.

Increases in the number of administrative levels, in highly specialized roles, and in the total number of personnel, also lead to more routinized procedures. Many persons are involved in each decision and phase of operation; they must be kept informed and their efforts coordinated. These requirements are typically met by standardizing activities which, under other conditions, remain less circumscribed. Manuals, job descriptions, multiple staff conferences, and administrative audits are among the devices used to ensure predictability of behavior.

The larger agency is, thus, in certain respects a different place in which to work than the smaller agency, although many of the particular tasks are the same. For some persons these are less satisfying conditions, and personnel turnover may increase. While the larger organization can efficiently undertake service responsibilities impossible for the small unit there may also be reduced effectiveness in terms relevant to social work objectives. The study of Aid to Dependent Children workers conducted in various sized units by Thomas revealed important differences in staff role conceptions and quality of performance.[23] Workers in smaller units, as contrasted with their peers in larger units, evidenced more consensus with their supervisors about important worker functions, greater breadth of role conceptions, and more commitment to the ethics of social work. Similarly, their performance was more effective, as measured in terms of diagnostic acuity and the appropriateness of treatment plans.

This analysis suggests that much of what is known through experimentation with small groups has relevance for social welfare administrative structures. However, other factors inter-

[23] Thomas, *op. cit.*

vene in the direct relationship between organizational size (as number of personnel) and the consequences noted. Cloward points out that certain emphases in professional practice (e.g., controlled relationships) contribute to formalized relations even in the small agency.[24] The extent to which social relations and staff member behavior may be related to differences in the *kinds* of persons employed in small and in large welfare organizations deserves intensive study. Agency and community size frequently vary together, and personnel available to agencies located in small towns and rural areas are different from workers available to large agencies in the big cities. Differences in personal characteristics of staff members in large and small units of the same state welfare department are related to differences pertaining among urban and rural residents.[25] It may be found that variations in these personal characteristics account for much of the observed dissimilarities among various sized agencies.

The impact of administrative or service unit size on clientele has received no systematic study. It has, however, been a matter of concern in the composition of different sized groups in, for example, group work practice and in the design of living units in residential settings. For child-caring institutions there is general recognition that smaller units provide greater intimacy and informality in relations among staff and clientele. Similar considerations have guided social group workers in composing small groups for various purposes, particularly when serving disturbed clientele. Most of this knowledge is derived from practice experience; it is often vitiated by the intrusion of other administrative considerations, as well as pressures to serve more clients. The disadvantageous effects of formalized staff-client relationships, due in part to increased agency size, have been reviewed by Cloward with respect to client recruitment, turnover, participation, and so on.[26]

[24] Cloward, *op. cit.*   [25] Thomas, *op. cit.*   [26] Cloward, *op. cit.*

The impact of agency size on clients can be seen most clearly by considering child-caring institutions. The small agency permits all clients and staff members to know each other and to develop intimate relationships. These patterns of interaction are especially crucial to attainment of agency service objectives. Decisions about clients and agency operations can be made by those immediately familiar with the individuals and the situational details. The development of such intimacy and familiarity is very difficult in the large institution. There are too many people to know them well, and decisions are made at levels more distant from both clients and line staff. The larger number of workers presents problems for the maintenance of consistency in treatment of clients and application of rules. Contending factions and dissimilar perspectives may develop.[27]

It is not asserted that these differences can be entirely attributed to size, or that largeness is undesirable. But there can be little question about the significance of size for the functioning of social welfare organizations. Without a body of tested knowledge, administrative decisions about the optimum size of organizational units must be made on the basis of intuition and experience. There is a high risk that the effects intended by administrative design are thwarted by unintended consequences which follow on unit size.

The Structure of Authority

All organizations create means for ensuring that cooperative action is oriented toward desired objectives. To avoid a state of anarchy among participating personnel, an explicit structure of authority and responsibility is defined in every social agency. However rudimentary this structure, it seeks to ensure pre-

[27] Robert D. Vinter and Roger M. Lind, *Staff Relationships and Attitudes in a Juvenile Correctional Institution* (Ann Arbor: School of Social Work, University of Michigan, 1958), pp. 20–30.

dictable behavior of workers in conformity to policy. It co-ordinates diverse individuals and their manifold activities within the agency. And it guides decision-making, resolves overt conflicts, and orders new issues and problems that emerge through time. Such controls are especially important to social agencies that spend "others people's money." In addition, policies and practices of governmental agencies are imbued with sociopolitical meanings of significance to many interest groups. The responsibility, accountability, and sensitiveness of social welfare agencies, therefore, pose special requirements for the maintenance of organizational controls.

The agency's structure of authority typically takes the form of a hierarchical ordering of personnel in official positions. Every position is subordinate to some position, and superior to others, with differential responsibility and authority being allocated to each. This ordering of personnel denotes "command authority," as superior-subordinate relations between levels are based on administrative sanctions; it may also denote "functional authority" if special competence is required for occupancy of superior positions.[28] Both types of authority often characterize differences between position levels in social agencies. Staff members exercise their responsibility for the activities of personnel at lower levels through decision-making, giving advice and instruction, communicating information, and reviewing performance. Production in social agencies is directly accomplished by practitioners, who constitute the second lowest administrative level (above clerical staff) in the hierarchy of employed personnel.

An agency's official system of policies, rules, and procedures comprises another dimension of its authority structure. This system establishes patterns of expectations that direct and proscribe staff members' activities. Furthermore, the official

[28] This distinction is drawn from Chester I. Barnard, "The Functions and Pathology of Status Systems in Formal Organizations," in William F. Whyte, ed., *Industry and Society* (New York: McGraw-Hill, 1946).

structure becomes elaborated and supplemented with informal patterns: work norms develop and persist, subordinates in one department are granted more discretion than in another, or warm and friendly relations rather than cool formality exist between administrative levels.

This statement of the structure of authority provides only a very general description of agency reality. In particular agencies there may be two or many levels of authority, with diverse patterns of responsibility, and differing rule systems. Aside from such specific variations, there are common features of agency authority structures which distinguish them from certain other types of organizations. Reference has already been made to the operational relevance of norms and values originating in the culture of professional social work. Thus, social agencies are characterized by a strong emphasis on harmonious and satisfying relations among co-workers; ability to form "positive relationships" with co-workers is perhaps more valued in social agencies than in many other organizations. The proliferation of specialized personnel outside the chain of command (e.g., consultants of all kinds) poses added problems in achieving coordination of effort.[29] New means for integrating influences and perspectives, and for arriving at decisions, are necessary when the functional authority of the specialist is segmented from the command authority of the supervisor. The administrative level at which certain types of decisions are made about service and clients may substantially condition the nature of these decisions. Janowitz and Delany have shown that individuals' positions in the administrative structure condition their knowledge and their perspectives.[30] Accuracy of knowledge about clients depends partly on degree of contact with them; workers at lower levels develop some-

[29] This phenomenon has been discussed by Lloyd E. Ohlin, "Conformity in American Society," *Social Work*, III, No. 2 (1958), 58–67.

[30] Morris Janowitz and William Delany, "The Bureaucrat and the Public: a Study of Informational Perspectives," *Administrative Science Quarterly*, II (1957), 141–63.

what different perspectives toward clients, with whom they interact frequently, than do higher administrative personnel, who interact more frequently with the general public. Further study is needed to explore the consequences for decision-making stemming from the perspectives of diverse agency personnel.

The nature of a social agency task conditions the type of authority structure that can be established. When tasks are complicated, require deliberation, and cannot be concretely defined in advance, greater authority must be delegated to personnel in the lower ranks. When appropriate action can be specified in advance, rule systems are more likely to emerge, and authority retained at higher levels.[31] The prevalence of technically trained personnel in an agency's lower ranks also tends to produce a downward delegation of authority.

The significance of agency authority structure can be seen by examining supervisor-practitioner relations in social work. The professional literature reveals great emphasis on the role of the supervisor. Some of this emphasis characterizes all "production" organizations: objectives are tangibly achieved at the practitioner level and administrative control must be exercised at the next highest level, the supervisor. Similarly, the foreman is the focus of concern in manufacturing organizations. A high proportion of untrained personnel in the field of social welfare impels administrative attention to supervision. But professional considerations appear to reinforce administrative concerns regarding this single aspect of the authority structure. Thus, supervision has afforded one means of upgrading practice, thereby validating the profession's claims to technical competence.[32]

[31] For an analysis of these patterns in the context of a hospital, see Rose L. Coser, "Authority and Decision-making in a Hospital," *American Sociological Review*, XXIII (1958), 56–64.

[32] Wilensky and Lebeaux suggest that traditional patterns of supervision impede public acceptance of claims to professional status, and

The traditional status of the supervisor involves a combination of prestige, power, and expertness. Supervisors in many agencies are chosen because of their knowledge and skill, thus enhancing the prestige and authority officially invested in the position. The power of the supervisor accrues from the informational vantage point provided by the position, and from whatever special competency is possessed, as well as the authority to make decisions, offer rewards, and evaluate performance. In these respects supervision in the social agency does not differ markedly from the patterning of authority in many other types of organizations. Yet a distinct note of disquiet can be discerned in the literature, suggesting special strains are associated with supervision. Discrepancies between professional orientations and administrative requirements seem to be one source of difficulty. All occupational groups claiming professional stature assert the competence and ethical commitment of their members (or of the profession's right to certify and enforce conformity with its standards). Professionals take considerable pride in their technical skills and prefer initiative and self-direction in the use of these skills.[33] Limits are placed on practitioner initiative and autonomy through supervision, however able the supervisor may be in exercising her authority.[34]

This analysis suggests that claims to autonomy are greater

hinder effective relations with other professionals under certain conditions. Wilensky and Lebeaux, *op. cit.*, pp. 237–38. Ohlin points to the role of supervision in professional preparation as another reason for continuing emphasis given it. "Conformity in American Society," *op. cit.*

[33] See Parsons's discussion of this orientation in "The Professions and the Social Structure," in *Essays in Sociological Theory, Pure and Applied.*

[34] A recent survey disclosed that practitioners' major objections to supervision include: "limitations on initiative," "being kept dependent," etc. Robert W. Cruser, "Opinions on Supervision: a Chapter Study," *Social Work,* III, No. 1 (1958), 18–26.

among fully trained and experienced practitioners. Under such circumstances it is expected that strain between professional and administrative orientations increases, and alternative arrangements are sought. The literature tends to confirm this inference, indicating most doubts refer to the supervision of fully trained and experienced practitioners.[35] Terms employed in referring to the problem are suggestive of the extent to which close supervision is perceived as a denial of professional autonomy: "emancipation," "independence," and "self-dependent practice." When male practitioners are assigned to female supervisors it seems probable that additional stress develops in the authority relations. As Caplow points out, this situation traverses the social norm that women should not be in positions of authority over men.[36] Furthermore, because success and achievement aspirations are more strongly held among men, the presence of a female supervisor in the promotional chain may be especially stressful.[37]

Strain also arises from juxtaposition of the nonauthoritarian ideology of social work and the exercise of authority and control within the administrative context. Valuation of autonomy

[35] Albert H. Aronson, et al., Administration, Supervision, and Consultation (New York: Family Service Association, 1955); Ruth E. Lindenberg, "Changing Traditional Patterns of Supervision," Social Work, II, No. 2 (1957), 42–47.

[36] Theodore Caplow, The Sociology of Work (Minneapolis: University of Minnesota Press, 1954), pp. 238–44. He also refers to the custom of choosing male executives for social agencies except those associated directly with feminine interests. In this connection it is interesting to note that in the professional literature, the supervisor is typically referred to as "she," while the subordinate practitioner is referred to as "he."

[37] In a study of personnel who had left agency positions, the writer found that larger proportions of men than of women cited salary reasons as affecting decisions to leave; larger proportions of those with professional degrees than of those without such education cited problematic staff relations, particularly with supervisors, as affecting departure decisions. Vinter, "Report of the Personnel Turnover Study," op. cit., pp. 3–4.

and self-determination for the client has pervaded the administrative structures of social welfare, reinforcing distinctively
professional claims to independence. Other conditions may
contribute to authority and control problems: larger agencies
include more separate functions, roles, and units to be coordinated; and higher proportions of untrained or inexperienced personnel reduce assurances that performance will meet
acceptable standards. Under these conditions controls must be
increased through closer supervision and more elaborate rule
systems. Staff resistance to more tangible controls is partially
attenuated by the obvious coordination requirements posed
by the larger agency. And among untrained and inexperienced
personnel, according to this analysis, professional autonomy
values are less fully developed. It is in the small agency with
a high proportion of skilled personnel that the traditional pattern of close supervision is expected to create greatest strain.
And it is precisely for such agencies that alternative patterns
are proposed in the literature.

The more prominent of these alternatives, consultation-
supervision (not to be confused with consultation of the specialist), may be examined in the light of the foregoing analysis.
Consultation as a mode of practitioner supervision seems intended to minimize the former educational focus, to share
some of the supervisor's power with the practitioner, but to
maintain the administrative authority of the supervisor. Reduction of the educational focus may be interpreted as removal
of an implication that, because he has more to learn, the
practitioner has not yet achieved full professional status. Strain
between administrative procedure and valuation of professional competency is thus minimized. Modification of the
supervisor's role only in these terms would probably have little
salutary effect, however, since the worker is restive not only
with the assertion that he has more to learn, but with the
process which reduces his autonomy. This second objection is

met by redefinition of the supervisor's role as "consultative," inducing a more advisory and collaborative relationship with the practitioner. This redefinition, if effected in supervisors' functioning, probably distributes power more equitably between supervisors and workers, as the latter obtain a greater share in decision-making. Maintenance of the supervisor's administrative authority presumably is intended to exercise, at least minimally, the responsibility to review performance, and so on. If the proposed changes have been correctly interpreted, consultation-supervision seems designed to reduce the strains in present supervisory limitations on professional autonomy. Educational supervision, effective during a period when upgrading of practice was a crucial task, is now a hindrance to professional morale and self-esteem where both are well developed and substantiated.

Difficulties which may result from such changes deserve brief mention. A significant downward shift of decision-making power reduces the effective authority of the supervisor and thereby alters the existing structure. Changes of this order sometimes have extensive effects neither intended nor anticipated in the initial design. One such effect may be to reduce the esteem and gratification of the supervisor. The emphasis in the literature on supervisors being "ready" for these changes can be interpreted as meaning they must be able to tolerate such deprivation. Another effect may be delegation of decision-making to a level below that required for effective communication and coordination in a given agency. For example, the breadth of information reaching supervisors through the present structure may be curtailed by the consultative pattern. The accumulative effects of this change could be to deny supervisors the flow of information essential to coordination between units and among staff specialists.

Attention should be given to the status of the client in the authority structure, and its effects for him. Three significant features characterize the relation of clientele to social agencies. First, many social agencies have an absolute or near monopoly of the services they render. Since clients can seldom "shop around," their preferences do not have the same weight as in a competitive market. Furthermore, individuals have little or no control over whether they shall remain as clients of some agencies (e.g., correctional institutions and mental hospitals). Second, the specificity and duration of client relations vary among agencies, usually being dependent upon the type of service. Relations with some agencies require only limited participation and involvement, the service being relatively specific and the contact transitory (e.g., administration of unemployment compensation). For other agencies (e.g., most residential settings), extensive involvement and commitment are characteristic, the service being diffuse.[38] Third, clients usually comprise the lowest status level, having no authority over others in the organization.[39] The consequences of low status and no authority will have greatest import for the client who participates maximally in the agency, and who has little choice of agency or even whether he shall remain a client.

Much more "happens" to clients than is denoted by the activities specifically designated as service or treatment. Moreover, even these activities are themselves conditioned by the entire character of the organization. The diverse influences operating on the client may be partially discerned by consideration of his status and the expected role behaviors associated with this status.

[38] For an elaboration of this point with regard to the mental hospital, see Talcott Parsons, "The Mental Hospital as a Type of Organization," in Milton Greenblatt, Daniel Levinson, and Richard H. Williams, eds., *The Patient and the Mental Hospital* (Glencoe, Ill.: Free Press, 1957), p. 116.

[39] "Membership" agencies are sometimes exceptions to this general rule. Even in such agencies, however, control by clients is exercised indirectly through annual meetings. Lay control of policy does not provide most client members with operating authority.

The phenomena of low status and no authority are impressed on clients by several features of agency organization. There exists a distinct and caste-like cleavage between staff and clients. The recipient of service may not aspire to the status level of professional personnel, though he may move upward within the hierarchy of clients. Many agency decisions affecting clients involve considerations relatively incomprehensible to them, and are made at distant levels. The rules and routines of an agency frequently occasion delays and denials for clients; these may be viewed as unfair and as negations of the agency's service goals. Interpretations by staff are helpful but often involve reasons irrelevant in the client's perspective.[40] The potent sanctions agencies may employ provide further confirmation of the client's subordinate status and relative powerlessness. Service may be denied or privileges withheld from the "uncooperative" client. On the other hand, the cooperative client (like the model patient) may receive many symbolic rewards of praise and recognition, in addition to actual privileges and services.

Permanency of lower status, exclusion from decision-making, and application of powerful sanctions are circumstances (stated in extreme form) usually regarded as unattractive in other areas of life. Customary responses to these conditions are alienation and disaffection, withdrawal, submissive dependency, or covert rebellion. None of these responses is considered desirable for the effective use of social services, yet all are evidenced in various degrees among agency clientele. Nonparticipation and drop-outs from the leisure-time services, nonreturns to the family casework agencies, and "prisonization" and covert hostility in the correctional setting, are familiar phenomena. Furthermore, it is well known that many persons and groups who may need the services most are often least

[40] Alvin W. Gouldner, "Red Tape as a Social Problem," in Merton, *et al., op. cit.*, pp. 410–19.

willing to become clients. The fact that the rates of such behavior are not greater suggests that compensatory conditions
exist. Several of these may be identified.

First, in an era of large bureaucracies—governmental, commercial, educational, and even religious—citizens have become
accustomed to client status. They may comprehend the nature
of "the organization" and have developed response patterns
that vitiate the negative consequences of such status. They
expect to be treated as they are. Some of the findings presented
by Maas and his associates substantiate the notion that client
expectations of being authoritatively dealt with are widespread
and do not result in service failures.[41] The transitory and
specific nature of many client-agency relations minimizes the
negative implications of this pattern. Indeed, it seems primarily
when the client role pervades the client self-image (i.e.,
permanency of low status and diffuseness of involvement) that
the pattern becomes problematic.

A second compensating condition is created by practitioners'
mediation of the adverse effects of agency structure on clientele. Professional dicta to be friendly, interested, and responsive in relations with clients are probably crucial in
offsetting the arbitrariness of rules and administrative decisions, and the impersonality of agency routines.[42] Also significant is practitioner emphasis on service rather than procedure, even at points where this may conflict with official
agency practices. To ignore or cut through rules is professionally disapproved, yet is probably frequently done.[43] The

[41] Henry S. Maas *et al.*, "Socio-cultural Factors in Psychiatric Clinic
Services for Children," *Smith College Studies in Social Work*, XXV
(1955), 56–75. Cf. Francis and Stone, *op. cit.*, chap. iv.

[42] Edwin Thomas, Norman Polansky, and Jacob Kounin, "The Expected Behavior of a Potentially Helpful Person," *Human Relations*,
VIII (1955), 165–75.

[43] For example, see Wilensky and Lebeaux, *op. cit.*, pp. 245–46;
Francis and Stone, *op. cit.*, chap. x.

actual incidence of such mediation by practitioners is not known. And it should not be assumed, as noted earlier, that all professional norms serve to ameliorate negative structural effects.

A third and potentially more promising compensatory pattern is now emerging. This is an explicit recognition of the effects of organizational structure on service, and deliberate modification of agency patterns to resolve the dilemmas encountered. The concept of a "therapeutic milieu" being developed in mental hospitals is, in large part, movement toward designing organizational arrangements so as to enhance rather than hinder service effectiveness. This approach seeks to re-examine every feature of the institutional structure, and the interrelations among staff and clients which are governed by it.[44] Specific modifications envisioned in this approach are directed at minimizing the status differentials between higher professionals and lower echelon staff and patients, reducing the powerlessness of the patients, and increasing their participation in decision-making. Particular attention is given to the roles of all participants in the institutional system in order to maximize the therapeutic contributions of each. This leads to assessment of the actual and potential influences of every echelon of staff (e.g., from psychiatrists to ward attendants) on patients, and of the influences of patients on each other.[45] Similarly, every policy and procedure—even physical arrangements—must be reexamined with regard to criteria of both therapeutic effectiveness and administrative efficiency. It is important to note that such an approach requires attention not only to particular organizational conditions, but to the interrelation and integration of all components. Among the more

[44] Morris S. Schwartz, "What Is a Therapeutic Milieu?" in Greenblatt, Levinson, and Williams, *op. cit.*, pp. 130–45.

[45] William Caudill, *The Psychiatric Hospital as a Small Society* (Cambridge, Mass.: Harvard University Press, 1958).

problematic conditions, from this viewpoint, have been the segmentation of treatment personnel and their services, and the emergence of informal patterns (among and between staff and clients) which conflict with official therapeutic purposes and procedures.

The rationale that, in so far as possible, the whole of organizational operation should be governed by the criterion of therapeutic or service effectiveness can be applied to every type of health and welfare agency. It is most relevant for those agencies which have the characteristics of small communities, such as mental hospitals, child-caring institutions, and residential camps. In such agencies client involvement is typically extensive and diffuse, and the client's role pervades his self-image. But the central focus of this paper has been to indicate some of the ways in which structural features are relevant to all agencies, however limited or transitory the client's contact. The notion of a therapeutic milieu suggests, although in limited terms, the utility of organizational analysis. With this perspective it becomes possible to comprehend more adequately the structures of social welfare, and their conditioning of social work services.

A SCIENTIFIC BASIS FOR HELPING

JOSEPH W. EATON

Professional social work is expanding. Many people in trouble need help as a substitute for the informal mutual aid that was available to their forebears in times of stress. They turn to technically prepared persons who are regarded as "expert" by virtue of their training and experience.

Social workers, along with such other social practitioners as clinical psychologists, psychiatrists, home economists, and vocational counselors, are engaged in helping people and groups with the resolution of complex social, psychological, and economic difficulties.[1] These helping professions share certain common characteristics:

1. They are relatively new. Most of them have developed since the turn of the century. When they first emerged, they were viewed as experimental or luxury services. Now many are regarded as essential to community welfare.

2. The helping professions assert that their work requires knowledge and skill not likely to be found in any ordinary citizen. Their professional role involves more than the application of wisdom and experience. It also requires the application of scientific methods.

3. The helping professions assert the need for minimum standards of training and experience.

4. They are active in man's biggest "do-it-yourself" industry: his personal and social life. They perform many social functions

---

[1] Joseph W. Eaton, "Whence and Whither Social Work?" *Social Work*, I, No. 1 (1956), 11–26.

which were at one time fulfilled exclusively by lay persons without professional training. Some still are performed by laymen, on their own terms.

5. Their services are most highly developed in large urban centers of industrially advanced countries with a relatively high standard of living.

The Scientific Approach to Practice

The belief that scientific procedures should be applied to action distinguishes professionals most clearly from their non-professional competitors, such as palm readers and the advice-to-the-lovelorn columnist. This process of inquiry, of applying science to helping people, can be viewed as a sequence of seven interrelated steps. The logical model of procedures is quite similar whether a child is placed for adoption on the basis of casework or the adoption process is studied to describe it conceptually and to evaluate its consequences. Research and practice differ largely in the general thoroughness and the proportionate emphasis placed on one or the other analytical step:

PROBLEM DEFINITION

Practice	*Research*
1. *Choice of problem* to be acted upon in a specific case	1. *Choice of problem* to be studied generally
2. Identification of *policies* to be taken for granted	2. Identification of *values and assumptions* to be taken for granted

PROBLEM ANALYSIS

3. Identification of *alternate theories* that could be applied by the practitioner	3. Identification of *alternate theories* that could be tested by the researcher
4. *Accumulation of relevant evidence* by scientific methods	4. *Accumulation of relevant evidence* by scientific methods
5. *Diagnosis:* formulation of an explanation of the evidence	5. *Analysis:* formulation of an explanation of the evidence

PROBLEM RESOLUTION

6. *Treatment:* action to deal with the problem on the basis of the diagnosis

6. *Prediction:* projection of the analysis on a new situation to test its validity

VERIFICATION

7. *Follow-up study* to check on the treatment plan and the facts and theories from which it was derived

7. *Follow-up study* to verify the prediction and the facts and theories from which it was derived

The similarities of research and practice are easily lost sight of by persons who use the concept of "research" as if it were limited to statistics and experimental design, a not uncommon misconception. Research can be done with a great variety of methodologies. Intensive case study is as respected a behavioral science method as is the analysis of quantified information. Anthropologists, for instance, proceed very much like caseworkers and psychiatrists in their intensive use of informants. The anthropologist usually has more time and training to be concerned with verifying information obtained from a dryland bean farmer about the folkways of Homestead village [2] than a social worker might have when interviewing the same farmer regarding an Aid to Dependent Children application. In both types of inquiry, there is a reliance on analytic induction [3] or on discernment, as Mirra Komarovsky has labeled this method of analysis.[4] It is especially well suited to the way social practitioners approach their work—case by case, group by group, problem by problem.

[2] Evon Z. Vogt, *Modern Homesteaders* (Cambridge, Mass.: The Belknap Press of Harvard University Press, 1955).

[3] Florian Znaniecki, *The Method of Sociology* (New York: Farrar and Rinehart, Inc., 1934), pp. 249–311.

[4] Mirra Komarovsky, *The Unemployed Man and His Family* (New York: Dryden Press, 1940), pp. 136–46; reprinted in Paul F. Lazarsfeld and Morris Rosenberg, *The Language of Social Research* (Glencoe, Ill.: Free Press, 1955), pp. 449–57.

The process of analytic induction can begin with a single case. It is not necessary to select it at random or to know how representative it may be of a given category of phenomena. The initial description of the situation is the beginning of a spiral process of making inferences about empirical, unconscious, or latent meanings and of testing them against subsequent cases. To be valid, a theoretical inference must fit them all. When it fails to fit, a reformulation is indicated. The procedure can be logically summarized as follows:

1. Description of the evidence to make it as specific and complete as is possible for the problem under consideration.

2. Checking the evidence for its internal consistency with other situations in the life of the respondent and, generally, with human reactions observed in similar situations.

3. Testing an inference about why and how something happens against plausible alternative explanations. Here again there is a reliance on the internal consistency of one or another explanation with what is known in the life of the respondent and with general knowledge concerning human behavior in similar situations.

This method has been used productively in such studies as Alfred R. Lindesmith's *Opiate Addiction*.[5] It can also be used by caseworkers in making a diagnosis of a particular drug addict in order to formulate a treatment plan.

To sum up: Research is a general procedure which in its simplest form can be thought of as a sequence of four operational steps:

1. The asking of researchable rather than policy or normative questions

2. The use of appropriate scientific methods to explore these questions

[5] Alfred R. Lindesmith, *Opiate Addiction* (Bloomington, Ind.: Principia Press, 1947). A similar methodology was employed by Donald R. Cressey, *Other People's Money* (Glencoe, Ill.: Free Press, 1953).

3. Theory-oriented interpretation of the data

4. Verbal and written communication of findings.

This procedure is as relevant to practice as it is to the systematic verification of generalized knowledge.

The Nonscientific Aspects of Practice

The methodological parallels of looking at a problem from a "research" and a "practice" point of view should not blind us to the fact that practice decisions must also be related to some extent to nonscientific considerations. No group worker can decide what to do with a teen-age group entirely on the basis of scientific knowledge. He must respond to artistic and policy considerations of what he thinks members will like, their parents will regard as useful, and the community will consider morally sound.

There always are several policy alternatives when a practitioner has to act. For instance, those concerned with a problem involving two mutually consenting homosexual adults can choose between ignoring this relationship or treating it as an offense against the criminal law. Even when the latter choice is made, there are still alternatives: offenders can be given probation; sent to a hospital; jailed and then paroled; or be made to "pay their debt to society" by hard labor in a chain gang. Choices like this have to be made daily by judges. Even within any given policy, there always are several discretionary alternatives. The criminal charge against the sex offender can be at the felony or misdemeanor level of severity. Imprisonment can vary in length. Casework can be intensive or supportive.

The boundary between clinically discretionary and morally prescribed action is rarely precise. This fact provides practitioners with opportunities to experiment with ideas that might be quite controversial. For instance, certain ex-felons in California must be involved in psychotherapy as a condition of probation. Is this requirement ethical or is it akin to brainwashing? This policy question about ethics can be investigated scientifically when formulated as a series of researchable questions:

Does such coercive treatment lead to socially desired changes in behavior?

Is the cost of this form of treatment lower than the cost of maintaining offenders in prison without paroling them prior to the expiration of their sentence?

What variations in parole officers' qualifications facilitate the exercise of the psychological treatment, the social service, and the surveillance aspects of parole supervision?

These questions can be investigated,[6] even if research cannot resolve the policy issue of whether it is right to expend public funds for "coercive" psychotherapy of criminal offenders, particularly when many mental patients and disturbed children in state institutions remain untreated for lack of available resources.

Evaluation: a Bridge between Research and Practice

Once policy choices are made, science can contribute a great deal to practice. It provides us with a methodology for estimating the probability that a desired objective can be reached with a given procedure. For instance, parole officer-caseworkers vary greatly in what they wish to accomplish with a given client, but their casework process can be de-

[6] Albert Labin and Joseph W. Eaton, "Group Psychotherapy for Criminal Offenders," *California Medicine*, LXXXVIII (1958), 22–26, pose these and other questions on the basis of an examination of a particular "aggressive" treatment program for criminal offenders on parole. See also Lloyd E. Ohlin, Herman Piven, and Donnel M. Pappenfort, "Major Dilemmas of the Social Worker in Probation and Parole," *National Probation and Parole Association Journal*, II (1956), 211–25.

scribed, analyzed, and interpreted when there is a specific criterion of "adequacy." This may be the parolee's self-judgment of his mental health, the worker's report of what progress was made, the judgment of the parolee's family or of observers uninvolved in the treatment process, or the achievement of specified objectives such as avoidance of new law violations.

This type of research concerning the outcome of an action program is welcomed by rationally oriented practitioners as an aid to making data-related choices between alternate policies. It is evaluative research: research about the consequences of rendering or not rendering a given type of service. It involves exploration of the null hypothesis, i.e., the likelihood that a particular purposive social action is of no consequence for a given problem.

It is the deliberate addition of criteria for measuring effectiveness which distinguishes an evaluative study from one undertaken primarily to contribute to the expansion of the frontier of knowledge. Policy objectives are viewed as having a legitimate and appropriate bearing on the research design, on what questions are asked, on what methods are used to explore it, on how the results are interpreted, and on the choice of audience to which the findings are communicated.[7]

One should not overdraw the distinction between basic research and studies undertaken primarily for administrative purposes, for applicability is rarely ever irrelevant to research planning. It motivates the investigator; it often helps to get him support and to maintain interest on the part of the general public and certain scientific reference groups. For in-

[7] See for instance, Louis J. Lehrman *et al.*, *Success and Failure of Treatment in the Child Guidance Clinics of the Jewish Board of Guardians, New York City* (New York: Jewish Board of Guardians, 1949); Edwin Powers and Helen Witmer, *An Experiment in the Prevention of Delinquency: Cambridge-Somerville Youth Study* (New York: Columbia University Press, 1951); Carl R. Rogers and Rosalind Dymond, eds., *Psychotherapy and Personality Change* (Chicago: University of Chicago Press, 1954).

stance, Clyde V. Kiser and T. K. Whelpton report that their comprehensive study of twenty-three hypotheses about the low birth rates in American cities during the late 1930s was undertaken because "it was believed that further knowledge of the social and psychological factors affecting fertility would be needed if this country were ever to attempt any form of legislation designed to encourage larger families." [8] The study was not evaluative, for it did not actually analyze or test any particular type of legislation. But the possibility of an application of its findings was noted by the investigators, who devoted more than a decade to the assembling of information and its gradual interpretation. It is probable that the utilitarian potential also affected the Board of Directors of the Milbank Memorial Fund, which financed the study and the publication of its findings. But while it is doubtful that any behavioral science research is undertaken without the presence of at least unavowed "practical" purposes, the hope of applicability in so-called "basic" research is more incidental to the research design than in evaluative studies.

Evaluation as a Ritualistic Symbol of Professionalism

Evaluative research is rarely supported institutionally merely because of concern with adding to the total body of human knowledge. It also has several unavowed and latent functions for the scientist and those who support his efforts. Among them is the fact that research is symbolic of professionalism. It may be advocated ritualistically by agencies that are not really interested in research and are actually fearful of its findings. They will have a "research department" which accumulates service statistics but will be discouraged from in-

[8] Clyde V. Kiser and T. K. Whelpton, "Resumé of the Indianapolis Study of Social and Psychological Factors Affecting Fertility," *Population Studies,* VII (1953), 95.

terpreting them. Such agencies may hire a "research social worker" who will have a moderate case load, will make extensive reports, but will ask few researchable questions about what he does.

Avowal of concern with questions about the results of work done is among the key differences between a professional calling and the nonprofessional rendering of services, between marital counseling by a social worker and by a self-styled mental "healer." The latter's work is largely governed by the ethics of *caveat emptor*—"let the buyer beware." The nonprofessional mental healer offers his services, like any other business man, to any person willing to pay for it. The classified advertisements of the daily paper of a large metropolis regularly contain advertisements [9] placed by such operators:

> Self-hypnosis for self-help. 45 years experience. Lessons private. Results.

> Institute of hypnosis. We offer more—man of physics also. Lecture each Wednesday—8:00 p.m., Saturday 2:00—donation.

> Madam Jane—Psychic reader. Advise love, marriage, business. This week $1.00.

> Intimate problems solved—private appointments. Also groups.

Ideological Attributes of Evaluation

Professionals generally take it for granted that they are more capable of superior accomplishment than these commercial "counselors." [10] While there is no doubt that persons who are trained therapeutically function with strong positive social

[9] Identifying information has been changed. Telephone numbers were always given but have been omitted here.

[10] Lee R. Steiner, *Where Do People Take Their Troubles?* (New York: International Universities Press, 1945); Earl Lomon Koos, *Families in Trouble* (New York: Kings Crown Press, 1956).

sanction, society's decided preference for their services cannot now rest on demonstrated efficacy of their methods or of their theories. Some of the most highly regarded techniques, like social casework and psychoanalysis, are used with only limited knowledge of how they affect particular clients in specified circumstances. Evaluative data are sparse.

The question needs therefore be asked: What supports public confidence in these professional services? One major factor is public confidence in the ideology of evaluation. The belief that there can be such a function in professional practice includes two major axioms:

1. *The axiom of knowability.*—This is the belief that knowledge can be applied to the solution of human problems. It is the implication that practitioners have a moral responsibility to apply knowledge, irrespective of how this might affect their personal interests in prestige or monetary reward. The client must be able to view the practitioner as primarily interested in his welfare. Only secondarily can the practitioner be concerned with his own personal benefits.

2. *The axiom of testability.*—Scientific methods can be used to test validity—the degree to which an application of knowledge meets the expectations of a specified criterion. This belief also has certain implications for practitioners. They are expected to test the efficacy of what they do whether the client asks for such testing or not. Professionalism implies that any practice be examined with reference to available knowledge.

An overt commitment to this ideology is not usually shared by nonprofessional helping occupations. Self-styled mental "healers" tend to evade occasions for evaluation.

Evaluation and Methodological Compromising

Sponsorship of evaluative research documents a professional commitment. But it will be pursued seriously only when this function is supported for more than ritualistic or ideological reasons. There must be a genuine interest in knowing the outcome of social practices. Professionals are actually far more ambivalent about evaluation than is consistent with their beliefs in its importance. Extensive participant observation in two professional subcultures, social work and medicine, reveals much verbal support for the ideology of evaluation but only occasional attempts at other than haphazard implementation.

There is a decided preference for the use of research methods which rank low on a scale of scientific adequacy but promise "some usable results soon." This is not to say that evaluative research studies fail altogether to apply methods of conceptual analysis and prediction to practice problems. Objective methods of knowing, such as observation of data, index and scale analysis, and experimentation, are used extensively. But there is also a good deal of naïve overconfidence in the training, experience, and status of the practitioner as indices of effectiveness of the work he can do.

There tends to be more confidence than is warranted in results derived exclusively by subjective methods. No human science can exist without their use. All hunches, intuitions, and serendipities begin with someone's thought or feeling, sometimes with little or no externally perceivable supporting evidence. Subjective methods are used in professional practice in a number of ways:

1. *Expert self-judgment.*—An expression of opinion by a person acting in a professional role, on a question about which he is presumed to be an "expert" because of his training and experience.

2. *Judgment by an expert jury.*—A group decision by several "experts" on a question about which they have interrelated responsibility. All of them may be persons with different but related professional roles.

3. *Client judgment.*—An expression of opinion of the per-

son or group who is the primary subject and object of a professional intervention by social practitioners.

4. *Client associates' judgment.*—An expression of opinion by individuals or groups (who are a significant component of his social world) in reciprocal interaction with the client.

No practice or social action is possible without subjective methods, but they must be employed with a sophisticated awareness of their many limitations. They do not, in and by themselves, permit the making of distinctions between the subjective inferences of men of knowledge, mystics, or quacks. They can suggest explanations about casual relationships, but they never prove them or even indicate the degree of their probable validity.

The contrast beween a strong ideological investment in evaluative research and its spasmodic implementation is well recognized within the helping professions. Robert P. Knight, in his presidential address to the American Psychoanalytical Society in 1952, summarized a state of affairs that has changed little during the intervening years:

Analysts have tended to hide behind the curtain of professional secrecy and have been loath to participate in sufficient numbers in any attempt at collection of data on age, sex, marital status, previous treatment attempts, diagnoses and outcome of therapy of patients' psychoanalytic treatment over the country.[11]

Readiness to participate in well-designed evaluative research is somewhat greater in social work and perhaps most highly developed in the field of clinical psychology. In all these fields, however, there is far more resistance to the idea of really doing evaluative research than one would expect. For it must be stressed that these professions justify their right to practice by

[11] Robert P. Knight, "The Present Status of Organized Psychoanalysis in the United States," in Robert P. Knight and Cyrus R. Friedman, eds., *Psychoanalytic Psychiatry and Psychology* (New York: International University Press, 1954), p. 25.

citing their ideology of evaluation. This is a major way in which they differentiate themselves from amateur counselors and the less educated.

The Controversial Nature of Problem Posing

Inconsistency between ideology and action is a commonplace social phenomenon. To the preacher, it may serve as a basis for a fiery sermon. But to the social scientist, it is a clue to the existence of conflicting forces in the social structure. Technically satisfactory evaluative research is difficult because it is more than a normatively neutral concern with problems of knowledge; it has highly predictable social consequences that tend to inhibit the enthusiasm for such research of persons who profess a commitment to it "in principle."

Evaluative research involves more than a choice of methods of inquiry. It is done for a particular purpose. Data are assessed in terms of relevant measurable standards. There are always several, and they are often mutually exclusive. Is marriage counseling successful if a feuding couple decides to get a divorce? Is release from a mental hospital evidence of cure, or does it reflect a good deal about how crowded our hospitals are and how little can be done there for mentally ill persons?

The posing of evaluative problems requires the researcher to take a stand on which of alternate criteria he regards as measures of success. This choice involves inescapable elements of controversy. It tends to bring to the surface certain latent issues, which are viewed as "disturbing" by many social practitioners and those who support them. Is closing a case by agreement of the therapist and the client equivalent to having helped him? Or is it merely evidence of "sociological seduction," the establishment of a shared system of beliefs among persons who have come to like one another? Do parole officers enhance statistical evidence of "success" by failing to note in their reports many "technical" violations of parole conditions which come to their attention?

The program of every social agency is based on certain operational faiths, such as belief in the rightness of the agency's program or of the therapist's clinical judgment. The details of practice are kept secret to protect them from outside criticism. Even before a research is undertaken, the mere formulation of a problem for evaluative study requires that everything about the agency be examined rather than taken for granted.

Research and Practice Are Somewhat Competitive Functions

Our faith in the value of science is in part supported by evidence that discoveries made through research have practical consequences that are greatly cherished. This utilitarian potential of research is not always self-evident, particularly in advance of the planning of a single study. It is easily lost sight of when research is sponsored by an agency primarily devoted to a practical program. Research requires the time and attention of professional workers. Good research psychoanalysts could earn from fifteen to fifty dollars per hour in private practice. Social work agencies could use research funds to hire additional workers, to serve more people now on their waiting lists. Money actually invested in research often leads to findings that raise a lot of questions and answer very few. Research may be understandably viewed as "waste" by persons who are devoting their professional lives to the task of helping particular people in trouble, and who are frustrated by the knowledge of how few of their potential clientele they are actually able to reach.

Research is by definition an ancillary rather than a primary function in a practice agency. Yet in one unpublished pilot study of 137 Veterans Administration social work supervisors, social workers, and nurses, research and higher salaries competed for top priority when respondents were asked to choose among five alternatives (which also included hiring a psychiatric consultant, raising custodial officers' salaries, and improving buildings, facilities, and food for patients) for the use of an annually renewable $10,000 gift. While the possibility need be considered that some respondents gave a higher priority rating to research than they might have had they not known that the questionnaire was mailed to them from a university and was part of a research project, their relatively strong preference is in harmony with the previously mentioned hypothesis that research has symbolic and ideological meaning for practitioners. But before agency funds are actually spent for such a purpose, the desirability of research has to be weighed against many more choices than those allowed for in our questionnaire.

Interpretation Has Consequences

Facts have more ascribed status in the field of social practice than they deserve on the basis of their achievement. They are collected, recorded, and tabulated energetically in every social welfare agency. They may be paraded in annual reports as symbols of documentation of the nature of the agency's services or the number and types of cases dealt with. But there rarely is much theory-oriented interpretation of their meaning. The social workers in the Veterans Administration stations who gave research a high priority in budgeting were reluctant to suggest that evaluative research data about their work be incorporated "with detailed interpretation in an article about their agency prepared for publication in a professional journal." They had been asked to read four simple, factual statements of a plausible, but imaginary, outcome of social work practice in a hospital like their own. They were then asked to indicate two types of attitudes:

1. Did they view the data as encouraging or discouraging evaluative evidence, or are their meanings unclear without more information?

2. Which of ten formal, informal, written, and oral methods of communication would they agree to employ, disagree to use, or be doubtful of using, if they were the first to make the findings?

Opposition to publication was most pronounced when facts were regarded as "discouraging" or their meaning seemed "unclear without more information." Even when findings were viewed by social workers as "encouraging evaluative evidence," only 38.6 percent of the responses favored publication. The reluctance to suggest publication of findings was even more pronounced in 106 responses of social work supervisors but was slightly less in 62 responses of nurses. Similar results were obtained in pilot studies conducted in social work departments of a prison, a mental hospital, and a university hospital.

Could this professional censorship be a reflection of the fact that interpretation usually raises controversial questions? It is one thing to report that "the average patient referred to the social service department of a mental hospital was seen three times a month." It is another to seek interpretation of these facts which would inevitably lead to the asking of policy questions such as: Is three times enough for intensive treatment? For how long are they seen and for what purpose? What can be accomplished? Why do these patients get less frequent service than certain prisoners in California state penitentiaries?

When facts are interpreted publicly, agency board members, journalists, and social scientists have a basis for asking these and other critical questions about prevailing policies. Data can, at best, only lead to tentative conclusions. And tentativeness creates a problem for practitioners who must act as if they were more than moderately certain.

The Anxiety of Tentativeness

Practitioners are asked to give help to persons in trouble, often under complex circumstances. The outcome of none of their treatment alternatives can be predicted with more than moderate confidence. This dilemma of uncertainty is anxiety provoking.[12] It is of concern to the practitioner and the agency which employs him, and it would worry most clients if they were aware of it.

The security needs of practitioners are met best by knowledge of a high degree of certainty. Much support for evaluative research comes from the hope that it can reduce the degree of uncertainty by adding to our general knowledge. But evaluative research results are at best only moderately valid; they only approximate the state of being correct by some designated criterion. The complexities of social life, the limitations of our research methods, and the paucity of resources that can be applied to the study of any question impose a quality of tentativeness on what we think we know.

Research can help the practitioner to substitute guesswork and ignorance for moderately probable generalizations. But it can never give an absolutely certain basis for decision-making. The most skilled professional who can make good estimates of the probability of being right versus the probability of being wrong is, therefore, at a public relations disadvantage when compared with certain self-styled "experts" ready to give more definitive answers with confidence.

There are many sources of error and limitation, even in the

[12] Joseph W. Eaton, "Science, Art and Uncertainty in Social Work," *Social Work*, III, No. 3 (1958), 3–10.

best research design. Findings derived from the application of social casework in one family agency are not necessarily relevant to another, with different practitioners, organizational expectations, and clients. In social life as in physics, the Heisenberg principle of indeterminacy applies. Heisenberg indicated that the making of minute measurements of small particles moving at great speed would be distorted by the device used to measure it. "The mere asking of questions as Socrates found long ago can have reorganizing and occasionally distressing consequences. Indeed the mere listening may have profound effects upon the person listened to . . ." [13] Social caseworkers and psychotherapists can never presume that they have a stable program. Clients and their workers change as they become involved in a study of their relationship.

The executive of a bureaucracy, who has to defend departmental budgets at least once a year, is understandably more reluctant to share with the public data that could be used by others to question his workers' practices. But the interpretation of research does much to help the secure, imaginative, and flexible social practitioner, who is more identified with achieving the professional objectives of his work than with being "right" or "safe."

Status Prerequisites for the Encouragement of Evaluation

The virtual nonexistence of research laboratories for the study of many social practice problems is perhaps more a symptom than a cause of this state of ambivalence about really doing evaluative research. Such inquiries are often absent even in organizations avowedly designed for this purpose,

[13] Nelson Foote and Leonard S. Cottrell, Jr., *Identity of Interpersonal Competence: a New Direction in Family Research* (Chicago: University of Chicago Press, 1955), p. 214.

such as university hospital social service departments, university psychiatric clinics, and far too many university-connected psychological and educational counseling services.

One important reason for this absence of a research function in institutions which are explicitly maintained to encourage it may be the subtle shift in role which occurs when a professional person is made the object of research. His status changes from that of a man of knowledge to that of a "subject." There is a status dysfunction in being an object of study.

Sound evaluative research has flourished in certain social work agencies with high professional standards, such as the Community Service Society of New York,[14] the Family Service Society of Philadelphia,[15] the Jewish Family Service Association of New York [16] and of Cleveland,[17] the Philadelphia Marriage Counseling Clinic,[18] and the Chestnut Lodge mental hospital near Washington.[19] Administrators and practitioners

[14] J. McVicker Hunt and Leonard S. Kogan, *Measuring Results in Social Casework* (New York: Family Service Association of America, 1952); Leonard S. Kogan, J. McVicker Hunt, and Phyliss F. Bartelme, *A Follow-up Study of the Results of Social Casework* (New York: Family Service Association of America, 1953).

[15] John G. Hill and Ralph Ormsby, *Cost Analysis Methods for Casework Agencies* (Philadelphia: Family Service Society of Philadelphia, 1953).

[16] Bernard Berelson, "The Quantitative Analysis of Case Records," *Psychiatry*, X (1947), 395–403; Elizabeth Herzog, Irving Lukoff, and Judith Lieb, *A Study of the Return Interview* (New York: Research Department of the Jewish Family Service Association, 1956; mimeographed).

[17] Helen L. Glassman, *Adjustment in Freedom* (Cleveland: United HIAS Service and Jewish Family Service Association of Cleveland, 1956).

[18] Emily Mudd, *The Practice of Marriage Counseling* (New York: Association Press, 1951); Malcolm G. Preston, Emily H. Mudd, and Hazel B. Froscher, "Factors Affecting Movement in Casework," *Social Casework*, XXXIV (1953), 304–11; Lyn Sellers *et al.*, "Pretesting Methods for Follow-up to Validate Measures of Movement in Casework," *Social Casework*, XXXV (1954), 285–91.

[19] Alfred H. Stanton and Morris S. Schwartz, *The Mental Hospital* (New York: Basic Books, 1954).

in these agencies apparently felt sufficiently secure to participate in studies that could be predicted to document the fact that their best efforts fall somewhat short of their aspirations. Investment in knowing more about how and why these shortcomings exist was very great. Careful precautions were taken there to protect the status of individual practitioners from being affected by the nature of the research findings. Research data were not used to evaluate personnel. Individuals were given organizational recognition for being willing to serve as "subjects" of research by having the analysis of results focused on a problem rather than on themselves as individuals.

Types of Evaluative Research

The pursuit of knowledge is more common than is generally recognized. A primitive type of evaluative study is made, for example, when administrators analyze their impressions and experiences prior to deciding to authorize hospital attendants to attend diagnostic conferences, thus to involve them more actively in the treatment process. They may then proceed from service-oriented inquiry to more systematic studies, such as those by Stanton and Schwartz [20] and Greenblatt, York, and Brown.[21]

The writer has found it useful to distinguish three overlapping types of evaluative research: (a) service-oriented evaluative research; (b) administrative evaluative research; and (c) basic evaluative research.[22] Each type of inquiry can begin with the asking of researchable rather than normative questions. In all cases there is an appropriate use of scientific methodology. Theory-oriented interpretations are made of the

[20] Ibid.

[21] Milton Greenblatt, Richard H. York and Esther Lucille Brown, in collaboration with Robert V. Hyde, *From Custodial to Therapeutic Care in Mental Hospitals* (New York: Russell Sage Foundation, 1955).

[22] Joseph W. Eaton, *Knowledge for Use* (Los Angeles: University of California Press, 1959).

data, and the results are communicated in some fashion. But these types of research differ in the extent of probability to which practitioners are justified in relying on the findings in making a decision.

Service-oriented evaluative research thinking is engaged in by every good practitioner. It is never a primary purpose but a by-product of professional practice and good administration. It is evaluation which takes place when a worker formulates a plan of treatment, a staff conference reviews a case, or an administrator accumulates evidence needed to prepare a memorandum for a proposed policy. It is pragmatic decision-making after analysis of whatever knowledge can be made quickly available to those who must act. For instance, a case-work director may decide to use money budgeted for psychiatric consultation to hire another caseworker on the basis of crude statistics of the agency's case load:

1. The workers carry an average of 100 active cases a month.

2. The workers report an average of seven hours a week overtime.

3. The agency waiting list includes 120 names—more than enough clients to make up a case load for a new worker.

Administrative evaluative research, like service-oriented study, is undertaken primarily to serve an action program rather than to accumulate knowledge. But it involves a formal assignment of agency personnel and resources to make an extensive survey of relevant facts and make interpretations. Studies can be described as administrative to the extent to which they are characterized by the following five attributes:

1. The formulation of specific administrative questions to be answered by research

2. A clearly stated administrative mandate to devote designated resources to doing a study

3. The official assignment of personnel to engage in research as one of their major functions

4. An explicit administrative commitment to examine the findings in terms of their relevancy for present practice and to implement them when indicated

5. A procedure for written or oral communication of the results and their distribution to designated persons within and/or outside the agency

Basic evaluative research, like the administrative type, requires that there be an appropriate collection of facts and plans for their interpretation. But a study tends to be viewed by academicians as basic to the degree to which it asks theoretically relevant rather than momentarily pressing administrative questions. The pursuit of knowledge must be the primary goal. There should be emphasis on quality of research design rather than on operational expediency. The findings should be interpreted on the basis of theory. The focus is less on the making of operationally useful decisions and more on the formulation and systematic testing of hypotheses.

Most evaluative studies in action agencies are of the service or administrative type. Many have been methodologically more shoddy than those undertaken for more basic research purposes, but methodological myopia is not an inherent attribute of the evaluation process. The aforementioned studies of social casework, of mental hospitals, or the "basic" research of how voters make up their mind, *The People's Choice* by Lazarsfeld, Berelson, and Gaudet,[23] do not lose any of their scientific status because they dealt with avowedly operational questions such as: What can be accomplished by social casework? How can mental hospitals become more therapeutic than they now are? How can voters be influenced?

[23] Paul F. Lazarsfeld, Bernard Berelson, and Hazel Gaudet, *The People's Choice* (2d ed.; New York: Columbia University Press, 1948).

Conclusion

No discussion of evaluative research and social obstacles to doing it should conclude without noting the fact that these difficulties are not and have not been "fatal." Behavioral scientists and social practitioners are ready to deal with the methodological problems of evaluative research and have made important contributions to our knowledge. Modern man's stake in the value of science has always been sufficiently strong to support a small group of practitioners to regard their work as something more than the rendering of service to people with problems, practitioners who also view their practice as a laboratory for the experimentation and the investigation of results. They have proceeded to question their own practices, even though the application of scientific methods to practice is anxiety-provoking. The inevitability that some consequence of action will be regarded as erroneous raises no special problem for the professor writing a textbook or a researcher making an inquiry, since neither has to act in situations which are vital to the happiness of another human being. However, the adoption worker who places the baby of an unmarried worker does not like to think of the occasional family which, after getting the baby, cannot meet the responsibilities of parenthood. The roles of researcher and practitioner are not easily combined in the same person at the same time. Only the more secure practitioners can act without needing to believe in what they do with more definitiveness than justified.

Science is neither a faith nor a panacea. It can be helpful when institutions and professionals who work there are able to tolerate some degree of uncertainty. It thrives when people can find satisfaction in the great though limited power that knowledge can give: the power of helping some of the people some of the time—of playing against fate with loaded dice.

THE PROFESSIONAL IDENTITY
IN SOCIAL WORK

NORMAN A. POLANSKY

Some years ago we reported on a study of social workers as an identifiable group within the American society.[1] In that study, a variety of evidence was examined regarding the objective and subjective status of social workers in one large city. The attitudes which social workers held on a number of issues of the day were compared with those of other groups. We found that to be a social worker represented a somewhat anomalous condition, if one accepted the usual theory that class membership determines attitudes. Our sample, at least, seemed located solidly within the middle class. Yet, attitudes held on a number of significant social issues were those to be expected from persons in the working classes of the culture. We speculated, therefore, that some of the restlessness and misgivings then current among social workers might be explained by this form of social marginality. And we concluded that more research was needed.

In this paper, I shall continue the social psychological analysis, although from a different vantage point. A number of papers subsequent to ours have served further to elucidate the role of the social worker viewed "from the outside." [2] If we

[1] Norman Polansky, *et al.*, "Social Workers in Society: Results of a Sampling Study," *Social Work Journal*, XXIV (1953), 74–80.
[2] Cf. *inter alia*: Ernest Greenwood, "Attributes of a Profession," *Social Work*, II, No. 3 (1957), 45–55; Joseph W. Eaton, "Whence and Whither Social Work?" *Social Work*, I, No. 1 (1956), 11–26; R. Clyde

treat the occupation of social worker as a role, we see that there are two sets of foices influencing the behavior and ideation of those in that occupation. One set derives from the fact that a role represents a position in a social structure. Hence, persons in a role are susceptible to the complex series of expectations, prohibitions, and demands of the others in the system with whom they interact. The other group of forces derives from the inner psychology of those occupying the position. It is this second set of forces which contributes so much to the color, variety, and individuality with which the same role, if it is of any complexity, can be and is filled by persons with differing make-ups.

There is reason to believe that as time passes a role as encompassing as one's occupation begins, for the individual, to blend into a single whole. Outer expectations and inner impulse merge, if one is fortunate, into an integrated unit which one might term his "professional identity." The processes by which this merger may occur, the social and intrapsychic vicissitudes which determine individual variations in professional identities, the sublimational and defensive opportunities which our occupational role may provide, are the subject matter of this discussion.

It is a truism to many who work in an interdisciplinary context that one field's gossip is another field's datum. The translation takes place when theories and concepts exist by which one can attempt to make something out of the facts before one. For a long time it did not seem possible to make very much out of the individual variations in role-assumption visible among social workers, since conceptual linkage of role-theory to an adequate dynamic psychology did not exist. It is only since being influenced by Erik Erikson that I have felt

---

White, "Social Workers in Society: Some Further Evidence," *Social Work Journal*, XXIV (1953), 164–72; Alfred Kadushin, "Prestige of Social Work—Facts and Factors," *Social Work*, III, No. 2 (1958), 37–43.

emboldened to continue, at least in the form of hypotheses and formulations, the work laid down some years ago. My hope is that we are by now in position to develop a more general statement from which we can understand more about ourselves and guide the development of our students.

Erikson on Ego-Identity

The over-all theory underlying this paper is taken largely from the work Erikson has been doing on the concept of ego-identity.[3] His work is noteworthy because of its rich measure of shrewd acumen, without which no substantial contribution ever emerges in the psychological sciences. It is also significant because of the peculiar systematic position it occupies. A major advance in Erikson is the fact that he has brought the whole framework of psychoanalytic psychology to bear on a number of problems which have always fascinated students of society. There is by now, for example, a good deal of information about the effects of social position, and of structures of positions, on the participants involved. But when we viewed these actors from the *inside,* as it were, we had previously been equipped with a psychological model which was all too simple, and all too pallid, to fit what any social worker could recognize as human. Finally, it becomes possible to talk psychologically about social positions and social roles without committing what Fritz Redl would call "an insult to the complexity of nature."

Nowhere does Erikson explicitly define "ego-identity":

I can attempt to make the subject matter of identity more explicit only by approaching it from a variety of angles—biographic, pathographic, and theoretical; and by letting the term identity speak for itself in a number of connotations. At one time, then,

[3] Erik H. Erikson, "The Problem of Ego Identity," *Journal of the American Psychoanalytic Association,* IV (1956), 56–121.

it will appear to refer to a conscious *sense of individual identity;* at another to an unconscious striving for a *continuity of personal character;* at a third, as a criterion for the silent doings of *ego synthesis;* and, finally, as a maintenance of an inner *solidarity* with a group's ideals and identity.[4]

Obviously, he has in mind a Gestalt with a number of different aspects. Perhaps the easiest way to take hold, and one most germane to this analysis, is to summarize his view of identity from the genetic standpoint.

As a contribution to ego-psychology, Erikson has prepared a chart showing the process of psychosocial maturation in the individual. This direction of maturation parallels, and is of course interdependent with, the usual image we have been taught in terms of organ zones. It is not essential to the present discussion to give more than a sketch of Erikson's thinking, with which many readers will be familiar in any case. Let me merely indicate a few of his assumptions.

One is that there is a sequence in development in terms of libidinization of organ zones, for example, which appears universal to all cultures and can be presumed to be innate. Second, he assumes there may be variations in the way energies released at each of these stages are handled by the people in the child's environment; the learnings from interaction of this inner push with outer handling leave permanent marks on the personality. Third, and in common with all developmental psychologies, he notes that learnings which are prior in time polarize the mental field, as it were, so that they, in turn, predetermine how later events will be experienced.

Erikson has formulated his image of what can happen at each psychosocial stage into a series of "bipolarities." Thus, the child's assumption about whether this is a reassuring or a threatening world (trust *vs.* mistrust) begins with the experience of receiving oral gratification in infancy. Whether

[4] *Ibid.*, p. 57.

in the long run a healthy development occurs, depends, one might say, on whether the wisdom of the body is met by a concomitant wisdom of society. The latter is expressed in the earliest years by way of parental handling.

The notion of identity is introduced by Erikson as the "phase-specific psychosocial crisis" of adolescence. It is out of this phase that the determination is made whether the individual will move in the direction of acquiring a workable identity or suffer its opposite, identity-diffusion.

Basic to the conception of identity is a sense of wholeness. According to Erikson, "its most obvious (conscious) concomitants are a feeling of being at home in one's body, a sense of 'knowing where one is going,' and an inner assuredness of anticipated recognition from those who count." Such a sense results from a successful integration of inner and outer forces and structures important in one's life:

From a genetic point of view, then, the process of identity formation emerges as an *evolving configuration*—a configuration which is gradually established by successive ego syntheses and resyntheses throughout childhood; it is a configuration gradually integrating *constitutional givens, idiosyncratic libidinal needs, favored capacities, significant identifications, effective defenses, successful sublimations,* and *consistent roles.*[5]

Finally, I should like to emphasize the key part which, in Erikson's view, a person's work plays in the evolving configuration:

Man, to take his place in society must acquire a "conflict-free," habitual use of a dominant faculty, to be elaborated in an *occupation;* a limitless *resource,* a feedback, as it were, from the immediate *exercise* of this occupation, from the *companionship* it provides, and from its *tradition . . .*[6]

Erikson sets the psychosocial frame, and indicates the place of one's work in his over-all integration.

[5] *Ibid.,* p. 71. [6] *Ibid.,* p. 65.

The Meaning of Work

We had been accustomed to regard the capacity to work mostly as a dependent variable when we considered personality dynamics. The ability to be productive, to invest energy, was regarded as the result of one's general state of psychic health. In Erikson's formulation we see that a more complex relationship is involved. The capacity to work and one's general ability to function are interdependent. Put another way, one's work does more than reflect that one is held together; it can help to hold one together.

The tendency of a neurosis to spread and to invade more and more of the ego is well known. Equally familiar is the stubbornness with which the work life holds out against encroaching pathology, so that when a previously effective adult begins to lose his ability to work, this is taken as a particularly ominous sign. Indeed, we sum up the set of insights involved in the telling phrase, "work, the last bastion of defense." Why should this be so?

Let us begin with a case illustration from the literature which points up in an intriguing way some of the key issues involved intrapsychically.

Some years ago, Bergler reported the case of a man who had been taken into analytic treatment.[7] This man was a successful lawyer. He continued to be a successful lawyer, even as his neurosis crippled him increasingly in a variety of other life spheres. The interesting thing, however, was that the law, in his case, was not really his chosen vocation in the sense of a calling. He practiced law almost automatically and without great interest. Indeed, he had drifted into the law out of convenience, following in the well-established footsteps of his

[7] Edmund Bergler, "Work, the 'Last Bastion' Engulfed in Neurosis," *Diseases of the Nervous System,* VIII (1947), 317–19.

father. The career which really fascinated him was gambling. He gambled with pleasure, with dedication, and with excellent skill. He lawed to eat, but he loved to gamble. And it was the capacity to gamble successfully which was first invaded by his neurosis. Indeed, his mounting losses were one reason for his entering treatment.

Erikson, it will be recalled, uses the phrase " 'conflict-free,' habitual use of a dominant faculty." [8] We recognize that in this patient the ability to gamble did *not* remain "conflict-free," but instead was invaded by the tensions attending his psychic distress. The ability to practice law succumbed much later. This odd example is of interest not only because it points up the general principle of spread of neurosis into activities of major investment by the person. It encourages us to go farther and to try to answer the question: Under what conditions is the sphere of work likely to become damaged?

This is a question well worthy of a research project in itself. However, it is my impression, based in part on Bergler's conclusions, that the research would yield results somewhat like the following:

1. *The more directly work is libidinally invested, the more is it susceptible to invasion by inner conflict.* It is a paradox, but it is evidently true, that just those people who get the greatest emotional "charge" out of their work, and often those who have had to struggle persistently against great odds for the opportunity to do a kind of work which was very much self-chosen, are the ones most likely to encounter periods of inability to perform even minimally or at all. It is as if the directness of connection to unconscious impulses which make work keenly pleasurable implies, by the same token, the existence of a channel that is dangerously open to unconscious conflicts and depression. Related to this is a second principle.

2. *The more one's work operates in the service of significant*

[8] Erikson, *op. cit.*, p. 65.

defenses, the more susceptible it is to neurotic invasion. Here, we should include the large group of people whose working is characterized by enormous energy but rather little satisfaction, except in that pallid form which in academic psychologies is called "tension-reduction." For such people the threat lies in the potentiality that what began as a successful defense may develop into something pathological. The example often visible in my own field is the investigator whose original healthy skepticism, which subserved curiosity and motivated studies, deteriorated into a penchant for criticism of the work of others which was hostile and essentially destructive in attitude. Severe crippling occurs at the stage when this same attitude also floods a person's own ideas and efforts, so that finally he is unable to project or energize a study of his own but can at best only pass judgment on the work of others. Since such people, incidentally, usually continue to teach, they may constitute impoverishing role-models for whole generations of graduate students. Fritz Redl used to say, "It ain't your neurosis, it's how you use it." Unfortunately, it may get away from you.

3. *The less one's work is structured by insistent routines, and obvious reality-requirements of the system or materials with which one works, the more it is at the mercy of inner conflicts.* The outstanding examples here, of course, are found among artists, writers, and other creative workers. Many of these suffer mightily unless they become, like Picasso, apparently able to reduce the process of creativity itself to a relatively systematic, intellectualized, and even routinized work life. The opposite pole, revealing the secondary defenses which can arise, is reflected in the shifting foci and quasi-amateurism of that obsessive genius Leonardo.

The last hypothesis may be subsumed under the more general principles recently advanced on the level of metatheory by David Rapaport.[9] Rapaport believes that the id, the ego, and the field of external stimulation *as experienced* may fruitfully be regarded as interdependent systems. No one dominates the others in any simple way, each is also relatively independent (autonomous) of the others. The ego's relative autonomy from the id rests on certain adaptive apparatuses (e.g., memory, perception, control of the motor apparatus) which are its own constitutional equipment. These do not merely subserve drives, but remain reality-adapted by virtue of continued "stimulus nourishment" from the outside, to which they also respond. So, in a broad way, we might say that the more one's work is oriented to external reality, and stabilized into relatively automatic, clearly structured, and relatively neutralized patterns of performance, the safer it is from the id's vicissitudes.

The Energy of Treatment

What motivates social work? Where does the energy come from? To say that one's work life is the safer if it succeeds in harnessing drive-energies and modulating them in stable ways in an intimate relation to external reality is not, nevertheless, to deny the necessity for strivings which do find satisfaction in one's work. By way of illustration let me discuss two personality tendencies for which social work as an occupation may offer opportunities. On the one hand, as we shall see, a position in social work provides a chance for sublimation; on the other, it may be ego-supportive by assisting with binding anxiety. Both tendencies may contribute toward a kind of work in which one dedicates himself to helping others through a relationship.

The first of these, which is fairly prevalent in the personali-

[9] David Rapaport, "The Autonomy of the Ego," *Bulletin of the Menninger Clinic,* XV (1951), 113–23.

ties of many of us in the helping professions, might as well be blatantly called "oral-dependency striving." This is the need to be loved, let us say, or to be given to. Social workers as a group exhibit a vast amount of it. We eat, and we discuss food; we drink, and we discuss drinks; we smoke heavily. Whether we show more of this characteristic than some other occupational groups (e.g., nurses or dietitians), I do not know. As a matter of fact, the available statistics would be irrelevant in any case. The point is that oral-dependency strivings can and do energize concern for other people and their needs. Such energy has made a very useful transposition when it can find gratification in the vicarious pleasure of others' needs being met; it may still be very useful in our work when it is only partially transposed into a strong need to be loved which will make one work to earn affection. We recognize it as an interference in instances in which the need to be liked is present in such extreme form that a worker cannot stand up against a client's impulses, or in which the inability of the client to give to the worker makes the worker frustrated and angry.

If one assumes that oral dependency is a strong tendency among social workers, one can explain a number of problems for which "social science theories" offer far less parsimonious hypotheses. To cite a few, let me list: the unconscious factors which cause mature workers to remain in supervision; the tendency to talk, as if it were realistically equivalent to acting (a pattern we share with psychiatrists); the susceptibility to fads and fashions promulgated by authorities; the reticence to assume overt leadership in interdisciplinary situations; and so on. I should like to say specifically, however, that oral-dependency needs do not necessarily find their gratification only in passivity. The function of professional training is in part to harness them, and to give them appropriate outlets.

Secondly, we might note that there has been too little recognition in our field of the extent to which conflict is a source of energy for treatment. Some people, however, are fully aware that conflict is an asset to some of our best workers. I choose to drag it out into the open because there is a body of opinion which has succumbed to its own propaganda and believes that the best recruits to social work are psychologically healthy, "well-adjusted" individuals. Many "psychologically healthy" individuals who come into social work readily flee direct practice into administration, diversely titled public relations positions, research, and teaching. For some of these, of course, practice is too painful because defenses against their own problems which echo the clients' are too weak; for others, "adjustment" is maintained only at the cost of exceedingly rigid defenses, which they dare not let down long enough to empathize with clients' miseries. Finally, there is undoubtedly a group to whom practice is simply boring, in the sense that one cannot recall what one has never experienced. Practice may be less enjoyable if it pains too much—or even if it does not pain at all!

My own guess would be that topflight practitioners are likely to come from among people who are reasonably well-adapted but rather complex personalities. They are complex because they have experienced anxiety very much like that in the people who come before them, but they have apparently found a way to master it.

Each of us can cite illustrations from among his acquaintanceship. What comes to my mind is the talent for following the thought patterns of delinquents possessed by a number of professionals whom I know. Each of these people is gifted in dealing with delinquents. Each really enjoys hearing about their escapades, and is able to empathize with them and with their fantasies. The thing which both differentiates them from their clients and helps them be effective is a balance of attitudes which make them shock-resistant.

Part of what holds us to the task, then, is the experience of solving and resolving our own problems over and over again in the lives of our clients. This is the mechanism of incorporation by repetition, an attempt of the ego to assume an active stance in relation to the conflict. It is stated much better in a remark once made by Erikson regarding psychotherapy: "In treating them, we cure ourselves."

Jules Henry has written a noteworthy paper which tackles these issues. In considering the deep mutual involvement of counselors and children in a residential center for the treatment of emotionally disturbed children he raises the question "Given the exacting nature of the counselor's task, from where does she derive the necessary strength and incentive to carry on?" And he answers it by noting that "in the Orthogenic School, the return is the feeling of achieving autonomy . . . The counselor's energy is derived from her *need* to solve her own problems in working to become an autonomous human being.[10]

Henry goes on to say that "the counselor's incentive to work parallels the child's struggles toward sanity, and ultimate reward for child and counselor is similar."[11] He cites the interesting correlation that the maximum length of stay for counselors (six to seven years) is also about the maximum length for children in treatment. At the end of that time the counselor usually goes on to more monetarily rewarding positions or, if a woman, probably marries. That there seems to be an optimal work-span for people who must bear the direct brunt of child care in institutions utilizing very high emotional involvement has been noted in other places. Henry's explanation of one of the reasons for it is certainly believable.

Once again, we should note that a function of professional

[10] Jules Henry, "The Culture of Interpersonal Relations in a Therapeutic Institution for Emotionally Disturbed Children," *American Journal of Orthopsychiatry*, XXVII (1957), 727 f.

[11] *Ibid.*, p. 728.

raining and of the externally dictated structure of our work
; to channelize the energy inherent in this mechanism in the
ealistic service of others' needs which are related, in just the
ight degree of closeness, to our own.

The Professional Self

I introduce the concept of the "professional self" into this
aper with considerable reluctance. It has been used in our
ield far too often as a vehicle in which unsound or sloppy
sychological theorizing could be carried in concealment. Let
ne begin, then, by noting what I do not mean by the notion.

I certainly should not like the term to mean that a student,
or example, could acquire an addition to himself which was
ndependent of the rest of him, really, but could be summoned
vhenever he had to meet the public or his client. This version
f the professional self is what is likely to emerge largely in
he service of psychological self-defense. It may be inculcated
y an overexuberant conviction in teachers that one learns
rom being taught. Especially when it is founded on a long
eries of preachments and verbal reinforcement, it becomes all
oo readily a corruptible addendum to the punitive superego
he student may have brought along with him in the first place.
The result is a façade which lacks firmness, and a self to be
used" (another barbarism, by the way) which is not really
ery useful. This is the professional self of saccharinity; this is
low of cliché jargon in place of serious discussion; here is the
uthor of the supremely incurious, "How do you feel about
t?" Because so many of our students are dependent people,
nd eager to do right, it is particularly dangerous to preach at
hem. The threat lies in the potentiality of their becoming dis-
racted from *doing* into working at *being,* or, even worse,
ppearing to be. A social worker is someone who gets things
lone.

A professional self founded on the abstracted superego content of one's teachers or superiors is too likely to be inflexible stereotyped, and lacking in the appearance of sincerity—which, in the deeper psychological sense, it is. The situation is even worse when this part of the totality begins to dominate the whole personality. Then we give off the kind of impression which was summed up in the article "Social Work: a Profession Chasing Its Tail." [12] An overconscientious professional self, then, is unlikely to be helpful in dealings with other people.

From the standpoint of the burgeoning social worker, too such an image of himself is dangerous. One's work life becomes too charged with duty, and not enough with pleasure. In the long run, of course, this is frustrating, by definition. The distraction into narcissistic play with one's self-image endangers just that "feedback . . . from the immediate exercise of this occupation" to which Erikson refers. Only in the pursuit of goals external to the self can one find continuing potentials for a lifetime of fascination in one's work. Our concern, therefore, has to be a good deal more with the student's morale for social work than with his morals while doing it

There are, however, some respects in which a professional self has a good deal of meaning for adequate functioning and for total integration:

1. Because of the complex and varied nature of the material with which we deal in practice and social work, much of the structuring of the work must be internally imposed.[13] We have already indicated the need, in any kind of work, to be able to reduce one's operations to a routine. It is not only foreign to our professional ideology, but it would seriously hurt our

[12] Marian K. Saunders, "Social Work: a Profession Chasing Its Tail," *Harper's Magazine*, March, 1957, pp. 56–62.

[13] Indeed, so important is a structure to sustained effort that results with an incorrect theory may well be better than with none at all.

effectiveness if we were to propose at this stage that people or groups should be simply categorized and treated by prescription. How, then, to establish any fixed points by which a worker may have some security, literally, that he knows what he is about? I think that here the professional self comes in, in the form of a fixed body of principles, attitudes, and reasonably clear images of how one at least goes about the job. A theory becomes absolutely essential, of course, and one reason why we so avidly commit ourselves to sets of assumptions or hypotheses from Freud or the social sciences is to meet the need, somehow, to find a structuring for our own activity in the face of an ambiguous "need" in the client.[14]

2. Because the job of social workers requires so much emotional investment, it becomes necessary to have a sense of a self which operates in treatment but which is not totally involved. Here, I think, a feeling that the self one uses on the job, or in relation to the job, is a semiautonomous organization within the personality becomes very supportive. On the one hand, it frees part of the ego for its important function of participant observation. And, on the other, it helps with restraining the tendency toward obsessive self-observation which may carry over from work and interfere with the rest of living.

3. Finally, and related to the two points above, there is some value to the notion that, for any job, one may—indeed must— have an organization of responses and equipment which one can and does turn on at will when one is at work. This is what one would mean by assuming his role when he enters the office. The capacity to do this, as we have noted, is supported by the very reality of the work situation: its demands (even for conformity); its tradition, which gives one a sense of super-

[14] Alvin Zander, Arthur R. Cohen, and Ezra Stotland, *Role Relations in the Mental Health Professions* (Ann Arbor, Mich.: Institute for Social Research, 1957), pp. 43 ff.

personal continuity; and its ideology, which fills in when theory falters.

Some Directions of Faulty Integration in Social Work

Continuing the analytical task, let us turn next to some of the problems which face us in planning for our profession. We shall do so only briefly, to be sure, since our present purpose is simply to sketch the outline of what appears to be a promising theoretical model. Extended detail would require more research than is here represented, of course.

The illustrations chosen concern malformations of the professional identity. After all, a "workable professional identity" is a kind of synthesis which involves a harmonious equilibrium among elements. When things are working well, it is difficult to analyze what the elements are. Insights may be gained, nevertheless, from attempts to pinpoint the causes of what appear to be specific forms of dysfunctioning.

In making our applications of the theory, it is well to recall that we have in mind a psychosocial model. Hence, dysfunction can be located either in the inner psychology of the individual or in the social process which involves him.

1. *Role-rigidity.*—By this term is meant the inability of the person to alter his possible range of behaviors flexibly in response to changing situations. Clinically, we are most familiar with the pattern as an aspect of neuroses or character neuroses. A person may, for instance, bring his ambivalence toward his father into all authority situations, and so forth. In social work we are accustomed to looking for the explanation of this kind of problem in ourselves in our own neuroses, and I have no doubt that this frame of reference is correct in the vast majority of instances. Thus, the worker who is compulsively giving (or withholding), the authoritarian worker, the worker

who has difficulty in facing hostility—all reflect deeper personality problems.

It may be of more interest in the present connection to call attention to a few types of social situations which may produce similar rigidity in the professional self. We have situational dynamic equivalents to the neurosis, in the sense that they, too, severely limit behavioral flexibility.

Even relatively normal persons suffer role-rigidity on the job when involved in a tightly bureaucratic administrative structure. Indeed, one aim of bureaucratization is to induce just this effect in the professional identities of those employed, and especially in the lower echelons. Even in highly intelligent organizations, bureaucratization may appear necessary when one is dealing with personnel in whose judgment one can frankly place no great confidence. Thus, in social work, we may have to flatly forbid *all* rights to impose discipline to members of an institutional staff who might abuse the right, or use it impulsively. At the same time, we are aware that with many children a decisive intervention at the time of acting out, and before defensive maneuvering can come into play, might well be most strategic for treatment. Another illustration: It took some time before a psychiatric team could trust the social worker to accumulate history, as we now do, rather than follow a history outline. One could not be sure a decade or two ago that the average psychiatric social worker was sufficiently trained to be able to sense the significant leads in following a more free-floating approach. My own recollection is that when the history outline was in vogue it was followed with rather scrupulous attention by workers whose basic personalities could not have been greatly different from those now entering our field. An organization, after all, has a large battery of rewards and punishments with which to induce the kind of behavior it wants.

A kind of bureaucratization occurs whenever treatment is

standardized in detail. One thinks, for instance, of the Rankian movement (or heresy, as some would have it). In this approach, great emphasis was placed from the beginning in providing both client and worker with clear images of their respective roles. Similarly, there was the assumption that all, or nearly all, clients must move through a period of active struggle with the worker, and the notion that if pain frequently accompanies growth, pain may be taken as a sign of growth. Whether these steps, and these processes, may be appropriate to mobilize energy in at least some cases seems unarguable. But, that all cases will be found to fit a similar pattern of treatment, whether struggling, dynamic passivity, reflecting-back, or free association on the couch, seems extremely dubious in the year 1959.

Yet, the tendency is great in the psychotherapeutic professions to reduce individualized complexity by fixing on a technique. And, it is of interest that movements in our field more frequently organize themselves around adherence to a technique than they do around acceptance of a theory—especially if it is a complex theory. Once a movement is formed, of course, its semiliterates devote great energy to ensuring the purity of behavior of those being initiated into it. The result, as I have indicated, is the dynamic equivalent to a character neurosis among the practitioners in the movement, and the moral equivalent of war in relation to foreigners outside it.

In such social phenomena in our own and other professions, by the way, we undoubtedly see yet another example of the mannner in which social groupings are erected to subserve the needs of their members. In this case, the need appears to be the widespread desire to locate external supports to bolster the almost inescapable necessity for imposing a structure, ourselves, for treating people.

A related social phenomenon in our own field is the whole tendency to displace content with form in other ways. Thus, we have only recently emerged from a period in which the intensity of supervision and the amount of time freed for recording were, in and of themselves, taken as evidence of the quality of the agency. In the absence of more concise reality checks the tendency is to estimate the caliber of work by "the way that we do it," even though ordinary common sense tells us there is really no substitute for an independent measure of what actually gets accomplished.

2. *Distraction into the status struggle.*—The part to be played by one's job in securing a place within the social structure and the significance of this in one's total identity are, of course, part of the burden of this piece. A job affords satisfactions from the doing; a job should also produce a modicum of guaranteed acceptance and even approval socially. How does social work measure up on this?

It is by now quite firmly established that the status of social work, ranked against other professions, is at best marginal. This is a source of considerable dismay to some of us—indeed, to such an extent that it makes one wonder. For one may be dissatisfied, let us say, with the social status of his occupation without being obsessed with the issue. My point is that a problem which affects us all is felt most keenly by a minority within our group. Such issues are arguable, but one even has the impression at times that the relatively poor level of pay is presented more as an insult to status needs than as material deprivation.

Concern with the status of one's occupation, or overconcern with it, can also arise from either internal or external circumstances. Thus, we have on the one hand persons with power drives much too pressing to be adequately sublimated in a helping profession—if, indeed, they could in any other. In individual cases, one becomes aware of intense sibling rivalries never resolved, of masculine identifications producing pressure in women, of feminine identifications threatening male workers, and so forth. One can also piece out, from time to time, instances in which workers have chosen social work in a spirit of familial rebellion without having counted in advance, let us say, on simultaneously abdicating the class position into which they were born and whose attraction they have never quite been able to repress successfully.

We have, on the other hand, some indications of an obsession with status on the basis of the particular situation in which a person finds himself. Thus, one has the impression that in agencies where morale is high—where workers have a feeling that they have a difficult job to do, and they do it well—less energy is dissipated into the status struggle, more is invested in the job. There is some evidence, too, that concern about the status of social work is actually greater among those who have risen to positions of power within it.[15] Chief social workers may be more concerned about competition with psychologists than are their workers.

The dynamics here are reminiscent of observations made on underprivileged minority groups. That is, those individuals in a position of leadership, who are upward-mobile, are often more frustrated about their low status vis-à-vis the dominant majority than are the submerged remainder. The nearer the goal appears to be, the greater is the desire to achieve it. Therefore, the stronger is the potential frustration in being blocked at that phase. Frustration with the status of social work, one might conclude, is an occupational hazard of achieving leadership within it.

A similar seduction to frustration also seems inherent in some social work jobs which throw their occupants into frequent association with those in the higher socioeconomic ranks of the culture. I would include here executives and

[15] I want to express my indebtedness for a number of stimulating talks with Herman Stein who has recently been applying a similar approach to understanding staff relationships in industry.

subexecutives of agencies whose clientele is predominantly of the upper middle class, as well as the personnel of certain councils and other structures for community organization. The temptation is also great for those workers whose emotional, intellectual, and/or aesthetic equipment has qualified them for intimate access to the circles of Upper Psychiatry. In this group, the temptation to "pass" by virtue of a change in self-designation or job title (e.g., as therapist) has long been pressing. More recently, however, a countermovement has begun to occur, and the title "social worker" is in vogue once more. This shift may represent a gradual increase in the general prestige of the title over the past decade among the cognoscenti. Or, it may simply be the same kind of sophisticated snobbishness by renunciation out of which the title "doctor" is passing from usage in academic circles in the current generation.

Hence, we see that distraction into the American status struggle may be a product of individual or social vicissitudes, or of some combination of both. In either case, when it reaches obsessional proportions, it constitutes a malformation in the professional identity. The surest way to increase the prestige of a profession like ours is obviously to learn more and more about how to do the job well, and to police our own ranks so that a high standard of service is generally maintained.

3. *Overinvestment.*—Social work is an occupation which welcomes overinvestment of the work life. In few fields can the id and the superego strike such gratifying bargains for energy production as in our own. Two examples may suffice to illustrate this phenomenon:

a) Moral fervor in the service of attack: Social scientists frequently must, and do, attack the work of others in the service of the eternal verities of truth and science, but this is supposed to be an intellectual exercise. Social workers can mount an attack from an even more energizing body of experience with actual human suffering. Hence, when we level an attack those parts of it which represent private sources of aggression are all too easily masked under acceptable moral indignation. Quite probably, the capacity for converting in the direction of moral indignation is an important natural resource in a field like our own. But, I think we lose something if we choose to deny recognition of the true sources of energy harnessed for objectives of social change.

b) Distortions in the administrative process. This writer pretends to no expertise in the art of administration. Nevertheless, there are some features of social work which make it an obviously different kettle of fish from industry, law, or brokerage, and so on, and which would argue extreme caution in translating experience from field to field. What are these features?

One, which is outstanding, is the absence, still, of clear and objective standards of performance, despite the progress we continue to make in describing what we expect of a worker. This is no field in which one can count units of production, volume of sales, or even Trendex ratings. Consequently, it is extremely difficult to screen out personal reactions and motivations from the very significant process of evaluation. A second feature of social work administration derives from the degree to which each individual worker, in the lowest echelons, is required by the nature of the job to impose his own structure on the job to be done with clients or groups. As we have indicated above, this makes the use of criteria drawn from manner of performance shakier than we would like. A third difficulty comes from the subject of the work itself. The emotional content facing the employee is often extremely highly charged and uncomfortably "open." There must be few occupations which demand so much of the employee in the constant handling of his own anxieties and other feelings. There must be few, also, which so often require the administrator to function in a quasi-therapeutic relationship, as we must do in social work simply to get the job done. Finally, there is the indisputable fact that administration in a profession like ours is handicapped in comparison with industry, for example, in its use of simple rewards and punishments as incentives. We are the more dependent on such things as approval and inspiration to obtain production, in part because we have little inducement in the way of imposing monetary or prestige rewards. On the other hand, both our ideology about the handling of fellow humans and the difficulty in replacing personnel block our inclinations to discharge employees or to demote them out of hand.

Out of this combination of circumstances, social work has developed a proud tradition of shrewd and effective administrative practice which is probably its most significant independent contribution to the technology of the general society. It is noteworthy, however, that the nature of the profession forces this to be very much a government of men. The jobs are creative and certainly nonroutine, the work is highly charged, and the personality forces we exploit in getting it done require a careful balancing.

Under such conditions, it is no wonder that a number of specific malformations creep into the picture, when the social worker becomes an administrator. Thus, the new supervisor may attempt to preserve the stability of his own professional identity by establishing a casework relationship with his supervisees, no matter how clear he is intellectually about the difference. Here, of course, he is struggling with his own equilibrium. It probably is no coincidence that the same era in which it is becoming *de rigueur* for supervisors to continue to carry cases is also the one in which a strong effort is being made to reduce the intensity of supervision for experienced workers. Is it possible that as supervisors have more direct outlets for their need to do casework, they will have fewer impulses to introduce these elements into another context? We have every reason to believe, as I have attempted to show throughout this paper, that a good deal of the supervisor's total personality integration has rested on his concept of himself as "caseworker."

Another form of distortion comes from the necessary personalization of the leadership process, in a field with open emotional content. The tendency is strong to resurrect familial relationships in the agency. We may see, therefore, administrators whose position at the center of a team is reinforced by needs which do not derive from the rational necessity to maintain high morale. They become father-figures, or mother-figures. Some administrators actively encourage this, by the way, with such statements as, "In our organization we have no need for formality and a lot of red tape." No, indeed. Instead, everyone relates personally to them, everyone's security depends on them.

The same administrator then may complain about being harassed and overworked with details—just as he may fall into a truly shocked depression when the inevitable happens, the sibling feelings go out of control, and the staff finally resolves its problems by turning against the central figure. Related to this style of administration, of course, is the social system in which it becomes impossible for the younger members ever to grow up. One finds psychoanalysts in training in their late thirties referred to as "the boys," for example, or social workers of really impressive competence treated as if they were still grasping the fundamentals. And, of course, the emotional threat of introducing new staff members, especially in positions of responsibility, is far out of line with any objective dangers to the jobs of those already on the scene.

My aim in this paper has been to continue the social psychological analysis of social work as a profession and a culture.

The paper has explored some of the circumstances which determine individual variations in professional identities, and forces which may interfere with the emergence of a satisfying and effective one for the social worker. The analysis has rested heavily on the psychosocial approach represented in the work of Erikson. However, I have also tried to maintain a balanced concern with social as well as intrapsychic considerations, and an eye to the practical, as befits a social worker's approach.

The paper would be truncated for me, and perhaps for the reader, if I did not end it with some general comments on the positive meanings of the conception. The foremost, for me, is the exciting potentiality of social work as a profession in which a satisfying identity may be found. The variety of jobs and subspecialties is such that many different facets of one's personality can find expression in an integrated way at almost any stage of one's career. For example, as the initial fervor and impulse subside in the worker, as it must in all of us, there is still the chance of an abiding fascination with a kind of work which never becomes simple, and which always offers new intellectual fields to conquer. The drive and sheer physical activity of our youth, therefore, can be replaced with the quieter joys of study, teaching, research—or the utilization of accumulated judgment. Unfortunate is the field so standardized that one cannot reap within it the feeling of mastery we all come to need simply as a reward for having lived. Moreover, the personal identity, and hence the professional identity, is no static thing. We change as we heal old wounds, or life provides us with new ones; and so do the kinds of feedbacks we require in our work life. In this connection, the institution of sabbaticals and of advanced study, which is growing in our field, may in our own lifetimes come to be recognized as a major safeguard of our own mental health. Erikson calls the period of treatment a psychosocial moratorium for young borderline patients. Perhaps the period of time granted for study will some day also be regarded quite openly as an acceptable psychosocial moratorium for mature workers to learn while they rediscover themselves.

Because of the delicate balancing which it represents, no man can create his professional identity for another, even if he dared to carry such responsibility. Neither can so complex and largely unconscious an intrapsychic institution be molded "by taking thought." But we can provide for our students opportunities to invest their energies, whatever the source, models with whom optimistic identifications can be made, and a social role which offers realistic satisfactions. Above all, I suppose, we can welcome them with a tolerant acceptance of the processes through which we hope they will find their ways. If the tolerance is occasionally mixed with amusement, perhaps they will forgive us.

PROFESSIONALIZATION AND SOCIAL WORK

HENRY J. MEYER

Any discussion of social work as a profession in the United States today must face a number of ambiguities. These we shall meet as we examine some of the central characteristics of professionalization in social work. There need be no ambiguity, however, about the old question put to social work by Abraham Flexner in 1915: Is social work a profession? [1] The professional status of social work is generally acknowledged. Other questions remain. What kind of profession will social work become? How will its own professional structure affect its future? How will it meet the demands that society places on it as a profession?

It is to such questions as these that this chapter may serve as prologue. Despite the voluminous writings of social workers about professional problems, the detailed analysis of social work as a profession has just started. A number of sociologists and social workers trained in the sociology of professions have begun to mark out the framework of study, to gather together the stray bits of information now available, and to initiate the inquiries that will permit an analysis of social work.[2] In

[1] Abraham Flexner, "Is Social Work a Profession?" in *Proceedings of the National Conference of Charities and Correction* (Chicago: the Conference, 1915), pp. 576–90.

[2] Especially the work of Wilensky and Lebeaux and of Greenwood mark major steps in this direction. See Harold L. Wilensky and Charles N. Lebeaux, *Industrial Society and Social Welfare* (New York: Russell

this discussion we shall use these sources as the backdrop for some comments that may help to call attention to issues for social work today.

Professionalization in Industrial Society

It may be useful to characterize briefly the nature of professionalization before presenting a general discussion of the social work profession.[3] The tendency toward professionaliza-

Sage Foundation, 1958); Ernest Greenwood, "Attributes of a Profession," *Social Work*, II, No. 3 (1957), 45–55; Greenwood, *Toward a Sociology of Social Work*, Research Department, Special Report No. 37 (Los Angeles: Regional Welfare Planning Council of Metropolitan Los Angeles, 1953). Greenwood has embarked on a program of research on social work as a profession, and some of the results are included in student group research project reports at the School of Social Welfare, University of California. See also Joseph W. Eaton, "Whence and Whither Social Work?" *Social Work*, I, No. 1 (1956), 11–26; Herbert Bisno, "How Social Will Social Work Be?" *Social Work*, I, No. 2 (1956), 12–18; Otto Pollak, "The Culture of Psychiatric Social Work," *Journal of Psychiatric Social Work*, XXI (1952), 160–65.

Among discussions of the profession by social workers see: Nathan E. Cohen, *Social Work in the American Tradition* (New York: Dryden Press, 1958); Cohen, "Social Work as a Profession," in *Social Work Year Book, 1957* (New York: National Association of Social Workers, 1957); Ernest V. Hollis and Alice L. Taylor, *Social Work Education in the United States* (New York: Columbia University Press, 1951). See also, for earlier studies: Esther Brown, *Social Work as a Profession* (New York: Russell Sage Foundation, 1942); Helen L. Witmer, *Social Work: an Analysis of an Institution* (New York: Farrar and Rinehart, Inc., 1942); Robert M. MacIver, *The Contributions of Sociology to Social Work* (New York: Columbia University Press, 1931).

[3] The relevance of industrialization as a setting for professionalization, with particular reference to social work, is well documented in Wilensky and Lebeaux, *op. cit.* See also Wilbert E. Moore, *Industrial Relations and the Social Order* (New York: Macmillan, 1951); Theodore Caplow, *The Sociology of Work* (Minneapolis: University of Minnesota Press, 1954).

For other references on the sociology of professions see: Robert K. Merton, George G. Reader, and Patricia L. Kendall, eds., *The Student Physician* (Cambridge, Mass.: Harvard University Press, 1957), especially Merton, "Some Preliminaries to a Sociology of Medical Edtion is almost inevitable in a growing industrial society. Specialization within an elaborate division of labor must be increased with the shift from agricultural and other primary industries to the factory, to trade, services, and technical enterprises. The urbanization that accompanied industrialization has further encouraged the development of numerous occupations to serve the city and its people, and it has also increased the social isolation of occupational groups, making them conscious of their separateness and of their interdependency. Specialized occupational knowledge is thus coupled with specialized functions for occupational groups in an industrialized society. The occupation becomes, in part, a substitute for the traditional focus of group identification and common interest, such as the local community. Professionalization represents a tendency for occupational groups to acquire the attributes of a community and to seek a favorable position within the larger society.[4] In this process, increase both of authority and of responsibility marks the transformation of an occupation into a profession.

With science-based technology becoming more and more visibly the basis for important functions—not only in production, communication, and distribution but also in the provision of medical and other services—the prestige of the science-based professions has increased more rapidly than that of the professions based on scholarship, such as law and the ministry. The newer professions have clustered around the sciences, and all professions, including law and the ministry, make over-

ucation," pp. 3–79; William J. Goode, "Community within a Community: the Professions," *American Sociological Review*, XXII (1957), 194–200; Talcott Parsons, "The Professions and Social Structure," in *Essays in Sociological Theory* (Glencoe, Ill.: Free Press, 1954), pp. 34–49, and "A Sociologist Looks at the Legal Profession," *ibid.*, pp. 370–85; Parsons, "Social Structure and Dynamic Process: the Case of Modern Medical Practice," in *The Social System* (Glencoe, Ill.: Free Press, 1951), pp. 428–79; A. M. Carr-Saunders and P. A. Wilson, *The Professions* (Oxford: Clarendon Press, 1933).

[4] Goode, *op. cit.*, p. 194.

tures to science. The hazy line between science and technology has encouraged many occupational groups to aspire to professional status. Almost every cluster of occupations in the economy of industrial society is capped by an occupational group expected to conserve, develop, and apply the fund of basic knowledge required to perform the functions to which the occupations are directed. Such an occupational group is an existing, or an incipient, profession.

The advantages of professional status are real. Prestige is one such benefit, and occupational prestige in a society where individual statuses tend to be achieved rather than ascribed is of major importance. Further, however, the command of a socially assigned function by a designated occupational group confers the benefits of partial monopoly. Successful claim to professional monopoly has economic advantages visible in the higher incomes of members of professional occupations, compared with the incomes of those unable to boast the advantage of such membership. In return for these and similar benefits to individuals who can be considered professionals, society expects responsible performance of a socially required function.

Efforts to define what is meant by a profession usually emphasize, with greater detail and elaboration, three characteristics: (1) a body of knowledge, accumulated wisdom, doctrine, or experience; (2) technical competence in the use of this knowledge; and (3) publicly asserted responsibility in the exercise of this competence on behalf of society.[5] Ques-

[5] See Greenwood, "Attributes of a Profession," *op. cit.;* Robert M. MacIver and Charles Page, *Society: an Introductory Analysis* (New York: Rinehart & Co., 1949), pp. 476–83; R. Lewis and A. Maude, *Professional People* (London: Phoenix House, Ltd., 1952), pp. 55–71; Ralph W. Tyler, "Distinctive Attributes of Education for the Professions," *Social Work Journal*, XXXIII (1952), 55–62; Morris L. Cogan, "Toward a Definition of Profession," *Harvard Educational Review*, XXIII (1953), 30–50; Flexner, *op. cit.*

tions about what kinds of knowledge, how much competence, how codified the ethic of responsibility, and the like, constitute the substance of most discussion of whether an occupational group *is* or is *not* a profession. Arguments about whether social work—or nursing, or pharmacy, or any other occupation —is or is not a profession have often taken this line. A more productive question asks about the nature of professionalization in social work—or these other occupations—not whether it is a profession. As Greenwood says, social work must be considered a profession because it is not otherwise classifiable.[6]

Accepting social work as a profession, it is of some usefulness, however, to differentiate social work among the professions. We may follow Carr-Saunders for this purpose.[7] He identifies four major types of professions or would-be professions in the modern industrial society, and these types are distinguished by the extent to which they are based on the theoretical structure of a branch of learning:

1. The old, established professions, such as law, medicine, and theology, are founded on well-established bodies of knowledge.

2. A second type of profession is based on its own fundamental studies and represents largely the emergence of occupational groups and interests around bodies of scientific knowledge. Illustrative of this type of profession are chemistry, engineering, natural and social science. The occupational activity of the profession is primarily the development and application of its body of knowledge.

3. A third type makes use of technical skills and establishes as its knowledge base a body of experience derived from the

[6] Greenwood, "Attributes of a Profession," *op. cit.,* p. 54.
[7] A. M. Carr-Saunders, "Metropolitan Conditions and Traditional Professional Relationships," in R. M. Fisher, ed., *The Metropolis in Modern Life* (New York: Doubleday and Co., 1955), as summarized by A. J. Reiss, Jr., "Occupational Mobility of Professional Workers," *American Sociological Review,* XX (1955), 693.

occupational practice. Nursing, pharmacy, and social work are classified among the "semiprofessions" by this criterion.

4. The fourth type of profession consists of occupations that aspire to professional status, but consistency of technical practice and the development of a sufficient body of practice theory are so rudimentary that little claim can be made to a theoretical base for the profession. Examples of this type are found primarily in business; for example, salesmanship. Carr-Saunders calls these "would-be professions."

From this classification one should not infer that all occupations that tend toward professionalization will finally resemble the old established professions. Social work might remain a "semiprofession." On the other hand, where the scope for elaborating a profession's fundamental knowledge permits cumulative scholarship or science rather than the mere accumulation of recorded experience, the prestige of science and of the older professions provides strong impetus to emulate them. Social workers use the medical profession as a model more often than any other.

Other attributes of professionalization are so directly associated with knowledge base that their use as criteria to classify professions would yield approximately the same results. More differentiating among professions is the extent to which its members seek to validate professional standing by efforts to establish and maintain preeminence of the profession's knowledge base, its competence, and its social responsibility. This effort to claim preeminence is sometimes referred to, in discussions of social work, as the claim to an exclusive function. But it is the conjunction of competence with knowledge and responsibility, rather than exclusiveness, that gives a profession its authority, even though that authority may for some professions be confirmed in law or by other institutional means. One cannot claim health as the private concern of the medical profession or transmission of knowledge as that of the teaching profession. One cannot find an exclusive function for social work in "helping people to help themselves," in social reform, or in humanitarian concern. Paralleling other professions, however, social work lays claim to specialized experience and knowledge coupled with competence for responsible performance within these general areas. Social workers as well as those outside the profession may be uncertain about the validity of this claim, and this constitutes one of the sources of uncertainty about the status of the profession today.

Some students include as attributes of a profession those sustaining and facilitating institutions that are the products of professionalization. Educational processes, schools, and apprenticeships; procedures to validate the qualification to practice; associations for defense or promotion of professional interests, including economic ones; methods of proclaiming ethical commitments and of disciplining professionals to them; the special patterns of the occupational subculture—all these develop with professionalization. The character of these accompaniments of professionalization has a bearing on a profession's performance of its social function. Social work will be affected as a profession by its schools, associations, and occupational culture patterns.

It must be emphasized, in concluding this brief and abstract consideration of professionalization, that any particular profession—such as social work—does not have its character determined exclusively by what the profession itself does. Professionalization is a response in the process of societal change. External as well as internal forces are at play, and one may conceive of professions as institutions for fulfilling social needs or functions. The forms through which the profession carries out its functions and what these functions are will be affected by extra- as well as intraprofessional factors. It is in this sense that social work, and other professions, may be said to face demands that must be acknowledged and responded to. A discussion of the profession of social work must try to identify and to take into account some of these demands.

The Social Work Profession Today

It is of some interest to note, as we attempt to characterize the profession of social work today, that much of the information needed is not yet available. The knowledge base for social work has hardly been identified, much less subjected to content analysis. The large literature on practice has not yet provided clear descriptions of the technical competence that social workers may possess. There is incomplete specification of situations in which social work asserts that it has professional responsibility. This is not to say that social work must itself provide knowledge of the sort required. Rather, those social scientists who would understand the profession have to undertake investigations from the outside, looking on social work as a phenomenon for study in the same framework as other professions and occupations. There have been some excellent beginnings, and the discussion of this section will rely heavily on these works.[8] But our presentation will be tentative and speculative.

We may conveniently discuss the social work profession by considering the character of its knowledge base, its claim to technical proficiency, and the question of its area of responsibility. We may also refer to some of the structural features of the profession and to some of the ambiguities apparent in social work as a profession today.

We are concerned with the character rather than the content of the knowledge base developed and sought by social work. Two features seem most evident: (1) the emphasis on the primacy of experience in practice, on the one hand; and (2) almost paradoxically, the assertion of scientific knowledge as the foundation for professional competence. These are not un-

[8] Particularly, Wilensky and Lebeaux, *op. cit.*, chap. xi.

related emphases for any profession, to be sure, because scientific knowledge and practice experience are interwoven in the art of a profession. But they are different. Scientific knowledge aims essentially at generalization from theories to specific instances, whereas a body of experiential knowledge seeks to provide the widest possible range of specific instances from which to draw as new ones are presented.[9] Not the choice between them, but how science and experience are to be used is the unsettled question in social work.

Different segments of the profession show somewhat different attitudes with respect to its knowledge base. Casework, group work, community organization, and administration, in that order, range from asserting the need for scientific knowledge as an underlying base to relying primarily on practice experience. This appears to be true even though casework and group work are well known for the use of the case approach both in teaching and in practice. Caseworkers have been more inclined to support and justify their practice decisions by appeal to bodies of theory claiming scientific standing. Thus psychoanalysis, whatever reservations may be made about it, takes a scientific stance, and casework considers its use of this body of doctrine and theory as application of a scientific discipline. Casework and group work, also, are the fields within social work that have most deliberately imported concepts and terms from the social sciences. Community organization as a field seems least concerned with conceptualizing the theory underlying its activities or with seeking to base it on scientific knowledge.[10]

These differences have historical and situational roots. Case-

[9] See Ernest Greenwood, "Social Science and Social Work: a Theory of Their Relationship," *Social Service Review*, XXIX (1955), 20–33.

[10] The range of evident concern with the type of knowledge base among caseworkers, group workers, community organization and administrative social workers is reflected in the discussions of these methods in Walter A. Friedlander, ed., *Concepts and Methods of Social Work* (Englewood Cliffs, N.J.: Prentice-Hall, Inc., 1958).

work was developed by emphasis on the individual, his strengths and weaknesses, his psychological mechanisms, and his responses to the social situation.[11] It found in psychology and in psychoanalysis a ready body of ideas about the individual. Its practice setting in hospital, clinic, and agency fostered association with the medical and psychiatric professions, which accept scientific knowledge as basic. Neither group work nor community organization developed in situations where scientific knowledge was highly valued or, indeed, generally available.[12] Since prestige is identified with science, a tendency to give at least apparent support to a scientific foundation is widespread. But throughout all parts of the profession the commitment is ambiguous.

One outcome of this uncertainty is reflected in the educational content of professional training. Curricula of schools of social work, despite efforts to reach common agreements through association and accreditation procedures, mix science-related and practice-derived courses, and there appears to be widespread concern with the problem of the relationship of each to the other. Social work schools find it difficult to identify appropriate prerequisites in underlying bodies of knowledge or sciences. The place of research methods courses, stressing scientific methodology, is uncertain.[13]

Social work is not entirely at liberty to choose whether it will base its claim to professional standing on a body of scientific knowledge. So pervasive is public insistence on science

[11] See Wilensky and Lebeaux, *op. cit.*, p. 288.

[12] For a discussion of the relationship of social work and social science, see Grace L. Coyle, *Social Science in the Professional Education of Social Workers* (New York: Council on Social Work Education, 1958); Herman D. Stein, "Social Science in Social Work Practice and Education," *Social Casework*, XXXVI (1955), 147–55; Donald Young, "Sociology and the Practicing Professions," *American Sociological Review*, XX (1955), 641–48.

[13] See Ernest Greenwood, "Social Work Research: the Role of the Schools," *Social Service Review*, XXXII (1958), 152–56.

that social work will almost surely have to support its claim to a body of fundamental knowledge by appeal to science. This will require as a first step a serious effort to analyze the actual content of what social workers know, where they obtained such knowledge, and the extent to which that knowledge has been or can be subjected to test. This is a difficult task. Social workers will, among other things, have to become more explicit about their assumptions and more articulate about their bases of action. But it will provide a firmer claim to professionalization than at present.

In this task the behavioral sciences can be of service, but they cannot do the job for social work. Like medicine, social work will have to ask its own questions of the social sciences, and it will have to choose what is appropriate knowledge from the viewpoint of its own professional objectives. But it will have to respect scientific methodology as a basis for knowledge and tolerate skepticism about its knowledge. It will have to overcome the fear that this will inhibit its confidence to practice and its claim to authority. It must really know what is known and what is not. On this basis social workers, like other professionals, can justify the authority in fundamental knowledge that is a mark of professionalization.[14]

The assertion of competent use of its knowledge base is a second characteristic of professionalization. We have made the point earlier that it is not exclusive interest in an area of social concern but special competence to work in the area that characterizes professionalization. In few of the programs employing designated social workers are school-trained, professional social workers predominant. Thus, only in psychiatric social work in clinics and hospitals, in medical social work, and in the teaching of social work are approximately one half of those

[14] See Alfred J. Kahn, "The Nature of Social Work Knowledge," in Cora Kasius, ed., *New Directions in Social Work* (New York: Harper, 1954).

employed as social workers "fully trained" in terms of the customary standard of two or more years of specialized schooling.[15] This proportion is approached in some of the family services. But in the largest programs, such as public assistance, group work, and child welfare work, the proportion is far smaller. There is no question that what social workers are employed to do is also done by less professionally trained persons. A crucial question is, of course, whether those who claim professional training have competences based on knowledge that distinguish them from the less professional or the nonprofessional. This is a question for which there is no clear, factual answer.

Professional competence involves more than the assertion of knowledge not possessed by nonprofessionals. As Wilensky and Lebeaux imply, development of a "professional self" in social work, comparable to that of the established professions is a part of professional competence.[16] They suggest that the professional social worker, more than the nonprofessional, must exhibit an impersonal and disinterested relationship with his client, an emotional neutrality or objectivity in his concern with the client's problems, an impartiality among clients regardless of personal preferences, and a responsibility for service rather than exploitation. Such norms appear to be evident among trained social workers, but research comparing trained and untrained social workers in these respects is still limited.

The aspect of special competence of social workers that has to do with effectiveness of technique also lacks demonstration in research. It seems likely, but it is not yet demonstrated, that trained social workers have greater skill in counseling, in working with groups and with communities, than persons of equivalent experience but less training.

[15] *Social Workers in 1950: a Report on the Study of Salaries and Working Conditions in Social Work—Spring 1950* (New York: American Association of Social Workers, 1952).

[16] Wilensky and Lebeaux, *op. cit.*, pp. 298–303.

One difficulty in dealing with such questions lies in the fact that what social workers do has not yet been objectively described. The actual work of the caseworker, group worker, or community organizer is reflected primarily through self-supplied reports or recordings or general illustrations taken from experience. These become the content of the asserted skill of the social worker with only limited recognition that errors of perception, recall, and reporting as well as other subjective biases may create inaccurate or erroneous presentations. It is suggested that the claim to competence must be accompanied by a willingness to subject the practices of social work to scrutiny in order to see what the content of professional practice really is. Even if social workers accept such a necessity, it is by no means an easy task to observe practice because conceptual, measuremental, operational, and analytical tools for such descriptions are not well developed. Nevertheless, far more than at present could be attempted if social workers accepted the need to examine directly their technical competence. One indication of professionalization is willingness to make public the professional operations or techniques so that they can be described and tested.

Norms of intraprofessional relations in social work would seem to stand in the way of such a development.[17] These norms protect the profession against outsiders who might question the mystique represented in the "art" of the practitioner, or against the hostile attack on practice skills by those who deny the sincerity and good faith of the practitioner. These dangers exist, but they can be recognized and guarded against without depriving the profession of necessary tests of competence.

In a larger sense, the question of special competence is the question of objective evaluation. One should not underestimate the dangers that inhere in disinterested evaluation of effort by

[17] *Ibid.*, pp. 303–8.

social workers or social agencies. Nor should one underestimate the difficulties of making valid assessments. There seems to be no alternative, however, to the necessity that social work subject its competence to test, and there are signs that it is moving in this direction.[18] It becomes more professional as it does so.

That component of professionalization that we have referred to as an asserted area for which a profession takes social responsibility in using its knowledge and competence presents again a confused picture for the profession of social work.[19] In its history, social work has long had a double focus: on social reform, on the one hand; and on facilitating adjustment of individuals to existing situations, on the other. These two themes reappear in various forms: as environmental manipulation or promotion of psychological functioning; as concern with people through mass programs; or as casework with persons "one by one." Social workers have been conscious of these two approaches to social welfare and have often sought to reconcile them. Mary Richmond, symbol of the case-by-case approach, is reported to have said to Florence Kelley, symbol of reform in the grand style: "We work on the same program. I work on the retail end of it, but you work on the whole-sale."[20] These two viewpoints are still not integrated, and both are represented by acknowledged spokesmen for the profession.

There is little doubt that those who define social responsibility of the profession in terms of individuals rather than of reform and policy have the ascendancy. Most of the students

[18] As an example, see Henry J. Meyer and Edgar F. Borgatta, "Evaluating a Rehabilitation Program for Post-Hospital Mental Patients," *Public Health Report*, LXXIII (1958), 650–56.

[19] See Nathan E. Cohen, "A Changing Profession in a Changing World," *Social Work*, I, No. 4 (1956), 12–19; Harry L. Lurie, "The Responsibilities of a Socially Oriented Profession," in Kasius, *op. cit.*, pp. 31–53.

[20] Frances Perkins, "My Recollections of Florence Kelley," *Social Service Review*, XXVIII (1954), 18.

in schools of social work elect casework as their specializa-tion.[21] Knowledge of the history and the details of social wel-fare policies is not emphasized in the curriculum as much as "human growth and development." The requirement of a school of social work degree for qualification to membership in the national professional association favors those in private agencies over those in mass programs. This trend is countered, but not balanced, by growing demand for trained workers in the public programs and by the fact that even in those profes-sions traditionally committed to individual approaches—such as medicine and psychiatry—emphasis on prevention in ad-dition to amelioration or cure is forcing attention to public policy and large-scale programs.

Wilensky and Lebeaux suggest that the choice the profession makes in this dilemma will depend largely on the development of its knowledge–skill base.[22] But it also depends on what is demanded of the profession in present-day society. Social work as a profession may not be permitted to abandon either ap-proach, to choose between responsibility for social welfare policy or for direct service to individuals. Expertness in the one may well require expertness in the other, for the profes-sion as a whole if not for each professional social worker as an individual. In this respect it may be compared to the medical profession, which has been forced to concern itself with pub-lic health and the economics of medical care. Especially as public programs extend further and further beyond income maintenance into family life, facilitating optimum health, planning and providing for services to the aged, and the like, those concerned with the individual must become implicated.

The boundaries of a profession's social responsibility are al-ways unclear because social functions are interrelated and

---

[21] *Statistics on Social Work Education, 1957,* compiled by David G. French (New York: Council on Social Work Education, 1957), Table 10, p. 16.
[22] Wilensky and Lebeaux, *op. cit.,* p. 333.

changing. It would seem that social work must look sensitively to its "public image" to clarify its prestige among other occupations and professions,[23] and also to obtain clues as to what may be expected of it. Because positions are available for all trained social workers, the profession should not overlook the fact that there are many other jobs that go unfilled where there is an evident belief that professional social workers should be available.[24] A thoroughgoing study of what tasks the American people in their communities and in their governmental and voluntary agencies want the professional social worker to perform is yet to be made. Social work, like other professions, must *perceive* its area of responsibility as well as define it.

Other Features

We can briefly mention some of the important ancillary features of professionalization of social work. These deserve more extended analysis, and research on them has begun.

The problem of recruitment is affected by professionalization in social work. Greatly concerned with attracting more students,[25] social work schools have built up elaborate selection procedures that reflect some of the ambiguities already indi-

[23] See Alfred Kadushin, "Prestige of Social Work—Facts and Figures," *Social Work*, III, No. 2 (1958), 37–43; R. Clyde White, "Prestige of Social Work and the Social Worker," *Social Work Journal*, XXXVI (1955), 21–27; White, "Social Workers in Society: Some Further Evidence," *ibid.*, XXXIV (1953), 161–64; Norman Polansky, W. Bowen, L. Gordon, and C. Nathan, "Social Workers in Society: Results of a Sampling Study," *ibid.*, XXXIV (1953), 74–80.

[24] See Fedele F. Fauri, "The Shortage of Social Workers: a Challenge to Social Work Education," *Social Work Journal*, XXXVI (1955), 47–51, 61.

[25] The Council on Social Work Education has an ambitious recruitment program, and most schools of social work make recruitment efforts of their own as well. See *Recruitment for Social Work Education and Social Work Practice*, Fourth Special Recruitment Issue of *Social Work Education*, Council on Social Work Education VI, No. 2 (1958).

cated. How much emphasis should be placed on personal qualities, how much on intellectual, is a continuous question. The bases for appeal to college graduates tend to stress altruistic interests and personality characteristics rather than interest in knowledge and skills. There is evidence that those who become students particularly "like to work with people," "to help others." [26] This is in keeping with the historical background of social work where middle-class persons approached social welfare as a humanitarian cause. Recruitment may be affected also by the relatively low income of social workers and by its relatively low status among professions.[27] But, as Kadushin points out, this depends on the social level from which recruits come. Negro students and those with working class backgrounds appear to be increasingly attracted to social work. Recruitment is also affected by the fact that social work

[26] See Alfred Kadushin, "Determinants of Career Choice and Their Implications for Social Work," in *ibid.*, pp. 17–27. This article includes an extended bibliography.

[27] Because of the large number of nonschooled social workers, it is difficult to find data comparing the salaries of "trained social workers" with those of other professionals. In a study of starting salaries of June, 1956, women college graduates, social and welfare workers ranked eighth in the twelve occupations reported—lower than home economists, nurses, and teachers and higher than dietitians, librarians, secretaries, and stenographers. See *1958 Handbook on Women Workers,* Women's Bureau Bulletin No. 266, U.S. Department of Labor (Washington, D.C., 1958), p. 77. On the other hand, a study of former students in schools of social work who entered employment in 1957 reported beginning salaries of $4,565 for women with a master's degree and $3,905 for women without a master's degree. See David G. French and Alex Rosen, "Personnel Entering Social Work Employment from Schools of Social Work, 1957," in *Recruitment for Social Work Education and Social Work Practice,* p. 15. Trained social workers earn more than the less trained, on the average, and men with equivalent training earn more than women. See *Social Workers in 1950,* p. 17. Salary level may be the best index of prestige between professions and within professions (cf. Ward S. Mason and Neal Gross, "Intra-occupational Prestige Differentiation: the School Superintendency," *American Sociological Review,* XX [1955], 326–31).

is traditionally a woman's occupation. Identical appeals cannot be equally effective with persons of different backgrounds.[28]

During their schooling, future social workers begin induction into professional culture, its norms and values.[29] Such induction takes place both in the classroom and in the agency, where the student begins what is almost a lifelong pattern of intraprofessional relationship with "supervision." This relationship functions in part as an apprenticeship approach to learning the skills of the profession and in part as a pattern of intraprofessional dependency that carries through from the worker to the supervisor to the consultant, who is often in a related profession, such as medicine, psychiatry, or law.[30]

During his training period there is an implicit contest between the school and the agency for loyalty and commitment from the student; but this is less inherent in the system of field placement than in the ambiguities about what constitutes knowledge and competence. The average student spends at least a third of his time in the degree program outside the academic setting. One result of this is to encourage an early identification with the specific problems of practice rather than with intellectual conceptualizations of these problems. It is to be noted that for many students field work begins concurrently with their first classroom lecture. Another result of this method would seem to be an early and deep-seated sense of responsibility to the client. Also, strong identification with other professional social workers and an immediate sense of

[28] Kadushin, "Determinants of Career Choice . . . ," p. 20. With respect to sex ratio, 64 percent of the former students in schools of social work who entered employment in 1957 were women. See French and Rosen, *op. cit.*, p. 11. In 1950 nearly 70 percent of social work positions were filled by women. See *Social Workers in 1950*, p. 5.

[29] See Eaton, *op. cit.*, pp. 13–16.

[30] See Frances L. Beatman, "How Do Professional Workers Become Professional?" *Social Casework*, XXXVII (1956), 383–88; Robert W. Cruser, "Opinions on Supervision: a Chapter Study," *Social Work*, III, No. 1 (1958), 18–26.

being a practitioner seem to follow. The total school experience thus points toward an image of the profession that is visible in the firsthand and available models.

For most students this means that social work is equivalent to casework. Most students take their field work in casework, major in casework, and find that they can get financial backing if they study casework. Thus, they leave school with the idea that casework is the meaning of professional social work and that casework methods are the meaning of professional skill. This fact is widely recognized as an important influence on the definition of competence and responsibility for the profession as a whole. Taken together, less than 20 percent of the 1957 graduates majored in other fields.[31] Hence, individual services rather than mass programs or social policies are emphasized as the responsibility of the professional.

A sizable proportion of social work students is older than those found in most other professional schools. Social work schools, unlike law, medicine, and most other professional schools, require a college degree before entrance. Another reason is that women whose employment has been interrupted by family responsibilities may return to the labor market via the school. There is still, too, a good number of employed social workers who enter or return to school in order to become "trained social workers." [32] Their schooling is often subsidized by public agencies or programs.[33] It is of interest to note that schools do not generally regard the work experience

[31] The concentration of students in casework is documented in French and Rosen, *op. cit.*, and in the annual *Statistics on Social Work Education* published by the Council on Social Work Education.

[32] The survey by French and Rosen reports that 45 percent of all men students and 58 percent of all women students had employment in social work prior to entering professional training. Among women students, two thirds or more in all age categories above twenty-three years had such prior employment. Unpublished preliminary tables prepared by David G. French.

[33] French and Rosen, *op. cit.*, Table 6, p. 13.

of such persons as a substitute for field placement when they become students. The schools tend formally to apply the same training procedures to the inexperienced and the experienced student.

Graduates of the schools enter professional practice frequently as a continuation of their field placement; not usually in the same agencies but in similar ones. Thus schooling and professional employment tend to merge. The graduates tend to take casework jobs predominantly in those social work fields to which they are committed through financial support—child welfare, mental health services, family service programs, and medical and rehabilitation programs.[34]

Trained social workers practice their profession almost exclusively as agency employees rather than as independent practitioners.[35] Thus social workers, like teachers, must reconcile professional norms with organizational demands of agency, hospital and clinic, or government bureaus. Bureaucratic demands emphasize specialization, limited responsibility, and conformity to rules. These may encourage conceptions of professional practice in the same directions. The effect of the structure of organizations on practitioners as well as on services is an important area for further study. On the other hand, professional identification can reduce the effects of bureaucracy through emphasis on professional rather than organizational norms and responsibilities and through providing support external to the bureaucracy.[36]

[34] *Ibid.*, Tables 8 and 9, pp. 14 and 15.

[35] One study concludes, from interviews with thirty caseworkers in private practice in New York City, that they consider themselves for the most part as psychotherapists or analysts. Josephine Peck and Charlotte Plotkin, "Social Caseworkers in Private Practice," *Smith College Studies in Social Work*, XXI, No. 3 (1951), 165–97. Development of private practice is sometimes viewed as a sign of professional maturity. See Sidney Koret, "The Social Worker in Private Practice," *Social Work*, III, No. 3 (1958), 11–17.

[36] For discussion of agency structure and bureaucracy, see Wilensky and Lebeaux, *op. cit.*, chap. x and pp. 314–16.

Because a high proportion of trained social workers is employed in hospitals and clinics, the interprofessional team is a familiar setting for the practice of casework and, sometimes, of group work. Teamed with the psychiatrist and the clinical psychologist, the psychiatric caseworker in particular is in a setting where his specialization must be made more explicit and his competence affirmed. Usually a woman, the caseworker in this team faces problems of sex-role differences as well as differences in professional prestige.[37] In this situation, as in the larger bureaucracy, strong identification with the profession is stimulated as a defense against lower status and prestige.

Perhaps the elaborate system of conferences on the job among social workers, with supervisors, and with consultants, provides the protection of association with fellow professionals. Local social workers' clubs and the local chapters of the national association serve a similar function.

Professional associations in social work followed the development of specialties until 1955 when the various separate organizations merged into the single National Association of Social Workers (NASW).[38] Within this association the special interests of psychiatric social workers, medical social workers, group workers, and other specialties are preserved. If it retains its eligibility requirement, the NASW will in time speak for all school-trained professionals and for these alone. Other associations, such as the American Public Welfare Association, that include both trained and untrained social workers represent wider interests. The even broader National Conference on Social Welfare, whose annual meetings attract about six

[37] The psychiatrist–social worker–psychologist team has been analyzed in detail in Alvin Zander, Arthur R. Cohen, and Ezra Stotland, *Role Relations in the Mental Health Professions* (Ann Arbor, Mich.: Institute for Social Research, 1957).

[38] The history of professional associations in social work is briefly reviewed in Nathan E. Cohen, "Professional Social Work Faces the Future," *Social Work Journal*, XXXVI (1955), 79–86.

thousand persons, is the most diverse of all social work associations. It seems to serve primarily as a forum for the whole range of interests of social workers, whether trained or untrained, in whatever field of interest, and whatever their concept of the function and responsibility of social work as a profession. The variety of these associations tends to blur the public image of social work as a profession, but it also enlarges it beyond the image of the social worker as one exclusively concerned with an individual case.

The question of the direction that the profession of social work will take is a matter of lively concern and discussion today as it was at earlier periods.[39] The old dilemmas pose the issues: scientific knowledge *vs.* practical experience; person-to-person skills *vs.* organizational skills; social reform *vs.* treatment. The strongest emphasis of vocal leaders seems to be on broadening the perception of responsibility so that the trend since the Second World War toward a narrow professionalism of individual treatment services will be embraced within the traditional concern with social welfare policies. As Nathan E. Cohen has put it:

Part of the answer to this dilemma may be in recognizing the fact that greater acceptance in the community involves the status not only of the social worker but also of social welfare as an institution in the democratic society.[40]

He sees progress in this direction as dependent on cooperative efforts of schools, social work agencies, and the professional association.[41] But it is by no means certain that such cooperation would broaden rather than narrow the profession of social work. In any event, social work is sure to struggle with the concomitants of professionalization for a long time. Such a struggle is characteristic of a vigorous profession.

[39] For a discussion of some factors affecting the ways a profession may change, see Harvey L. Smith, "Contingencies of Professional Differentiation," *American Journal of Sociology,* LXIII (1958), 410–14.

[40] Cohen, *Social Work in the American Tradition,* p. 346.

[41] *Ibid.,* p. 348.

INDEX

THE PROFESSIONAL HOUSEPARENT

By Eva Burmeister

Children in institutions have had an overwhelming number of negative experiences. Houseparents in these institutions require understanding and skill to do their jobs effectively. This book shows how the houseparent can use everyday activities to make the institution a place where the child is given help, where he has fun, and—hopefully—where he can learn to trust those around him. This book will be valuable not only for houseparents but for foster parents, teachers, caseworkers, or anyone else who works with children.

$4.50

TEACHING THE MENTALLY RETARDED CHILD

By Natalie Perry

How can the severely mentally retarded child be encouraged to express himself? How can he become a useful and happier member of society? In this highly informative book, Natalie Perry shows how the home, school, community, can work together for the benefit of the severely retarded child. She presents the principles and practices of school programs and activities which can be offered to each child depending upon his level of maturation. *Illustrated.* *$6.50*

A PRIMER OF SOCIAL CASEWORK

By Elizabeth Nicholds

This book is designed specifically for untrained, nonprofessional or volunteer social workers and their directors. In simple, non-technical language, Mrs. Nicholds surveys the areas of social work open to these people. She describes methods by which the nonprofessional caseworker can help individuals adjust to the pattern of their environment, and lists community resources to which the caseworker can refer his client. Among the areas of casework considered are public welfare, child welfare, the problems of adolescence, and the aged. *$4.50*

Columbia University Press
New York and London